MW00981974

From The Channel Ports

Mike Smith

THE AUTHOR

Mike Smith spent seven years as headteacher of one of the country's leading comprehensive schools and three years as the proprietor of an antiquarian bookshop, before he became a magazine journalist and travel writer. He is the author of several topographical books and guidebooks.

Mike lives in the Peak District, but spends part of every year in France. He is also the author of the Landmark Visitors guide to the Dordogne.

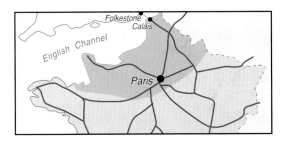

HOW TO USE THIS GUIDE

This guidebook covers an area of France whose perimeter is defined by the Channel coast, the Belgian border, and an arc that runs from Reims, through Paris and Chartres, to St Malo. It is designed for visitors who enter France through one of the Channel ports. Easy-to-follow car tours from the ports encompass all the well-known, and some lesser-known attractions to be found within three hours' drive of the coast.

A Top Tips section at the beginning of each chapter lists attractions not to be missed and things to do. Each chapter ends with suggestions for accommodation, eating out and shopping, not just in the Channel ports, but also in all the main areas covered in the itineraries. Telephone numbers and opening times of castles, show houses, museums, galleries and activity centres are listed, and details of all relevant tourist information offices are also included.

Feature boxes are specially designed to provide background information, which will help make all the visits in this fascinating region even more interesting. The guidebook also contains an entertaining 'Quick Guide' to the attractions of Paris.

The fact file at the end of the book lists useful general information for visitors to France.

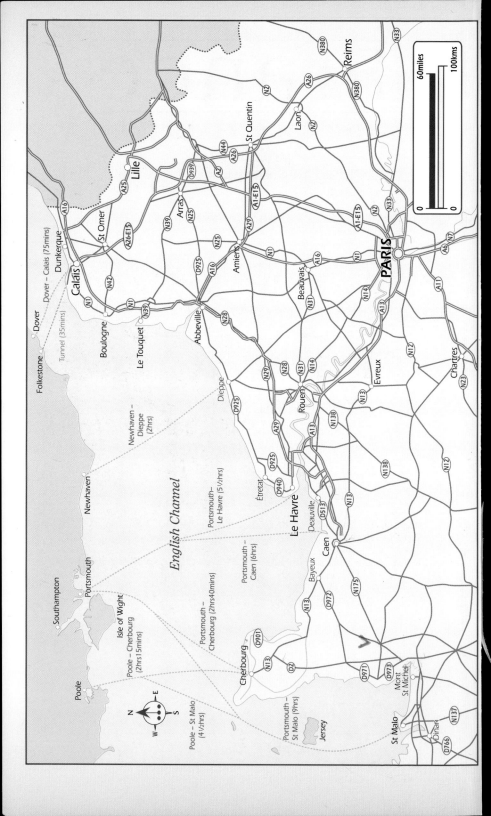

France

From The Channel Ports

Mike Smith

Contents

INTRODUCTION   **13**

1 CALAIS, THE OPAL COAST AND FRENCH FLANDERS   **17**

1.1 A tour of Calais	17
1.2 A drive along the Opal Coast	26
1.3 A tour of French Flanders	31
Additional Information	38

FEATURE BOXES

Getting there	19
Top tips for Calais	20
Cite Europe	21
The Burghers of Calais	23
Calais' two museums	24
Top tips for the Opal Coast	27
The Channel by plane	28
Marconi's hop across the Channel with radio waves	30
Top tips for French Flanders	31
Royal posturing	32
A palace of justice	34
Journey into space	35
The Dunkirk spirit	37

2 FOUR NORTHERN CITIES   **42**

2.1 Lille	43
2.2 St Quentin	48
2.3 Laon	52
2.4 Reims	56
Additional Information	62

FEATURE BOXES

Top tips for Lille	45
Getting there	45
Changing hands	46
Top tips for St Quentin	49
The Second Battle of the Somme	49
St Quentin Plage!	51
Top tips for Laon	53
Animal magic	54
Lively Laon	55
Devastation	57
Top Tips for Reims	58
Bubbly!	61

3 BOULOGNE, THE BELLE ÉPOQUE TOUR AND THE SOMME BATTLEFIELDS   **66**

3.1 Boulogne-sur-Mer	66
3.2 The Belle Époque tour	73
3.3 The Somme Battlefields	79
Additional Information	89

FEATURE BOXES

Getting there	66
Top tips for Boulogne	67
All sea-life is here	69
Say cheese	70
Boulogne's pasha	72
Top tips for Le Touquet round-trip	74
A golfer's paradise	75
Making a splash	77
Signs of the times	79
Top tips for the Battlefields tour	80
Science fiction or science prediction?	82
Ruskin's rapture	83
The Battlefields tour	85
Poppies in Flanders' fields	86

4 DIEPPE, THE ALABASTER COAST, ROUEN, GIVERNY, BEAUVAIS AND GERBEROY   **96**

4.1 A tour of Dieppe	96
4.2 The Alabaster Coast	103
4.3 The route of reconstruction	111
Additional Information	123

FEATURE BOXES

A Personal View of Dieppe	96
Getting there	97
Top tips for Dieppe	97
Don't give up the day job	100
Footnote!	102
Top tips for the Alabaster Coast	104
The artists' church	106
The monk's concoction	108
Homage to the liberators	110
Top tips for the Route of Reconstruction	112
Different impressions	114
The story of Joan of Arc	116
Flaubert's parrot	118
The artist becomes a gardener	119
The Monet of Gerberoy	121

Le Havre, the Côte Fleurie and Chartres **128**

5.1 Le Havre and the Cote Fleurie 128
5.2 A visit to Chartres 137
Additional Information 144

Feature boxes

Top tips for Le Havre and the
Côte Fleurie 129
Concrete proposals 130
A volcanic eruption 131
Silver ladies and ugly ducklings 134
Costume change 135
Top tips for Chartres 138
Pilgrims' progress 140
The sound of music 143

A quick guide to Paris **150**

6.1 A selection of dos 151
6.2 A few don'ts 154

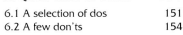

Cherbourg, Bayeux, D-Day landing beaches and Caen **160**

Additional Information 171

Feature boxes

Getting there 160
Top tips for Cherbourg, Bayeux,
D-Day landing beaches and Caen 161
Pipe down! 162
Elliptical thinking 164
D-Day landings 167
A man and a woman 170

St Malo, Dinard, Dinan and Mont St Michel **174**

Additional Information 180

Feature boxes

Getting there 174
Top tips for St Malo, Dinard, Dinan
and Mont St Michel 175
Popping to Britain for the day 177
Clones on the beach 178
Mirror image 179

FACT FILE

Accommodation 182
Disabled visitors 184
Driving in France 184
Electricity 185
Health 186
Measurements 186
Money 186
Outdoor activities 186
Passports for pets 187
Postage 187
Public holidays 187
Telephones 187
Time 188
Tipping 188
Tourist information offices 188
Travelling across the Channel 188

INDEX **189**

Above left: Beach huts, Calais. *Above right:* Looking down the Opal Coast from Cap Blanc-Nez. *Below:* Rodin's Burghers of Calais.

Above: Canal quarter of St Omer. *Below:* café culture, Lille.

Above left: Swimming pool in Town Square, St Quentin. *Above right:* The beach, St Quentin. *Below left:* Loan Cathedral. *Below right:* Joan of Arc, Reims.

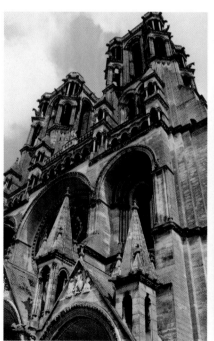

Above left: 'Reims Cathedral'.

Above right: The Basilica from Rue de Lille, Boulogne.

Below: View from the Town walls, Boulogne.

Above: Port de Plaissance, Dieppe.

Left: Pont d'Aval arch, Étretat.

Opposite page

Top left: British Cemetery.

Top right: Poppies.

Middle right: Houses in Arras.

Bottom: Amiens cathedral.

Above: Rouen. *Opposite page:* Monet's Garden, Giverney.

Introduction

From the very moment travellers step or drive into France from their train or ferry, they realise that they have entered another world. The patchwork-quilt appearance of the British countryside, with its network of hedgerows and walls, is replaced by a vast mosaic of unenclosed fields stretching to far horizons. Changes in the built environment are equally noticeable: almost every dwelling in France is characterised by elegant proportions and an imaginative use of local materials; mansard roofs make an appearance; shutters are far more common than they are in Britain and their purpose is functional rather than decorative.

Britain and France both have a wealth of castles and country houses, but the French make very little distinction between the two types of building, using the word 'château' to describe both the forts of the Middle Ages and the Renaissance houses of the aristocracy, many of which retain defensive elements, such as battlements and turrets, as ornamental features. The great Gothic cathedrals of Britain and France share a common ancestry, but they are very different in appearance. Whereas British cathedrals are long, French cathedrals are high; whereas British Gothic developed into a unique Perpendicular style; French Gothic evolved into the Flamboyant.

STYLE

Anyone driving through France cannot fail to notice that most French drivers, unlike their British counterparts, buy cars which are made in their own country. One can hardly blame them, because at a time when many of the world's leading car manufacturers are content to turn out characterless 'world cars,' French car designers continue to produce vehicles with unique features and quirky contours.

French people are much less inhibited than the British. They not only have a language that is wonderfully expressive, but they also make unrestrained use of gesture as a means of communication. They also dress well, have a natural sense of style and they are willing to set aside periods of the day for conversation with family and friends. Meals in France are rarely seen as snatched necessities, but rather as opportunities for an exchange of gossip and ideas, as well as the slow enjoyment of good food and wine.

All these differences highlight the fact that Britain and France have remained stubbornly resistant to infection in a world threatened by a plague of uniformity. Although the two countries are now linked by a tunnel, they remain worlds apart. Crossing the Channel may well have become easy and even common-place, but it is still an exciting experience, because it is a journey to another world.

THE CHANNEL COAST

All the French Channel ports are interesting places in themselves. Even much-maligned Calais has now been smartened up and is making the most of its historical legacy; Boulogne has a wonderful Old Town, completely surrounded by ramparts; Dieppe is not only France's oldest port, but also one of the oldest holiday resorts in the world; modern Le Havre is a famous example of planned post-War reconstruction and was designed by a very significant twentieth-century architect; Cherbourg has also risen again from wartime devastation and St Malo has a complete circuit of seventeenth-century ramparts which proved to be strong enough to remain intact after a sustained bombardment with twentieth-century weaponry.

The coastline that links these ports is known by a series of evoca-

Above: Laon, town gate.

tive names, such as the Opal Coast, the Alabaster Coast, the Flower Coast and the Mother of Pearl Coast, names that reflect both natural and man-made beauty. Natural formations, such as the headland of Cap Blanc Nez, near Calais, and the stack rocks and rock arches of Étretat are among the most spectacular coastal features to be found anywhere, but the entire coast has long been a magnet for artists, and the Alabaster Coast can even claim to be the cradle of Impressionism.

The craze for sea-bathing also had its origins on this coast, at a time when the coming of the railways allowed Le Tout Paris to migrate to the Channel coast. Purpose-built seaside towns, such as Le Touquet, Deauville, Trouville and Cabourg, were once among the most fashionable resorts in the whole of France. Even today, they retain the elegance and grandeur that characterised them in their heyday, but they also manage to offer every facility to the modern holidaymaker.

Above: Rouen cathedral.

INLAND FROM THE COAST

Splendid architecture is not confined to the coast. Superb man-made structures of all kinds are to be found in the hinterland. Within three hours' drive of the Channel ports are some of the greatest cathedrals in the entire world. Chartres, Amiens, Beauvais, Laon, Reims, Rouen and Paris (Notre Dame) are all very beautiful and highly influential examples of Gothic architecture, and they all lie within the scope of this guidebook.

The cities of northern France are magical places too. Paris is rightly celebrated as one of the world's most romantic and attractive capital cities, but other northern cities have surprising qualities. The atmosphere of Lille is a heady mix of Paris and Brussels; Laon has the largest architectural heritage area of any city in France, and the heart of one of the cities on our itineraries is converted into a vast sandy beach in the summer months, even though it is one hundred miles from the sea – such a metamorphosis could only take place in France!

The villages are surprising too. Most people associate beautiful French villages with the hot and sunny areas of Provence and the Dordogne, but there are some very special villages and small towns within three hours' drive of the Channel ports, including inland places like Gerberoy, Cassel, Cleres and Montreuil, and coastal settlements like Honfleur, Varengeville and Cancale.

15

SPECIAL ATTRACTIONS

The area included in this guidebook also encompasses three of the most visited attractions in France, outside Paris: Mont St Michel; the Bayeux Tapestry and Monet's garden at Giverny. Monet planted his garden in order to use it as a subject in his paintings, many of which can be seen in the art galleries of northern France. Almost every town and city on our itineraries has a splendid collection of paintings and other works of art, not least because so many of the world's greatest artists were born in France. Not just art galleries, but museums of all types, are found in abundance throughout northern France. Most are characterised by highly imaginative displays and many are devoted to the country's experience in the two world wars of the twentieth century.

Northern France was a major battlefield in both wars. The fields of the Somme became a graveyard for almost an entire generation from Europe's great nations, the Normandy beaches saw an assault that changed the course of history, and the V1 and V2 rocket sites, which are concentrated near the northern Channel ports, could so easily have changed the history of World War II if they had been used earlier. Visits to all these places and the many battlefields, memorials and war museums are evocative and moving experiences.

Many of the cities of northern France were battered, bruised and burnt in the two world wars, but they have all risen, Phoenix-like, from the ashes. Old buildings have been renovated, new ones have been erected, mostly with typical French flair, and welcoming and cheerful pedestrian areas have been created,

Northern France may not have the guaranteed hot and sunny weather of the South, but within three hours' drive of the Channel ports there is a wealth of art and architecture, coastal and inland scenery, historical sites and modern attractions that would be hard to match anywhere in Europe. Modern cross-Channel transport has brought this exciting region within very easy reach of Britain, but it remains a land that is so very different from our own country. Vive la Différence!

Above: An eclectic mix of posters, Rouen.

1
Calais, the Opal Coast and French Flanders

1.1 A TOUR OF CALAIS

Many readers will remember the days when cross-Channel travellers felt the need to prepare for their journey by taking a dose of sea-sickness pills and motorists entering France through the port of Calais emerged into a cloud of nasty-smelling smoke belching from a quayside industrial complex. Entry to the Route Nationale involved the negotiation of confusing road junctions and a tortuous journey through busy streets lined with tiny and somewhat shabby terraced houses.

Calais was hardly a promising introduction to France in those days and many first-time British visitors must have decided, there and then, that it would be the very last place they would ever choose as a base for a French holiday. However, times have changed: crossing the Channel is a very different experience today and the old town of Calais has acquired a bright new image.

Cross-Channel ferries have become larger, more luxurious and they are much less likely to roll with the waves. For those who prefer to avoid the sea completely, there is now the simple option of a 35-minute trip through the Eurotunnel. Getting to France has never been easier.

Entering France from the port is also much more straightforward these days. Motorists disembarking at both the ferry port and the Eurotunnel terminal can now gain immediate access to the A16 and A26 autoroutes and zoom off to the sunny South without touching the streets of Calais at all. As a result,

Calais is no longer the first port of call for most people taking Continental motoring holidays. However, many visitors to Europe do leave the autoroute on their return journey, in order to visit **Cité Europe**, the huge out-of-town shopping complex that has been constructed at **Coquelles**, near the Eurotunnel terminal.

Goods on sale at Cité Europe include : a big range of men's, ladies' and children's fashions; shoes; beauty products; home furnishings; gifts; toys; sports and leisure goods; spectacles and photographic materials. Very in-expensive wine and beer is in plentiful supply. There is a large selection at the Carrefour hypermarket and at a branch of Victoria Wine, but the Tesco Vin Plus outlet contains France's largest selection of wine from all over the world. Customers are known to queue at empty shelves in the hope of being first in line to grab bottles from the next delivery!

There is free parking space for 3,500 cars, but visitors towing their

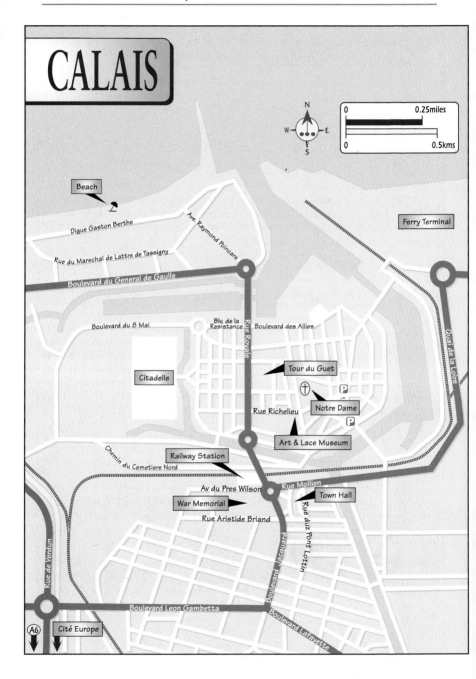

CALAIS

0   0.25miles

0   0.5kms

N
W   E
S

Beach

Digue Gaston Berthe

Ave. Raymond Poincare

Rue du Marechal de Lattre de Tassigny

Ferry Terminal

Boulevard du General de Gaulle

Boulevard du 8 Mai

Blv. de la
Resistance   Boulevard des Allies

Rue Royale

Quai de la Loire

Citadelle

Tour du Guet

Notre Dame

Rue Richelieu

Art & Lace Museum

Chemin du Cemetiere Nord

Railway Station

Rue Mollien

Av du Pres Wilson

Town Hall

War Memorial

Rue Aristide Briand

Rue duz Pont Lottin

Boulevard Jacquard

Rue de Verdun

Boulevard Leon Gambetta

Boulevard Lafayette

A6

Cité Europe

Getting there

Cross Channel ferries are operated by the following companies:

P&O Stena Line
Crossing time about 75 minutes.
Every 45 minutes at peak times.
☎ 0870 600600
www.posl.com

Sea France
Crossing time about 90 minutes.
Every 90 minutes at peak times.
☎ 0870 571 1711
www.seafrance.com

Hoverspeed operate a Super Seacat
Crossing time about 35 minutes.
Hourly.
☎ 0870 240241
www.hoverspeed.com

Eurotunnel operate car-carrying trains from Folkestone
Crossing time about 35 minutes
Every 15 minutes.
☎ 0990 353535
www.eurotunnel.com

Eurostar operate passenger-carrying trains through the tunnel, some of which stop at Calais.

In order to reach the town centre from the terminals, drivers should follow Toutes Directions and Centre Ville signs and foot passengers should board free buses from the ferry port to Calais centre.

TOP TIPS FOR CALAIS

Not to be missed
- Rodin's statue of The Burghers of Calais
- The Town Hall
- Museum of War
- Museum of Fine Arts and Lace
- Tour Guet

Things to do
- Take a walking tour from the Boulevard Lafayette to the sea-front
- Have a drink in one of the bars in and around the Rue Royale
- Have a meal in one of Calais' many restaurants
- Visit the Cité Europe shopping complex. Perhaps spend an entire day there!
- Fill up your car boot with bargain booze from one of the beer and wine and cash-and-carry outlets
- Tour the lighthouse
- Visit the Citadelle
- Shop for lace and other souvenirs
- Hire a bike (near the lighthouse)
- Visit the church where General de Gaulle tied the knot
- Watch the boats go by from the fishing jetty
- Relax or play volleyball or boules on the beach
- Walk along the promenade
- Eat ice cream while sitting on a seat overlooking the sea

own caravans are required to park in an uneven gravel-covered car park, where conditions for pushing a heavy trolley laden with bottles are far from ideal. The Caravan Club ought to complain about discrimination against caravanners. Visitors to France hoping to stock up with beer and wine on their journey home should remember that the centre is closed on Sundays.

The chance to buy, all under one roof, the very latest fashions, jewellery, perfumes, chocolates and coffees makes Cité Europe an irresistible attraction for hypermarket addicts, and even those people who normally hate shopping in huge out-of-town complexes are drawn to the place by the opportunity of stocking up with lots of good wine and beer at ridiculously low prices.

Except on Sundays, when it is closed, Cité Europe is always teeming, not only with returning holiday makers, but also with day trippers from southern England, who now seem to regard the place as their local supermarket. It seems certain that many visitors making one-day shopping expeditions to Cité Europe spend their entire day in the place and never set foot in the real France at all. But would shoppers find it worth their while to emerge from this warm, brightly-lit, well-equipped cocoon into the old French port of Calais?

Cité Europe

Cité Europe, the huge shopping complex which is located at Coquelles, 3 miles (5km) from the heart of Calais and close by the Eurotunnel terminal, is effectively an entire city centre under one roof. There are 11 supermarkets, a huge Carrefour hypermarket, 150 shops, 12 cinemas and 30 eating places ranging from fast food outlets to up-market restaurants. Designers of the complex have made rather kitsch efforts to produce a genuinely European centre. Many of the restaurants are set around Place de Lisbonne, a mock-Continental square, complete with pavement cafés and a fountain. Buildings along different sections of the perimeter represent, with varying degrees of accuracy, styles of architecture from a range of European countries. Large illustrated wall plaques near one of the first floor toilet blocks contain descriptions of the traditional cuisine of various European countries – the account of British food is not nearly as unfavourable as it might be, but this is probably a gesture of deference to the large number of British visitors.

Anyone prepared to make the effort of driving into the centre of Calais would immediately discover that the place has undergone a remarkable transformation. The narrow streets of terraced houses are still there although many of them have been pedestrianised. The town's main shopping street, which begins life as the Boulevard Jacquard and evolves into the Rue Royale, has been smartened up with the introduction of neat paving, splendid floral displays and the installation of wonderfully informative heritage boards, with descriptions in English, as well as French. Most of the town's architecture, which results from hasty post-war reconstruction, is far from pretty, but some remarkable individual buildings have survived the bombardments which Calais has suffered over the centuries, and the town's shops, bars and restaurants are very inviting indeed. There is much of historical interest in this ancient Channel port, which also contains two very interesting and unusual museums. In addition, Calais has a little known asset in its fine and very extensive sandy beach, which is backed by a splendid promenade with all the trappings one would expect to find in a French seaside resort

THE STORY OF CALAIS

Before paying a visit to this greatly underrated town, it is worth taking a brief look at its turbulent history.

Until 1885, Calais consisted of two distinct townships: the old **Port of Calais** and the newer industrial township, known as **St-Pierre**, immediately south of the old town. In the thirteenth century, the port area was developed as a fortified town and a conduit for the wool trade between Britain and Flanders, but it suffered greatly in the Hundred Years War at the hands of Edward III. He put Calais under siege after his victory at Crécy, in 1346. Faced with starvation, the citizens finally capitulated one year later and, it is said, were only spared from massacre by the bravery of six leading citizens who surrendered to the King in return for assurances that the people of the town would not be harmed.

By 1453 England had lost most of its possessions in France, but they retained possession of Calais until 1558. Then 30,000 troops, commanded by the Duke of Guise, captured the town for the French crown, much to the distress of Mary Tudor, who is said to have cried, "When I am dead and opened, you shall find Calais lying in my heart."

Given its strategic position, it is hardly surprising that Calais found itself in the thick of many subsequent conflicts. The town saw action during France's battles with Spain for control of Flanders. The Spanish army actually captured Calais in 1596 and there were further battles in the area in 1638 and 1651. Much greater horrors were to befall the town in the twentieth century, after it had undergone considerable industrial development in the nineteenth century and evolved into a centre for machine lace production, largely thanks to lacemakers from Nottingham who had settled in the town. In fact, the township of St-Pierre, with its factories and terraced streets of workers' housing, is largely a British creation.

The port area and St-Pierre were united as one town in 1885 and Calais became a thriving port and manufacturing centre. At that time, the town contained some unique vestiges of Tudor architecture from the two hundred year occupation by the English, but most of this was swept away in the conflicts of the twentieth century. Calais was an important British base in World War I and consequently suffered heavy bombardment in the bombing raids of 1917 and 1918, and it was once again in the thick of the action during World War II. In May 1940, just before the British Expeditionary Force was evacuated from Dunkerque, the Green Jackets fought an heroic last ditch battle alongside French troops, who were also besieged in the town. Four years later, Canadian troops spearheaded the assault that liberated Calais from the Germans.

The thirteenth-century **Tour du Guet**, which will be encountered on a tour of the town, has witnessed and suffered from many bombardments over the centuries. It remains standing as an evocative monument to Calais' turbulent history.

A WALK THROUGH THE TOWN

Parking is fairly easy in Calais. There is a good deal of on-street parking and there are car parks along the sea front, at the railway station, which is immediately west of the Town Hall, and also near Boulevard Lafayette, where the walking tour begins. The street, which has patisseries, charcuteries, bars and restaurants, leads to **Boulevard Jacquard**, which is where Calais' larger stores are found. The Royal Dentelle is excellent for lingerie, lace goods and other lace souvenirs, but the boulevard offers many other opportunities for buying souvenirs, clothes, household furnishings and, as one would expect in northern France, delicious cakes, bread and cheeses.

Boulevard Jacquard ends at the large **Hôtel de Ville** (Town Hall), overlooking a big open space, which

The Burghers of Calais

After his victory at Crécy on 26 August 1346, Edward III put Calais under siege for a whole year. Exhausted and facing starvation, the townspeople finally ended their resistance on 4 August 1347, but the English king, who was obviously determined to make the most of his victory, would only agree to spare the people of Calais if six leading citizens would come dressed as beggars to present the keys of the town to him.

Eustache de St-Pierre, Pierre and Jacques de Wissant, Jean d'Aire, Jean de Fiennes and Andrieu d'Andres bravely volunteered to meet the king's wishes and prevent a massacre of citizens. Rodin's sculpture shows them arriving in the king's presence dressed only in their nightshirts. Edward fully intended to execute them, but Queen Philippa d'Hainault pleaded for their lives and obtained their reprieve at the last minute. Although the citizens of Calais were saved from massacre by this brave act, they were evicted from their homes and their town remained in English hands for over 200 years.

once had the forlorn appearance of a no-man's land, but is now beautifully paved and adorned with colourful and well-tended gardens. The Town Hall, which has an elaborate, Flemish-style façade and a clock tower with an uncanny resemblance to Big Ben, forms an impressive backdrop to Rodin's great sculpture **The Burghers of Calais**, which depicts the six leading citizens who surrendered to Edward III in 1347, in order to save the townspeople from persecution. Rodin's sculpture, which makes deliberate and clever use of rough surfaces and uneven execution,

depicts the drama and emotion of the episode far more accurately than some standard heroic sculpture of the period could have done. Rodin's sculpture portrays a range of emotions: some of the burghers show despair, while others show defiance.

Immediately west of the Town Hall gardens, there is an interesting and highly informative **Museum of War**, which is housed in a German bunker and largely concentrates on depictions of life in Calais during World War II, but also has some exhibits from World War I.

Calais' two museums

Calais has two somewhat unusual, but very interesting museums. The Museum of War is housed, rather surprisingly, in a former command post of the German navy, situated in St-Pierre Park, close to the Town Hall. The exhibits, which include artefacts, models, reconstructions, posters, newspapers and videos, tell the story of Calais in World War II from the arrival of the British Expeditionary Force. Major episodes include: the last stand of the Green Jackets in 1940, the evacuation at Dunkerque, the Battle of Britain, the German use of the Lindemann long range gun from their Calais coastal defences and the liberation of Calais in 1944. One of the more macabre exhibits is a collection of fragments from aircraft shot down in the region. The wartime activities of General de Gaulle are recorded in the museum and there are some souvenirs of the World War I.

The Museum of Fine Arts and Lace, on Rue Richelieu, immediately east of the Rue Royale, has a large collection of lace produced by Calais' famous lace-makers. It is surprising to find that machine lace-making was introduced to Calais largely by Nottingham lace-makers in the nineteenth century. There are also paintings on display, but the collection is a rather odd mixture of seventeenth- and eighteenth-century paintings, pictures by local primitive artists and a few works by modern masters such as Derain and Picasso. Some sculpture is also on show and Rodin's preliminary studies for the *Burghers of Calais* are particularly fascinating to those visitors who have admired the great statue outside Calais' Town Hall, or even to those who have only seen the copy by the Embankment in London!

Eccentric topiary

The traffic island near the Town Hall is adorned with superb floral displays and highly eccentric examples of topiary, which bear an uncanny resemblance to the giant topiaries produced as works of art by the American artist Jeff Koons. In recent times, an enormous, highly colourful peacock, fashioned entirely from flowers and greenery has been sitting proudly on the traffic island.

By dodging the traffic that circulates almost incessantly at this intersection, enter the road known as Rue Clémenceau, soon evolving into the **Rue Royale**, which makes a long approach to the sea front. All the way to the front, there are restaurants, bars, souvenir outlets and both bargain and quality shops. Not surprisingly, seafood is a speciality of many of the restaurants in the port area, but all tastes and all pockets are catered for. Some eating places, such as fish and chip shops and bars that include "pub" in their name, are obviously aimed at those British visitors who have a fear of unfamiliar foreign food and drink. However, trippers would be well advised to avoid such places, not only because it seems rather absurd to visit France without sampling its legendary cuisine, but also because British food and drinks are generally more expensive in French restaurants and cafés than the Gallic options. There is an enormous choice of drinking and eating places on the Rue Royale and also on some of its side streets (see Additional Information at the end of this chapter).

A short diversion to the left of the Rue Royale goes to the **Citadelle**, a vast array of fortifications which was first constructed in 1560 by the Duke of Guise, but which was still being used for defence in 1940. A diversion to the right of the Rue Royale leads to the Rue Richelieu, and the **Museum of Fine Arts and Lace**, which contains work by local lace-makers and a number of preliminary studies by Rodin for *The Burghers of Calais*, as well as other interesting exhibits. The Church of **Notre Dame** is also located to the right of the Rue Royale. The building is unusual in that it is fashioned in the English Perpendicular style and clearly dates from the period when the English occupied Calais, although it has been much altered and extended over the ensuing centuries. It is surprising to find that General de Gaulle, the man who repeatedly rejected English membership of the early Common Market, married Mademoiselle Vendroux in this most English of French churches, when he was a young officer. The **lighthouse**, which stands to the north of the church and has a 167ft (60m) tower, was erected in 1848. Guided tours of the building are available.

Returning to the Rue Royale, there are more towers: a mock-up of the Eiffel tower outside the Café de Paris, and then a real tower in the form of the thirteenth-century **Tour du Guet,** where the terms of the town's surrender to the English in 1347 were announced from the first floor window by Jean de Vienne, Governor of Calais. The tower has suffered repeated batterings during its long history: it was split in two by an earthquake in 1580; hit by an English cannonball in 1696; struck by German shells in 1940 and bombed by the allies in 1944. An eighteenth-century bell stands at the base of the tower, which has variously been used as a pigeon loft, a lighthouse and as part of an optical telegraphic system.

The Rue Royale then continues past a lively funfair on the Place d'Armes to a tiny harbour picturesquely littered with small boats, before terminating at the sea front, where cross-Channel ferries come and go almost as frequently as planes at Heathrow. The ferries can be viewed at fairly close quarters from a long, well-used fishing jetty that divides the ferry port from Calais' extensive and greatly underrated beach area.

The beach

The golden yellow sands contain long rows of white beach huts, of the sort that figure so prominently in French films. Although it can be somewhat windswept at times, the beach is almost always crowded in the summer months with sunbathers, children making sandcastles, teams of volleyball players and knots of people playing boules. No dogs are allowed on the beach in summer and this is emphasised by regular announcements from loud hailers. The promenade contains the usual plethora of snack and ice cream stalls and is backed by restaurants, all with a commanding view of the sea and of the passing ferries, which provide a never-ending source of fascination. All in all, Calais' seafront provides an unexpected but highly evocative glimpse of France-by-the-Sea. It should not be missed by any visitor to the town.

Bargain booze trips

As already noted, Calais has much more to offer the visitor than the cheap beer and wine to be found at Cité Europe, three miles (five kilometres) from its centre. But

entrepreneurs are all too aware that many British visitors do use the town as little more than a source of cheap booze and, as a result, many cash-and-carry outlets for wine and beer have been built in and around the town. Details are given in the Additional Information section at the end of this chapter.

Street markets

Visiting markets is one of the joys of holidaying in France. Calais has two stall markets. The market at Place Crévecouer, near Boulevard Lafayette, is held on Thursday and Saturday, and the street market at Place d'Armes takes place on Wednesday and Saturday

1.2 A DRIVE ALONG THE OPAL COAST

INTRODUCTION

The French are fond of assigning evocative names to various stretches of their magnificent coastline. The coast which runs south-west from Calais is known as the **Opal Coast**, a name that is said to have been coined by the painter Edouard Léveque, who was inspired by what he saw as the unique and ever changing light of the region. However, some French publications dispute this version and suggest that the name is simply an evocation of the cream coloured waves crashing against the white sands.

Whatever the truth of the matter, the Opal Coast is a wonderful stretch of coastline which embraces long stretches of sand interspersed with areas of dunes, two magnificent chalk headlands with commanding views across the Channel of the white cliffs of Kent, Belle Époque

TOP TIPS FOR THE OPAL COAST

Not to be missed

- Cap Blanc-Nez and Cap Gris-Nez – both offering the chance to stare nostalgically at England
- Museum of the Atlantic Wall, Audlinghen, which houses the huge gun that was used to bombard Britain
- Museum of World War II at Ambleteuse
- Fort Vauban at Ambleteuse

Things to do

- Play boules on the beach at Blériot-Plage
- Water-ski at Blériot-Plage
- Go sand-yachting at Sangatte
- Go horse riding at Sangatte
- Walk on the path between the two Caps
- Take a guided walk from Wissant to discover flora and fauna
- Pause for refreshment by the dolphin statue at Wissant
- Enjoy the beach at Wissant or Wimereux
- Go sail-karting or kayaking at Wissant
- Hire a pedal car at Wissant
- Go rock-pooling at Wimereux
- Visit the Wimereux Mussel Festival in late July
- Stroll along the prom to get the feel of a Belle Époque resort at Wimereux
- Visit the Tuesday market at Wimereux

seaside resorts, old fishing villages, a number of fascinating museums and a superb coastal path. There are lots of opportunities for energetic pursuits such as water skiing, sand-yachting, karting and kayaking.

The cliffs are littered with former wartime defences, and a pioneer of aviation and a pioneer of wireless used the Opal Coast to perform some of their most crucial experiments.

THE TOUR

At the western end of Calais' long beach, flat sands are replaced by an area of dunes, topped by a picturesque collection of beach huts. This area is known as **Blériot-Plage**, in memory of the pioneering flight across the Channel undertaken from this point by Blériot in 1909. Some 550yd (500m) from the centre of the little resort, there is a monument to the aviator. The locals often play boules at the foot of the dunes and groups of tourists do their best to emulate them. Those who prefer more energetic pursuits can hire water-skis in the area.

The Channel by plane

Louis Blériot was an engineer who was born in Cambrai in 1872. After turning his attention to aviation design, he built various types of aircraft, but then decided to stick with and champion the merits of the monoplane, which he improved by adding adjustable wings as an aid to stability. On 25 July 1909, only five years after the Wright brothers had made their first successful flight, he set out to prove the worth of his monoplane by attempting the first flight of a heavier-than-air machine across the English Channel. After setting off from a spot on the Opal Coast now known as Blériot-Plage, he arrived in Dover 30 minutes later. His aircraft, which had a three-cylinder engine and a 25ft (8m) wing span, is preserved in the Conservatoire des Arts, in Paris, and on the ninetieth anniversary of the historic flight, there was a re-enactment by Swedish pilot Mikael Carlson.

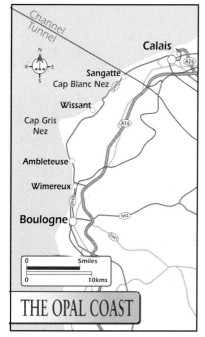

THE OPAL COAST

have made a dash for the Channel tunnel in an attempt to reach the UK. In the nineteenth century, Sangatte was identified as the French terminus of a projected Channel tunnel and some construction work actually took place near the resort, but the project was soon abandoned.

Water skiing and sand-yachting are both available at Sangatte and hiring details can be obtained from the tourist office.

After Sangatte, habitation gives way to wide rolling fields highly reminiscent of those which characterise the English Downs. Along this stretch of road it is easy to appreciate that France was joined to southern England until the waters swept in to create the Channel at the end of the last ice age, about 8,000 years ago.

The two Caps

The land rises dramatically to the magnificent chalk headland of **Cap Blanc-Nez**, which is crowned by a huge obelisk commemorating the Dover Patrol. On any fine day in summer, hundreds of people sit on the edge of the cliff and stare across at

Following the D904 along the coast to **Sangatte**, the beach huts gradually become grander until they evolve into beach villas. Recently, Sangatte has become well known as the site of a large refugee centre from where many displaced people the strange land of white cliffs, which is clearly visible across the Channel; others peer through the telescopes that are provided, perhaps even playing a little mental game of invasion planning.

The view westwards along the coast from Cap Blanc-Nez is just as dramatic as the view across the Channel to England. The neat, pretty village of **Escalles** occupies a hollow in the fields below the headland and the D940 can be seen twisting and turning as it drops down to the sea at Wissant. **Cap Gris-Nez** rises beyond the little resort and the coastline then snakes away to a misty horizon. It is a view to take the breath away.

Wissant

After taking the long descent to **Wissant**, enter the town by leaving the D940 and taking a narrow road littered with parked cars. Wissant is an old fishing village that has metamorphosed into a seaside resort. Some fishermen still operate from the town and search the seas for mussels, crabs, lobster and perch. Because the harbour silted up long ago, their boats have to be dragged up the beach by tractor. Many of the fishing boats are then parked in the back gardens of the fishermen's cottages and act as selling points for fresh fish. Wissant has a nice pavement café next to a prominent street sculpture of a dolphin. A long, tarmac-covered promenade is lined with flats, bars and cafés, all painted in light colours, and there is a fine, light-coloured sandy beach that gave the resort its name, which means "white sands". Pedal cars can be hired on the promenade and they are very popular with children and adults alike, with the result that promenading is somewhat hazardous for

pedestrians. At the eastern end of the resort, flat sands give way to dunes and there is a terrace café overlooking a yachting area. Sail-karts and kayaks can also be hired.

The resort, which is popular with French families, markets itself as the "Town Between the Two Caps", and it is possible to join guided walks from Wissant, which look at the flora and fauna of the two chalk headlands.

The road to Wimereux

The D940 now makes its undulating way to **Wimereux**, climbing past high dunes and the remains of wartime defences and dipping through coastal villages. A road off to the right leads to Cap Gris-Nez, which is the nearest point to England, with the Kent coast just 18.3 miles (29.5km) away. The headland, which contains a light-house and a coastal patrol station, is much favoured by "twitchers" who have a particular interest in monitoring the migration of birds.

Driving along the D940 two interesting war museums are encountered. The **Museum of the Atlantic Wall** at **Audinghen**, which is housed in a World War II bunker, contains, among many other items, one of the 35m-long guns that the Germans used to bombard the English coast. The **Museum of the Second World War** at **Ambleteuse** traces the history of World War II from the invasion of Poland to the Japanese surrender, through the use of over a hundred life-size models and thousands of objects from the armed forces.

Fort Vauban, a seventeenth-century fort constructed by Sébastien Vauban, Louis XIV's great expert in defensive fortifications, is also to be found on the sea front at Ambleteuse. It has an artillery tower and a horseshoe-shaped battery.

As the D904 drops into Wimereux, it passes some modern villas and flats, some of which have possibly been designed to resemble fishermen's cottages. Wimereux is a resort that was developed in the Belle Époque era and once had pretensions to be the "Nice of the North". The project was never quite completed but Wimereux does have a long promenade, some decent hotels and bars, and a beach, which is a mixture of flat sand, shingle and rock pools. There is a Tuesday market and an annual Mussel Festival in late July. Wimereux has the distinction of being the place from where Marconi made his first broadcast across the Channel.

The road to Boulogne

After Wimereux, the D904 climbs over a hill containing yet more remnants of wartime fortifications, before dropping down to **Boulogne**. Boulogne is entered past a long line of unattractive slab-like, sea-front buildings, many of which have obviously resulted from hasty and utilitarian post-war reconstruction. There is a good enough beach on the right, but it has a belching industrial complex as its incongruous backdrop. Upon reaching the middle of the lower town turn up the hill for the much more attractive and older upper town, which is described in the next chapter. Carry on past the Old Town, eventually to reach a new commercial centre and the access road to the A16 autoroute.

A quick return to Calais is possible along the autoroute, but the entertainment is not yet over, because the verges of this particular autoroute are adorned at frequent intervals with steel sculptures depicting people engaged in the various energetic pursuits on offer along the coast that has just been visited. All the sculptures are composed of inter-connecting two-dimensional surfaces covered in bright white paint. As a result, they look exactly like giant paper cutouts!

Marconi's hop across the Channel with radio waves

Guglielmo Marconi was born in Bologna in 1874, but he was half-Irish, his mother having been born in County Wexford. When he was in his early twenties, he became interested in wireless telegraphy and by 1895 he had succeeded in building an apparatus that could send signals over a few kilometres by using a directional antenna. After patenting his system in 1897, he set up his own wireless company in England and, two years later, gave a convincing demonstration of the value of his product by establishing a wireless link across the English Channel. Just two years after this success, he sent signals across the Atlantic. The Italian and British navies were quick to adopt Marconi's system and his ingenuity was recognized with the award of a Nobel Prize in 1909. During the World War I, when he was in charge of the Italian wireless service, he developed shortwave transmission as a means of sending secret messages.

1.3. A TOUR OF FRENCH FLANDERS

INTRODUCTION

This circular tour takes the visitor through land close to the Belgian border. The countryside and the towns take on much of the character of France's northern neighbour: the predominant building material is brick; there is a fair sprinkling of stepped gables and belfries with carillons; most towns have a Flemish-style central square and, near St Omer, there is a stretch of canal-side buildings that could have been lifted straight out of Bruges.

Even the people have adopted some Belgian habits: the most popular drink is beer; they consume heroic quantities of chocolate; they stage annual carnivals with giant papier mâché figures and they have a very definite fondness for living behind net curtains.

Although this border area has been under French rule since the late seventeenth century, it was ruled for a period by the Counts of Flanders and then by the Kings of Spain. During the last war, the region was under German occupation and it was here that the Germans built their bases for the VI and V2 rockets, weapons that had the potential to change the

---

TOP TIPS FOR FRENCH FLANDERS

Not to be missed

- The Field of the Cloth of Gold – just to get the feel of history taking place at this spot (there is actually nothing to see!)
- The German V2 bunker at Eperlecques
- The Square, St Omer
- The Cathedral, St Omer, especially the organ
- Exhibition of V1, V2 and space rockets at La Coupole
- 'View of the Five Kingdoms' from Cassel
- The walled town of Bergues
- The story of the 1940 evacuation told in the museum at Dunkerque

Things to do

- Go walking in Guines Forest
- Drink locally-brewed beer in St Omer
- Eat hand-made chocolates in St Omer
- Shop in the Saturday market at St Omer
- Eat traditional Flemish food in a St Omer restaurant
- See a re-creation of a Flemish kitchen in Musée Henri-Dupuis
- Watch the net curtains twitch in Cassel
- If you are here on Easter Monday, watch the traditional carnival in Cassel
- Drink Belgian beer at Cassel on a terrace overlooking Flanders' fields
- Cycle between Bergues and Dunkerque
- Inspect the seventeenth-century walls of Gravelines

course of the war, and the tour takes in two of these bases.

The journey also includes some major surprises. In the heart of this very flat land, there is a large village, built Provencal-style, at the top of a hill, and a town with an English-style cathedral close.

Although the tour takes the form of a car drive, it should be remembered that French Flanders is an area that is perfect for cycling and walking. If you are visiting this region, bring your bike and bring your boots!

A TOUR OF FRENCH FLANDERS

From Calais, take the D127 for **Guines**, a quiet, unassuming little place, but an excellent departure point for walks in **Guines Forest,** which occupies a large area of land between Ardres and Guines. There is an extensive array of footpaths that are very well marked.

FIELD OF THE CLOTH OF GOLD

The motor route follows the D231 from Guines in the direction of **Ardres**. Along the way, notice a simple plinth on the left which marks the **Field of the Cloth of Gold**, where Henry VIII and Francois I met for peace talks in 1520. Although this historic spot merits a large brown tourist sign on the nearby motorway, the commemorative stump of stone is very hard to spot and there is absolutely nowhere to park. In order to inspect the plinth, whose inscription is in English and French, there is little option but to pull onto the grass verge and then take one's life in one's hands to cross the road to the little monument by dodging the fast-moving traffic.

Royal posturing

In 1520, Henry VIII was invited to France by Francois I, who was keen to form an alliance with England against the Spanish. Henry stayed at Guines, then a border town in English-occupied Calais, and Francois stayed at Ardres, which was under French control.

Lavish tents were erected in "no man's land" between the two towns. Here the two kings met for several days, but the negotiations were fruitless and the two monarchs spent much of their time trying to outdo each other in a contest of flamboyant dress.

The field where the two kings met has become known as the Field of the Cloth of Gold and a re-enactment of the event takes place each year in Guines.

Eperlecques

At Ardres, join the N43 for St Omer. After passing through Nordausques, keep a careful look-out for a left turn to **Eperlecques**. After following a narrow country lane, lined with pretty cottages, eventually a sign on the left indicates the **Bunker d'Eperlecques**, where there is an interesting museum. A memorial at the gate commemorates the dead of all the nations who participated in the last war and the flags of Britain, France and Germany fly side-by-side at the entrance way. The theme of peace and reconciliation is continued inside the building, even though the museum is based around an enormous 72ft- (22m) high bunker which was

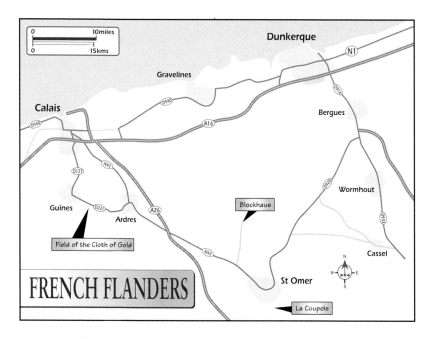

constructed by the Germans in 1943 to house the V2 rockets that were targetted on London. The bunker, which was built by POWs, was actually designed to be three times higher than its present height but, during its construction, the site was discovered by the RAF, who sent 187 bombers across the Channel to fatally damage the base that could so easily have changed the course of the war.

St Omer

Return now to the N43 and continue to **St Omer**. Many British visitors to France must have seen the sign to St Omer on the autoroute and dismissed the town as a northern industrial centre unworthy of a detour. In fact, St Omer is very worthy of a visit: it has a delightful central square, some flamboyant Flemish buildings, a superb basilica, two good museums and some very inviting cafés which dispense the excellent locally-produced beer.

The central square, **Place Maréchal Foch**, has plenty of pay-and-display car parking places (except on Saturday, which is market day). The square is overlooked by a large, four-square Classical **Hôtel de ville**, which has rusticated stone work and is topped, rather incongruously, by a wide, but squat dome, which in turn has a little tower supporting clocks on all four faces. The roof also carries a large neon-lit sign that beams out the name of the town. Many of the buildings that surround the square have very distinctive, steeply-pitched tiled roofs punctuated with dormers. There are also some Dutch gables and the eighteenth-century **Hotel de Bailliage**, which stands on the northern side of the square. Once the palace of justice and now a bank, it has a wonderfully elaborate façade, which is adorned with pilasters, balconies and sculptures.

33

A palace of justice

St Omer's Hotel du Bailliage, in Place Maréchal Foch, was originally the King's Tribunal, and was used in struggles against local aldermen. It then became a local court. The French tend to call such buildings Palaces of Justice and this St Omer building merits the title because it really is palatial: it has pilasters with Doric capitals, balconies, stone reliefs modelled in the shape of garlands of flowers, and four statues representing Justice (blindfolded and holding the Tables of Law in one hand and a rod in the other), Prudence (with a mirror), Temperance (with an upturned vase) and Strength (leaning on a column).

The building became a museum until it was bought by a bank in 1904. It is still in use as a bank.

La Belle Époque restaurant is tucked into the north-western corner of Place Maréchal Foch and there are many other cafés and restaurants on the perimeter of the square, all with pleasant pavement seating areas. Although Place Maréchal Foch has a distinctly Flemish appearance, the names on some of its cafés, including Le Dickens and the Queen Victoria, indicate a strong British link. In fact, the British army had its headquarters here in the first two years of World War I.

St Omer is France's largest brewing centre and, not surprisingly, plenty of excellent beer is available in the town's cafés, bistros and restaurants, another concentration of which can be found in Place Victor Hugo. Handmade chocolates are a local speciality and many restaurants serve up Flemish favourites, such as rabbit, dried fruits and eels. The town holds an extensive flea market in May and September and a flower market in May; there is a **Fine Arts Museum** (currently closed for renovation), with Flemish and Dutch paintings and a collection of earthenware, and a **Museum of Natural History** which, rather incongruously, contains a reconstructed Flemish kitchen.

Basilica of Notre Dame

A short walk from Place Maréchal Foch, down Rue Louis Martel, leads to the **Basilica of Notre Dame**, a massive church with a huge square tower and an unexpectedly English appearance and even an English-style "cathedral close". Unlike their English counterparts, most French cathedrals simply stand at the side of the street, along with every other building. One side of St Omer's basilica does indeed face the street, but the other side is quarantined from the bustle of the town by a picturesque English-style close, which is a haven of tranquillity.

The interior of the basilica contains one of the most fabulously ornate organs imaginable. It was constructed, from Danish oak, by the Piette brothers in 1717. Some gorgeous stained glass in the transepts and chancel compensates for a lack of stained glass in the nave, and there is an astronomical clock designed by Pierre Enguerran, who was a contemporary of Copernicus and Galileo. It has the Earth at its centre and the sun on the outside.

La Coupole

Three miles (5km) south of St Omer, on the road to Helfaut, there is another museum devoted to German rocketry. This modern museum, known as **La Coupole**, not only covers the development of the V1 and V2 rockets, but also traces Von Braun's subsequent career as the mastermind behind the American space programme.

Journey into space

Wernher von Braun was an enthusiast of space from his teens when he saw an article by the pioneer rocket theorist Hermann Oberth and came across an illustration of a rocket heading towards the moon. He became a member of Hitler's rocket development group at Peenemunde and designed the V2, which was, in effect, the world's first ballistic missile. The V2 rose into the stratosphere before plunging to its target and the only warning of its approach was the double boom as it broke the sound barrier shortly before impact. If RAF bombing of Peenemunde had not set back V2 development by some months, the V2 might have been ready before the Normandy landings and so changed the course of the war. RAF bombing of the launch pads in the Pas de Calais also meant that only mobile launchers could be used by the Germans. Even so, 1,000 V2s landed on Britain and another 2,000 were fired at European targets, particularly Antwerp.

At the end of the war, von Braun and 120 of his associates were taken to the United States of America and employed to develop weapons for the US Army. Von Braun went on to develop the Saturn V rocket that put the first man on the moon in 1969.

Cassel

After returning to St Omer, take the D928 towards Bergues. It is important to keep an eye out for road signs, because some of the junctions are a little confusing. This road runs alongside the canal on the northern edge of St Omer. The low, brick-built, canal-side houses are delightful and the whole scene, which looks like a cameo of Bruges, is very picturesque and highly photogenic. It is possible to hire boats or take a conducted trip along the canals (see Additional Information).

Before reaching Bergues, take a right turn towards **Cassel** (the sign is easily missed). When a cross-roads is reached, continue straight ahead, even though there is no sign to Cassel at the junction. After driving over a very bumpy level-crossing, begin the climb up to the large hill village, which is, of course, a totally unexpected feature in this largely flat land.

Approaching the summit, there are wonderful views over the surrounding countryside. According to an old local saying, five Kingdoms are visible from Cassel – France, Belgium, Holland, England and, above the clouds, the Kingdom of God. On a clear day, it is possible to see landmarks which are 37 miles (60km) away and there are even claims that the tower on Les Halles in Bruges can be spotted in the distance. Several viewing platforms in the public gardens give visitors ample opportunity to put these claims to the test.

The town is dominated by a massive, but very plain, brick-built church. In a manner typical of a Flemish Hallekerk, the interior has three naves, rather than a nave and two aisles. There is a distinct lack of decoration except for an elaborate organ, which is highly reminiscent of that in St Omer. The church has been much altered and re-built over the years and seems to be in need of constant renovation. The Jesuit church, nearby, has also undergone a recent wholesale renovation.

Cassel is a little run-down and rather shabby in places, but it has a reconstructed windmill, a nice cobbled market square and lots of whitewashed, brick-built houses, almost all of which have net curtains in their windows – look out for them twitching when walking past or, more especially, as you stop and stare. There is a stall market on Thursday and a carnival on Easter Monday, when giant papier mâché figures, which are a characteristic feature of local festivals, are paraded through the streets.

Given its strategic, hill-top location, it is hardly surprising to find that Cassel has often found itself in the thick of battle. The Romans built a walled encampment here; the town suffered in the wars between France and Flanders; the Duke of York marched 10,000 men up to the top of the hill and down again in 1793; Maréchal Foch had his headquarters in the building which now houses the **Museum of History, Art and Folklore** and Cassel saw some particularly bloody fighting in 1940 when the Germans were pushing the

British Expeditionary Force back to Dunkerque.

Turning away from bellicose matters, the T'Kasteelhof restaurant has lots of Belgian beers and a terrace with splendid views over Flanders.

From here drop down the D919 to **Wormhout**, which is less spectacularly located but much neater than Cassel. It too has a massive church and some nice houses – also with net curtains!

Bergues

The D218 arrives at **Bergues**, a walled and partly moated town with very impressive gates and a high belfry that was reconstructed after the original sixteenth-century tower was destroyed in 1944. There has been a great deal of reconstruction in Bergues but the neat buildings of pale brick give it the appearance of a very attractive seventeenth-century Dutch town. Sitting to enjoy a drink in one of Bergues' cafés and soaking up the atmosphere and appearance of the surroundings, it becomes very apparent that the border with the Low Countries is close by.

Dunkerque

The D916 passes through typical Flanders countryside to **Dunkerque**. During the twentieth century, this large coastal town was bombed to pieces on more than one occasion. Unfortunately, much of the post-war re-building work took the form of repetitive concrete blocks arranged in a monotonous grid pattern, and the more recent high-rise buildings have done little to improve the appearance of the place. But Dunkerque does have an impressive neo-Gothic church, a massive belfry, which contains the tourist office, an excellent **Musée des Beaux Arts**, with works of art by Flemish and Dutch masters, some models of ships, including an early paddle steamer, a Delft tile panel depicting the bombardment of the port in 1695, and a basement devoted to the evacuation of the British Expeditionary Force in 1940.

In the minds of most British people, the beach at Dunkerque is still associated with a heroic mass evacuation, but anyone whose knowledge of the place has been confined to black-and-white photographs of serpentine lines of thousands of troops queuing up on the beach for the little ships to arrive, will be amazed to find that Dunkerque is a very popular holiday resort with all the usual hotels, cafés, snack bars, ice cream stalls, amusement arcades and play areas. The beach is adorned with long rows of highly colourful beach huts, some with distinctive wavy decorations, and the resort seems to be particularly popular with young people, many of whom roller-blade at a terrifying rate up and down the long promenade. Lots of youngsters are in the habit of cycling to the promenade and parking their bikes on the beach, where they gather in pairs for canoodling or in groups for secretive conversation.

Visitors from Britain who have brought their cycles with them will find the whole area explored on the French Flanders tour ideal for cycling.

Return now to Calais by following the coast road, which passes through the town of **Gravelines**, with its ramparts and church from the sixteenth century, or take the fast option of the A16 autoroute.

The Dunkirk spirit

In May 1940, the British Expeditionary Force and the First French Army found themselves trapped between Bock's army group in the north and Rundstedt's in the south. The Germans planned to encircle the retreating armies, but they were thwarted by Operation Dynamo. This was the remarkable evacuation from the beaches of Dunkerque of 338,226 British and French troops between 27 May and 4 June. The troops were ferried across the Channel by a shuttle service of 765 ships of all shapes and sizes, but the escape was also aided by Hitler's bizarre decision to halt Rundstedt's tanks just a few miles from Dunkerque. Some believe that Goering had advised Hitler to take this step because he wanted the Luftwaffe to complete the victory over England rather than the army; others think Hitler wanted to save his troops for the battle for Paris, believing that the British would come to terms with Germany if France surrendered.

ACCOMMODATION

CALAIS

Hotels

***Le Copthorne
Modern, with health club and pool.
In woods near Cité Europe
☎ 0321 466060

***Le George V
Centrally located. Traditional, but
renovated and with reasonable
prices. Two restaurants
☎ 0321 976800

***Holiday Inn Garden Court
Near the port. Gym. Inexpensive
restaurant
☎ 0321 346969

***Métropol
Traditional hotel near Town Hall.
Reasonable prices.
☎ 0321 975400

***Meurice
Grand eighteenth-century hotel,
reconstructed after destruction in
1940
☎ 0321 345703

2-star hotels in Calais include the following:

**Belle Vue
On the Place d'Armes
☎ 0321 968890

** Climat de France
On Digue Gaston Berthe
☎ 0321 343539

**Hotel Ibis
on Boulevard Jacquard
☎ 0321 968989

**Hotel Pacific
Small, near Rue Royale
☎ 0321 345024

Budget choice

Also, those seeking budget
accommodation in small, but clean
rooms with TV and shower, could
choose:

Formule I
near Cité Europe
☎ 0321 968989

OPAL COAST

Wimereux

***Hotel Atlantic
Digne de Mer
☎ 0321 324101

**Hotel Speranza
Rue Général de Gaulle
☎ 0321 324212

Wissant

**Hotel Bellevue
Rue P. Crampel
☎ 0321 324108

*Hotel Normandy
Place de Verdun
☎ 0321 359011

Camp site

There is an excellent site for touring
caravans at Guines (10 miles [16km]
from Calais):

****La Bien Assise
with shop, swimming pool, take-
away restaurant, member of Castels
chain
☎ 0321 352077

FRENCH FLANDERS

Bergues

**Hotel du Tonnelier
Rue du Mondayt de Piété
☎ 0328 686037

**Hotel Amaris
Place de la Gare
☎ 0321 570767

DUNKERQUE

***Hotel Borel
Rue de l'Hermitte
☎ 0328 665180

***Europ'Hotel
Rue du Leugheaer
☎ 0328 662907

***Welcome Hotel
Rue Poincaré
☎ 0328 592070

SAINT OMER

***Hotel de Bretagne
Place du Vainquai
☎ 0321382578

ATTRACTIONS

CALAIS

Light house
Open: Oct–May: Monday to Friday 2–
5.30pm. Saturday, Sunday: 10am–
12noon, 2–5pm. June–Sept:
Monday–Friday 2– 6.30pm. Saturday,
Sunday: 10am–12noon, 2–6.30pm
☎ 0321 343334

Museum of Fine Arts and Lace
On Rue Richelieu, east of Rue Royale
Open: Monday, Wednesday, Friday:
10am–12noon, 2–5.30pm. Saturday:
10am–12noon, 2–6.30pm Sunday: 2–
6.30pm
☎ 0321 464848

Museum of War
In St-Pierre Park,
opposite Town Hall
Open: February, March, October,
November: Monday, Wednesday,
Sunday 11am–5pm April–September:
Monday, Wednesday, Sunday: 10am–
6pm
☎ 0321 342157

OPAL COAST

**Museum of the Atlantic Wall,
Audlinghen**
Open: February, March, October
9am–12noon, 2–6pm. April–
September 9am–7pm
☎ 0321 329733

**Museum of the Second World War,
Ambleteuse**
Open: April–October 10am–1pm,
2–6pm. November–March 2–6pm
☎ 0321 873301

Fort Vauban, Ambleteuse
Open: April–October Sunday 3–7pm.
July, August: Saturday, Sunday,
Monday 3–7pm
For information ☎ 0320 546154

Water-skiing, Blériot-Plage
☎ 0321 351570

Horse riding, Sangatte
☎ 0618 973304

Sail-karting, Wissant
☎ 0321 858678

Kayak centre, Wissant
For information ring ☎ 0320 091302

FRENCH FLANDERS

Cassel

**Museum of Art, History
and Folklore**
Open: Wednesday–Sunday 2–6.30pm,
May–October
☎ 0328 405285

Dunkerque

Musée des Beaux Arts
Place du General de Gaulle
Open: 10am–12, 2–6pm. Closed
Tuesday.
☎ 0328 592165

Continued overpage

St Omer

La Coupole, museum of rocketry
at Helfaut
Open: April–September: 9am–7pm.
October–March: 10am–6pm
☎ 0321 930707

Eperlecques

German Blockhaus
Open: March–November. Variable
opening times!
☎ 0321 884422

St Omer

Boat trips on the canals
☎ 0321 391515 or
☎ 0321 951019

Musée Henri-Dupuis
Natural history and Flemish food.
Wednesday–Sunday 10am–12noon,
2–6pm
☎ 0321 382413

Musée Sandelin
Rue Carnot,
Paintings and earthenware.
Currently closed for renovation
☎ 0321 380094

EATING OUT

Calais has a very large number of
bars and restaurants. The following
is a small selection:

Aquar'Aile
Good fish dishes, overlooking sea
Rue Jean Moulin
☎ 0321 340000

Le Channel
Sea views
Boulevard de Résistance
☎ 0321 344230

Cote d'Argent
Local poultry dishes, overlooking
ferries
Digne Gaston Berthe
☎ 0321 346807

George V
Rue Royale
Two restaurants at two different
prices
☎ 0321 976800

La Grand Blue
Rue Avron
Sea food, near fish port
☎ 0321 979798

Histoire Ancienne
Rue Royale
Traditional brasserie
☎ 0321 341120

La Pléiade
Rue Jean Quehen
Good sea food, well served
☎ 0321 340370

Le Sole Meuniere
Boulevard de Résistance
Sea views
☎ 0321 344301

OPAL COAST

Blériot-Plage
Les Dunes
☎ 0321 345430

FRENCH FLANDERS

Bergues

Au Cornet d'Or
French dishes in timbered
restaurant
☎ 0328 686627

St Omer

La Belle Époque
Flemish specialities
☎ 0321 382293

La Bretagne
French and Flemish dishes
☎ 0321 382578

Les Frangins
Reasonable prices
☎ 0321 987278

Au Petit Saint-Pierre
Quai du Haut Point
☎ 0321 938401

SHOPPING

The main shopping streets in Calais are Boulevard Lafayette, Rue Jacquard and Rue Royale.
These streets contain a very comprehensive range of goods, both quality and bargain, and a good choice of gifts – lace is something to look for.
Cité Europe, next to the Eurotunnel terminal, has a Carrefour hypermarket, 11 supermarkets and 150 shops. Beer and wine at bargain prices can be purchased at Carrefour, Victoria Wines and at Tesco Vin Plus.
Other bargain beer and wine outlets include the following:
Auchun (A26, Junction 12 or 14), includes Sainsbury's Wine store (also a Nike factory outlet)
Beer Lovers Cash and Carry (A26, Junction 14)
Boozers (A16,Junction 17)
Continent (A26, Junction3)
Eastenders (A26, Junction 18)
Franglais (near TGV/Eurostar Station)
Pérardel (A26,Junction3)
Pidou (A26,Junction3)
Wine and Beer Company (A26, Junction3)

MARKET DAYS

Place Crévecour, near Boulevard Lafayette – Thursday, Saturday.
Place d'Armes, on Rue Royale – Wednesday, Saturday

FRENCH FLANDERS
St Omer has a good selection of beers, cheeses and home-made chocolates. There is a Carrefour supermarket north of St Omer and an Auchun supermarket south of the town.

INFORMATION CENTRES

Calais
Boulevard Clemenceau (near Town Hall)
☎ 0321 966240

Opal Coast
Sangatte/Blériot-Plage
☎ 0321 349798

Wimereux
☎ 0321 832717

Wissant (2 Caps Tourist Office)
☎ 0321 851562

French Flanders
Bergues
☎ 0328 687106

Cassel
☎ 0328 405255

Dunkerque
☎ 0328 687106

St Omer
☎ 0321 980851

Wormhout
☎ 0328 628123

2 Four Northern Cities – Lille, St Quentin, Laon, Reims

INTRODUCTION

British visitors to France can now join the A26 at Calais and make the 700-mile (1126km) drive to southern France without leaving the autoroute at any point. The first part of the journey, from Calais to Reims, is monotonous for long stretches, but the boredom of drivers is temporarily relieved at intervals, because the autoroute passes close by three great churches and provides motorists with spectacular and memorable views of these ecclesiastical masterpieces.

Although St Quentin's massive church is actually located in the middle of the city, it appears in the fields to the north of the autoroute as though it were an isolated basilica in open countryside. Some miles further east, drivers are treated to a spectacular view of Laon Cathedral, which appears in silhouette at the summit of a bold hill, much like Lincoln Cathedral from the plains of eastern England. When drivers reach Reims and take the Dijon spur, a motorway loop takes them right by the city centre and provides a spectacular view of the stunning cathedral at the head of one of the city's streets. Reims is a popular destination because it is at the heart of France's champagne industry. Unfortunately, very few motorists make the effort to leave the motorway in order to explore St Quentin or Laon. Both are very worthy of visits.

Between Calais and St Quentin, a number of junctions connect with a succession of N-roads and autoroutes, all of which converge on Lille. After years of neglect by British visitors to France, Lille has been converted into a popular short break destination by the introduction of the fast Eurostar link from London.

I must confess to having avoided the place myself for many years – perhaps I considered it was hardly worth making a detour to a textile manufacturing town in the heart of a coalfield or perhaps I still associated the city with an embarrassing episode from my schooldays, when I was allocated a pen friend who was described on a typed document issued by my French teacher as "Boucq, Marcel, Lille.". In my naivety, I began my first letter to my new correspondent with the words "Cher Boucq....". When Marcel wrote back to me, he gently pointed out that Boucq was actually his surname; whereupon I cringed with embarrassment and promptly terminated our

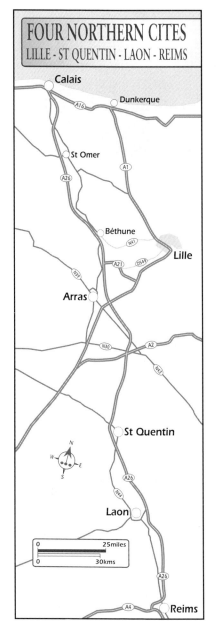

FOUR NORTHERN CITES
LILLE - ST QUENTIN - LAON - REIMS

Calais

Dunkerque

A16

St Omer

A1

A26

Béthune

N41

D549

Lille

A21

Arras

N39

N30

A2

N43

St Quentin

N
W———E
S

A26

N44

Laon

| 0 | 25miles |
| 0 | 30kms |

A26

A4

Reims

correspondence. When I finally made the effort to visit Lille, I was surprised to discover that it is one of the most vibrant and exciting cities in France.

This tour of four northern cities will cover short detours from the A26 to Lille, St Quentin, Laon and Reims. It is hoped that many readers who take the trouble to sample these places for the first time will be sufficiently seduced by their charms to add them to their list of future short break destinations.

2.1 LILLE

INTRODUCTION

Lille is France's fourth largest city and a thriving commercial and industrial city at one of the major transport crossroads of Europe. The city has some fine assets including: a number of very ornate, Flemish-style buildings at its core; wonderful opportunities for shopping, particularly for antiques, fashionable clothes, food and beer; a vast choice of cafés, bars, restaurants and night spots; and one of France's greatest art galleries. Thanks to all these attractions and its high student population, Lille seems to have a higher concentration of young people, both residents and visitors, than any other French city, and, although it will be seen as politically incorrect to make the observation, it would be very hard to find a place with more pretty girls than Lille.

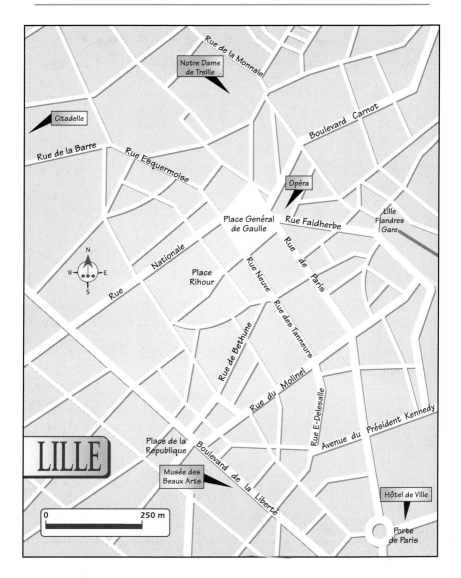

LILLE

Rue de la Monnaie

Notre Dame
de Treille

Citadelle

Rue de la Barre   Rue Esquermoise

Boulevard Carnot

Opéra

Place Genéral
de Gaulle

Rue Faidherbe

Lille
Flandres
Gare

Rue Nationale

N
W   E
S

Rue

Rue de Paris

Place
Rihour

Rue Neuve

Rue des Tanneurs

Rue de Bethune

Rue du Molinel

Rue E-Delesalle

Avenue du Président Kennedy

Place de la
Republique

Boulevard de la Liberté

Musée des
Beaux Arts

Hôtel de Ville

0   250 m

Porte
de Paris

TOP TIPS FOR LILLE

Not to be missed

- Place du Général de Gaulle
- The old hospital (Hospice Comtesse)
- Vauban's Citadelle
- General de Gaulle's birthplace
- Palais de Beaux Arts, with great art from many periods

Things to do

- Watch the world go by in the Place du Général de Gaulle
- Have a drink in a pavement café in Place Rihour
- Dine on Flemish or French food
- Search for second-hand books in the Old Stock Exchange
- Wander the cobbled streets of Lille's Old Town
- Spoil yourself on chocolates, cheeses and breads
- Check out the juxtaposition of old and new architecture at Notre Dame de la Treille
- Treat yourself to some new clothes in Rue des Chats Bossus
- Shop till you drop in Euralille shopping mall
- Climb to the top of the 320ft (98m) belfry of the Town Hall
- Visit the great Lille clearance sale

Getting there

L ille is about 62 miles (100km) from Calais and can be reached by taking the A16 autoroute to Dunkerque, followed by the A25 to Lille. Alternatively, several exits from the A26 (Calais–Reims autoroute) give access to roads which lead directly to Lille: the N42 from St Omer; the N41 from Bethune; the A21 or A1 from the Lens area.

Eurostar trains from London run through the Eurotunnel to Lille. Journey time is two hours. (for information and booking, ☎ 0990 186186).

Changing hands

Lille's prosperity was founded in the fifteenth century, during the rule of the Dukes of Burgundy. The city was ruled by Spain in the sixteenth and seventeenth centuries, until it was captured by the French in 1667. However, Lille's troubles did not end with its incorporation into France. The city was put under siege by Marlborough in 1708 and by the Austrians in 1792, it was occupied by the Germans for most of World War I and suffered repeated bombardment during World War II.

Like Paris, Lille has a very busy *Peripherique* and also a metro, but the metro system in Lille, which was introduced in 1983, is unusual in using unmanned, automated trains. Like Brussels, the city has a magnificent central square that is surrounded by tall, ornate town mansions. The similarities that Lille shares with the two capital cities do not end there, for the general atmosphere of the city is perhaps best described as a heady mix of Paris and Brussels. In recent years, brash new buildings have been erected and the Old Town has been renovated, so adding to the attractiveness of this vibrant city.

A TOUR OF LILLE

Trying to find on-street parking in Lille is like enduring an unending nightmare, but there are some underground car parks close to the main area and these should be used by visitors who wish to retain their sanity. The middle of Lille is characterized by a series of interlocking squares and a somewhat complex street pattern. Visitors are advised to begin their walking tour of the city by establishing compass directions from the main square. The tour will begin in the square, which is the city's most magnificent set piece, and then visit Lille's other sights by following a series of radiating spokes in a clockwise rotation.

General de Gaulle was born in Lille in 1890 and the city's central square bears his name. **Place du Général de Gaulle** is a magnificent, pedestrianised open space that is always teeming with life and movement. A tall column at the hub of the square commemorates the townspeople's resistance in the siege of 1793 and there is a large fountain with a circular perimeter wall, which is popular as a location for meeting, chatting, relaxing and watching the world go by. The square is surrounded by tall, colourful and highly decorated Flemish-style town houses.

Clearance sale

Local tourist documents advertise an annual clearance sale in Lille that takes place over two days in early September. The sale has its origins in a medieval law, which allowed servants to sell off their masters' old clothes once a year, but anyone visualizing a church jumble sale needs to think again. The Lille clearance sale, known as the Grand Braderie, is the largest antiques and flea market in Europe. Dealers descend on the city from all over Europe and the Place du Général de Gaulle and the Place Rihour are both crammed with stalls.

The city also stages a Flower Market in April, a Balloon Festival in May, the Lille Festival in June and a Christmas Fair, which features a large Ferris wheel in the central square.

The most famous building in the Place du Général de Gaulle is the **Vieille Bourse**, or old Stock Exchange, of 1652, which is fashioned in a very ornate Flemish Renaissance style and set around a courtyard that once contained over 20 merchants' shops, but now accommodates flower sellers and second-hand book dealers. The Vieille Bourse is over-shadowed, in size at least, by an edifice that was built in the thirties to house the offices of **La Voix du Nord**, the regional newspaper. The building, which was designed by Albert Laprade, is a bizarre Art Deco interpretation of Flemish Renaissance. It has a high, stepped gable whose apex is topped with bronze statues representing the three provinces of Artois, Flanders and Hainaut. Next door to the newspaper offices, there is an attractive theatre that was once an army garrison.

Follow a short road westwards from Place du Général de Gaulle to arrive in Place Rihour, a square with a huge war memorial, a plethora of cafés and bars, and the tourist office, which occupies one of Lille's oldest buildings.

Musée de l'Hospice Comtesse

By walking northwards from Place du Général de Gaulle, it is possible to enter Lille's **Vieille Ville** (Old Town), which is a maze of narrow, cobbled streets containing lots of bars and restaurants in the ground floors of tall Flemish-style buildings, many of which have elaborate façades. The Rue de la Monnaie, which has some of the best town houses, leads to the **Musée de l'Hospice Comtesse**, housed in a former hospital, which was founded in the thirteenth century by Jeanne de Constantinople, Comtesse de Flanders. The fifteenth-century barrel-roofed hospital ward has an attached seventeenth-century chapel, which was constructed to allow the patients to worship without leaving their beds! Since 1969, the building has housed a collection of furniture, wood sculptures, Lille earthenware, tapestries by Guillaume Werniers (a Lille weaver) and some seventeenth- and eighteenth-century art from the Low Countries.

While wandering in the old town, visitors are also likely to come across **Notre Dame de la Treille**, a nineteenth-century Gothic edifice with an incongruous all-glass facade which was added in 1999.

The Citadelle

Beyond the Old town, appears the massive **Citadelle**, erected when Lille and Pas de Calais were captured by the French in 1667. Vauban, Louis XIV's military engineer, was responsible for the design of the fortress, which is pentagonal in shape and surrounded by a ditch that can be flooded to form a moat. The Citadelle, which is generally regarded as the greatest of all Vauban's defensive structures (and there are lots of them throughout France), was once a self-contained town, complete with its own water supply, accommodation blocks and shops. It is still used by the military but can be visited on Sunday afternoons.

Immediately east of the Citadelle, is the **Birthplace of General de**

Gaulle. Some of the rooms are open to the public and there is an exhibition of photographs and documents charting the General's life. The car involved in the assassination attempt on de Gaulle at Petit Clamart is also on view.

Return to the main square by walking in a southerly direction. On the way, pass through the Place du Théâtre, which contains two remarkable buildings by Louise-Marie Cordonnier: the vast and highly ornate **Opera House**, which was begun in 1914 but only completed in 1923, and the **Chamber of Commerce**, completed in 1920 and featuring a prominent Flemish belfry which is very visible from the adjacent Place du Général de Gaulle.

Having returned to the Place du Général de Gaulle, take a walk in an easterly direction along Rue Faidherbe to **Euralille**, a huge triangular, glass and steel shopping mall, erected in 1994 and containing a very comprehensive range of retail outlets.

After returning once more to the central square, locate the **Hotel de Ville** by walking in a southerly direction along the Rue de Paris. The building, which was completed in 1932, has a 320ft- (98m) high belfry which is accessible to the public (100 steps). The view from the top extends for 31 miles (50 km).

Palais des Beaux Arts

North-west of the Town Hall is the **Palais des Beaux Arts**, with a collection which is second only to that of the Louvre. The museum contains Egyptian, Greek and Roman antiquities, a fine collection of French sculpture, ceramics, altar pieces, medieval art, paintings from the golden period of Dutch and Flemish art, as well as examples of Impressionism and Cubism. Artists represented in the gallery include Raphael, Tintoretto, El Greco, Goya, Van Dyck, David, Courbet, Delacroix, Manet, Monet, Sisley, Toulouse-Lautrec, Delauney, Léger, Braque and Picasso.

The visits to the various sights and museums of Lille could only be achieved in any meaningful way by spreading the itinerary over several days of a short break holiday. A walking tour of the city also requires stamina, but has the advantage of taking in lots of bars and cafés, which allow punctuations for relaxation and refreshment, and also lots of retail outlets, which provide plenty of opportunity for some serious shopping. It should also be emphasized that the tour has only taken in a select sample of Lille's many attractions.

2.2 ST QUENTIN

INTRODUCTION

St Quentin is located close to the A26 Calais-Reims autoroute, some 100 miles from Calais. The huge basilica of St Quentin is clearly and dramatically visible from the A26 autoroute, but very few tourists are seduced into the town by this great apparition. Given the fact that **St Quentin** is a textile town, which was heavily bombed in World War I and is now twinned with Rotherham, one can hardly blame motorists for not breaking their journey.

However, anyone who does take the trouble to leave the motorway is in for some surprises, particularly if their visit is made during July or August, when the town is utterly transformed in the most surprising

TOP TIPS FOR ST QUENTIN

Not to be missed

- The Basilica, with its Flamboyant-Gothic porch, flying buttresses and stained glass
- The highly decorative Hôtel de Ville
- The Entomological Museum, with Europe's largest collection of butterflies
- Lécuyer Museum, with its superb pastel portraits

Things to do

- Relax at a café in the town square and admire the highly decorated façade of the Town Hall and listen to its carillon
- Enjoy a walk in the woods in the heart of the town
- Have a Portuguese meal at the Vasco de Gama
- If you pay a visit in July or the first two weeks in August, take your children to St Quentin Beach, in the Town Square (!), where they can play in the sand, splash in the pool, play on the swings and roundabouts, enjoy a game of volleyball or tennis, ride on the donkeys etc. etc.

way imaginable (see feature box). Even at other times of year, St Quentin is worthy of a visit, because it contains two remarkable museums and two outstanding examples of Gothic architecture. There are also some good examples of Art Deco buildings resulting from the wholesale reconstruction that took place after the bombardments that devastated the town in World War I.

The Second Battle of the Somme

St Quentin was behind the German lines for the majority of World War I. After the collapse of Russia in late 1917, the Germans were able to turn their attention to the battle for France and, for the second time in the war, the valley of the Somme became a major battleground. In March 1918, 45,000 British soldiers were taken prisoner by the Germans at the Battle of St Quentin, and the Allies were unable to recover the town until September 1918.

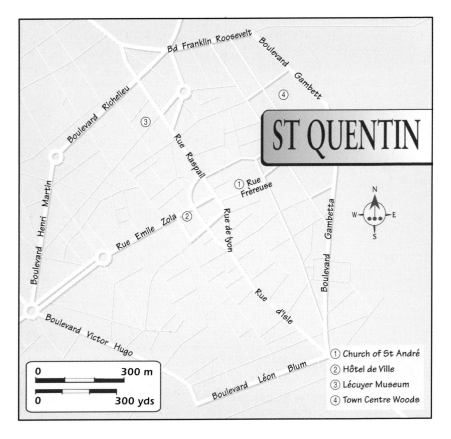

① Church of St André
② Hôtel de Ville
③ Lécuyer Museum
④ Town Centre Woods

In recent years, extensive and imaginative regeneration work has transformed the heart of the town into a very attractive area, and a large wood on the fringe of this area also adds to St Quentin's appeal.

A VISIT TO ST QUENTIN

Approach the town on the link road from the motorway, passing through some shabby suburbs, but appearances improve dramatically after crossing the Somme bridge and arriving at a large roundabout topped by an impressive statue. The long, sloping Rue d'Isle runs from this traffic island to the middle of the town, which is located at the summit of a hill. The street is lined with attractive shops and its neat pavements are adorned with large planters, which unexpectedly contain palm trees.

Gothic masterpieces

The **Basilica of St André** crowns the hill. The church, which is 370ft (113m) long and 130ft (40m) high, was built between the thirteenth and sixteenth centuries. The tower is partly Romanesque and there are some impressive flying buttresses, but the great glory of the exterior is the porch, which is an outstanding example of Flamboyant Gothic. The interior, which has aisles stretching right up to the apse, contains superb stained glass windows, some of which date from the thirteenth and fourteenth centuries. Without doubt, St Quentin's church is an outstanding, but much underrated piece of Gothic architecture.

After taking a short walk along the Rue St André to the large central square, visitors come across another superb Gothic edifice in the shape of St Quentin's highly ornate **Hotel de Ville**. Construction of the Town Hall began in 1331 but a highly decorated, arcaded and triple-gabled façade, which was added in 1509, converted the building into one of the most astonishing secular examples of late Gothic architecture to be found anywhere. In the eighteenth century, a slate, tile-hung clock tower was added. The carillon, which has no less than 37 bells, peels out a merry tune every 15 minutes.

Museums

The square itself is very large and lined with shops and cafés. Just one block away, to the south, there stands the **Entomological Museum**, which will appeal to anyone who can stomach the sight of thousands of brightly patterned and rare butterflies being pinned to show cases. The museum has the largest collection of butterflies in Europe, with a staggering 600,000 in total. 15,000 exhibits are on permanent display, 80 per cent of which are butterflies, the rest being insects.

Walk along the Rue Raspail, north from Rue St André, to a museum that is much more congenial. This is the **Lécuyer Museum**, which contains almost 100 exquisite pastel drawings by Quentin de la Tour, who was born in St Quentin in 1704 and became

St Quentin Plage!

Driving in the St Quentin area in July or during the first two weeks in August, visitors will encounter signs which are very reminiscent of those classic "Skegness is so Bracing" advertisements that once tempted them to the Lincolnshire seaside town. But these St Quentin signs would appear to be inviting visitors to a beach in a town that is 100 miles (161km) from the sea!

When we drive into the town, the first signs of a beach appear in Rue St André, just opposite the Basilica, where we find a street covered in sand, with children happily making sandcastles or playing beach-tennis, but this amazing sight is nothing when compared with the view that awaits us in the large Place du Général de Gaulle, where we find that the huge square has been covered in a very thick layer of splendid golden yellow sand and converted into one of the liveliest beaches you are ever likely to see. There are beach cafés where parents can relax as they keep a watchful eye on their children, beach huts, a swimming pool with diving boards, water slides, a paddling pool, a fountain, swings, roundabouts, outdoor chess boards, table tennis tables, volley ball courts, donkey rides etc., etc., etc.

It would be difficult to envisage a more drastic or more imaginative transformation of the heart of a town than St Quentin's summer make-over. Take your children and let them enjoy one of the most unexpected opportunities for a day on the beach they are ever likely to come across!

the official portrait artist of Louis XV. The gallery also houses some seventeenth- and eighteenth-century French and Italian paintings and some eighteenth-century furniture.

Aside from its museums and fine architecture, St Quentin has some other surprises in store for visitors. One surprise lies immediately east of the Basilica, where there is an extensive wooded area with some very pleasant walking paths, another surprise takes the form of the Vasco de Gama hotel and restaurant on Place Cordier where Portuguese cuisine is on offer, but the biggest surprise of all greets visitors who come to the town in July or the first two weeks in August, when an industrial town some 100 miles (161km) from the coast is converted into a beach resort (see feature box).

2.3 LAON

INTRODUCTION

Laon is situated close to the A26, 123 miles (198km) from Calais. The view of **Laon** from the A26 auto-route is awesome. The town's great cathedral stands in silhouette against the sky at the eastern edge of a 300ft- (91m) high plateau that rises abruptly from the plain. The open arcading in the top two tiers of each of the four towers is clearly visible, as are the ramparts and rooftops of Old Laon, which straggles westwards from the cathedral along the summit of the plateau.

It is hardly surprising to learn that this bold hill was regarded by the Romans as a strategically important site and that they built fortifications here. Laon became a Bishopric in 497 and the Carolingian kings later made the city their capital and

enclosed it in ramparts. Laon (pronounced 'Long' by the locals) continued to prosper in the Middle Ages, when the great cathedral was built.

The town was put under siege on a number of occasions during the Hundred Years War and saw action in the Napoleonic Wars and also in the two world wars of the twentieth century. Bombing in World War II was largely confined to the lower town and the area around the station, so the old hill city of Laon, with ecclesiastical and vernacular architecture stretching across nine centuries, has managed to survive intact and is now the largest protected heritage site in France.

A VISIT TO LAON

On the approach to Laon, the black silhouette of the cathedral meta-morphoses into a three-dimensional, stone-built edifice at the summit of a 300ft (91m) hill and the old city appears in front like some enormous *village perché*.

The lower town, at the foot of the hill, has all the messy paraphernalia of a modern city, with fast-food outlets, supermarkets, bypasses and bus and rail terminals. There are plenty of parking places in the lower town, but anyone leaving their car here is faced with two alternative routes to the summit of the hill, known locally as the "Plateau". The first option is to tackle the daunting climb up the steep sides of the plateau by walking up the *"grimpettes"*, the narrow alleys and paths that squeeze between the buildings clinging to the side of the plateau. The alternative route to the summit is by the POMA 200 mini-metro train, which ascends and descends the hill at alarming speed.

TOP TIPS FOR LAON

Not to be missed

- Laon Cathedral, a masterpiece of Gothic architecture
- Laon Museum, with its outstanding collection of antiquities
- The ramparts of the town

Things to do

- If you are feeling energetic, walk up the *grimpettes*, the steep, narrow alleys that lead up to the Old town
- If you are feeling lazy, take the POMA 200 mini-metro train up to the Old town
- Walk slowly around the outside of the Cathedral, in order to fully appreciate the revolutionary twelfth-century architecture
- Spot the animal sculptures on the Cathedral's west front and the oxen which lean out from the towers
- In the interior of the Cathedral, admire the proportions, the great height of the nave, the rose windows and the consistent style
- Book a guided tour of the Cathedral at the Tourist office
- Go on an eerie evening guided tour of the walls
- Admire the twelfth-century chapel in the grounds of the museum
- Shop in Rue Chatelaine
- Pause for a coffee at the Lamphi Theatre in Place Général Leclerc
- Visit the church of St Martin, with its transitional-style architecture
- Have a picnic and enjoy the view from the ramparts near the Abbey of St Vincent

Anyone willing to take a chance on finding a parking place in the upper town, can drive up to the plateau by taking a road which reaches the summit via a series of hairpin bends.

Cathedral of Notre Dame

The **Cathedral of Notre Dame**, at the eastern edge of the plateau, is hugely impressive, from a distance and from close up, and from without and from within. It was built, between 1160 and 1230, to replace a church that had been destroyed by arsonists. It is the earliest purely Gothic church to be built in France and it incorporates several features, such as deep-set portals in the west front, western towers and rose windows, which were highly innovative in the twelfth century and became a model for the other Gothic cathedrals that were subsequently built in Paris, Chartres and Reims.

Animal magic

Sculptured forms of sure-footed oxen famously emerge from the open arcades of Laon Cathedral's great towers. The story goes that an ox fell while hauling stone from the quarries of Chemin des Dames to the hill-top building site for the cathedral. The unfortunate beast was then replaced by a sure-footed and inexhaustible divine ox.

The west front also contains carvings of many other animals, including a goat, several horses and even a rhinoceros and a hippopotamus.

The west front has splendid portals and an array of sculptured animals. The cathedral's tall towers have open arcades in their top two tiers and are the first Gothic towers to be built on any European cathedral. Seven were originally planned but the four that materialized are impressive enough and give the cathedral a superb profile, which is further enhanced by its dramatic setting.

There were once 2,000 stained glass windows in the church but most of the stained glass is now confined to the rose windows at the east and west ends and in the north transept. However, the huge areas of plain glass in the main body of the building allow light to flood into the church and illuminate the four-

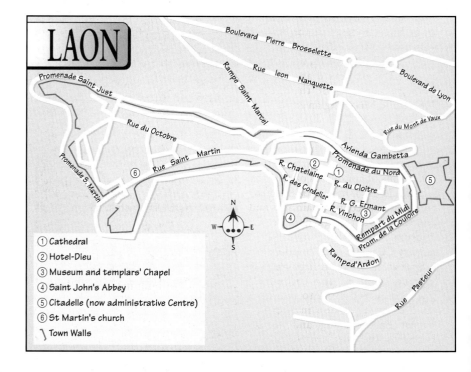

LAON

① Cathedral
② Hotel-Dieu
③ Museum and templars' Chapel
④ Saint John's Abbey
⑤ Citadelle (now administrative Centre)
⑥ St Martin's church
〴 Town Walls

storey nave, which has perfect proportions and wonderfully consistent architecture. During the Revolution, the cathedral was stripped of much of its furnishings and decoration, 100 paintings were destroyed and some of the altars were white-washed over, but there is much to enjoy, particularly the superb unity of the design, the striking lantern, the rose windows, the sexpartite vaulting and the elaborate gilt gates which front the chancel. (I am particularly pleased to note that the altar is dedicated to St. Thomas à Becket, simply because the parish church in my own Peak District town is similarly dedicated.)

The museum

Near to the cathedral, there is a **Bishop's Palace**, which is now the Palais de Justice, and also a former hospital. The town's **Museum** stands in the Rue Georges Ermant, a short walk south-east of the cathedral. It was established in 1851, in order to exhibit the objects d'art coming from excavations of the Gallo-Roman and Merovingian graveyards in the region. The museum then acquired some 1,700 Greek vases, statuettes and sculptures, to complete one of the most extensive collections of antiquities outside the Louvre. There is also a collection of pre-twentieth-century paintings and sculpture. In the garden of the museum, there is a splendid twelfth-century **Chapelle des Templiers**.

Staff at the tourist office, which is located close to the cathedral, organize guided visits to the cathedral every afternoon in July and August. Each evening, and also on Saturdays, they also provide guided walks around the town and rather eerie, guided walks along the walls.

The town

These guided tours are an excellent option for visitors, but Laon is also a perfect place for aimless, unguided wanderings, which will inevitably uncover many quaint corners, decorated doorways and old alleys. The cathedral is linked to the heart of the town by Rue Chatelaine, which has been pedestrianised since 1986. The street contains some nice shops in some picturesque premises but, recently it was disappointing to find some degree of shabbiness and a surprising number of empty premises, perhaps a sign of too few visitors. Surely a town of Laon's historical and architectural importance deserves more tourists.

Lively Laon

Visitors to Laon would be very unlucky if they were to arrive at a time when there are no festivities in the town such as:

Youth Film Festival in March;

vintage car hill climb and a display of early planes in early June;

Jazz'titudes Festival in early July;

Medieval Weekend, including a Medieval Market, also in July;

Festival of French Music in late September.

At other times, there is often street theatre of one sort or another, in the square in front of the cathedral. It is obvious that thespians cannot resist performing in front of the wonderfully theatrical backdrop of the great church.

Walking along the Rue Chatelaine, visitors can catch sight of a curious little clock tower on the Centrale Pharmacie and a nice shop front on the adjacent Patisserie Royer, but take care when photo-graphing these buildings, because the road ceases to be pedestrianised at this point and cars are apt to arrive unexpectedly from a side road.

The Rue Chatelaine leads to the Place Général Leclerc with the **Hôtel de Ville** and a nice spot for a coffee in the Lamphi Theatre. Continue westwards along the Rue St Jean and the Rue St Martin to the **Church of St Martin**, which is of particular interest because it was built just before work started on the cathedral, at a time when Romanesque was evolving into Gothic.

Old Laon is surrounded by 4.4 miles (7km) of ramparts and it has three surviving fortified gates. If visitors follow the walls eastwards to their southern extremity, they arrive at a Morlot gun emplacement. The views from this area are excellent and ideal for a picnic. Follow the Promenade de la Madeleine, to the walls that encircle the eighteenth-century **Bishop's Residence**, with its impressive Classical façade. Before descending from the plateau and heading back to the autoroute, most people will certainly wish to walk back to the cathedral and take a last look at a building which is not only a landmark for miles around, but also a landmark in the history of architecture.

2.4 REIMS

INTRODUCTION

Reims is close to the A26 autoroute and 168 miles (270km) from Calais. Unlike St Quentin and, to a lesser extent, Laon, the last city on the A26 tour is well established as a tourist venue. Even though the city is well known in the UK, there is uncertainty about the spelling of its place-name. Is it Rheims? Or is it Reims? Given that the city was the capital of the Celtic tribe known as Remi, the spelling "Reims" will be adopted here.

Reims became a Bishopric in the fourth century and later the seat of an Archbishop. St Remi baptised Clovis, the first Christian King of France, here in 496 and Reims has hosted the coronation of most of France's kings, from August Philippe in 1180 to Charles X in 1825. The most famous coronation of all took place on 17 July 1429 when Charles VII was crowned King in the presence of Joan of Arc, who had led his armies to victory over the English.

The great cathedral, which was built between 1211 and 1430, was so badly damaged in World War I that it remained closed for 17 years while renovation work was carried out. The city itself was all but destroyed and suffered again in World War II, but it has risen from the ashes to become a suitably bubbly tourist venue for the Champagne region. It has a fine shopping area, a vibrant nightlife and some good museums and art galleries, but tourists are largely drawn to the city because it possesses a large number of champagne manufacturers and one of the world's great cathedrals.

Devastation

Reims was in the battle zone for almost the entire duration of World War I. 12,000 homes were destroyed and many people sought refuge in the champagne caves but, in the end, it was necessary to carry out a mass evacuation. During Easter 1917, 25,000 shells fell on the city in one week.

During the war, the cathedral suffered 300 direct hits and was so badly damaged that it had to be closed to the public until 1937, in order to allow painstaking and costly renovation to take place.

The city suffered again in World War II, when a further 6,000 homes were destroyed.

A VISIT TO REIMS

Situated on the north bank of the river Vesle, Reims divides neatly into three areas: the shopping, hotel and restaurant area in the north-west, the cathedral and museum area in the centre and the champagne caves and basilica of Saint-Rémi in the south-east.

The Cathedral

Begin an inspection of Reims in the very heart of the city by taking a seat at a pavement café in the cathedral square, angling it to face the great church and taking time over a drink,

in order to stare as long as possible at the breathtaking west front, with its stunning rose window, its splendid symmetry (quite rare in French cathedrals), its lavishly decorated portals and its dazzling array of hundreds of sculptured figures, including the famous smiling angel on the north-west portal, who once lost her head but is now fully recapitated.

Many of the figures are replacements of the originals, and postcards with photographs taken in World War I of the badly damaged cathedral show that a very great deal of restoration work must have been carried out on the façade, but there can be no doubting that the west front of Reims Cathedral is a fabulous sight which makes a most tremendous impression on visitors of all ages.

When my youngest daughter made her first visit to Reims at the age of six, she took out her drawing pad, asked me to draw an outline of the west front and then spent the next hour in deep artistic concentration as she tried to sketch in all the detail she could see from her seat at the pavement café in the square.

The interior of the cathedral is no less impressive, not only because it contains hundreds more sculptures, but also because it has dazzling stained glass windows, fine proportions and a remarkable unity, even though its construction spanned three centuries.

After walking half way down the nave, turn to look back at the west end of the church and take in the full magnificence of this great set-piece. Above the interior of the west doorway, there is a tall, pointed, stained glass window with a huge

TOP TIPS FOR REIMS

Not to be missed

- The great Cathedral of Reims
- The Tau Museum, which houses the original sculpture and tapestries from the Cathedral
- Musée des Beaux Arts, with Cranachs, Corots and much else besides
- Third-century Roman gate at Porte de Mars
- The building where the Germans signed the surrender in 1945

Things to do

- Sit in a café in the Cathedral Square and take time to soak up your drink so that you can soak up the beauty of the Cathedral
- Find the sculpture of the smiling angel on the north-west portal
- Turn in the nave to admire the great western rose window
- Enjoy Chagall's stained glass window in the Lady Chapel
- Tour old Reims, on a petit train, or in a horse-drawn carriage, or on foot, with a guide or cassette guide, or simply wander through the streets
- Go to one of the free summer promenade concerts
- Shop in modern Reims
- Give the kids a go on the carousels
- Eat in one (or more) of Reims' many restaurants
- Go on a guided tour of a champagne cave
- Follow the tourist drive around the vineyards and wine villages
  See the sound and light show at Saint-Rémi

inset rose. The door and window are framed by rows of sculptured figures arranged in seven glorious tiers. Above the window, there is a row of nine Gothic arches, all inset with stained glass windows, and above this, there is the great rose window, with a dazzling, kaleidoscopic composition of highly colourful stained glass and with so many radiating stone ribs that it almost seems to rotate before one's eyes.

Walking to the east end, it is seen that the church has virtually no transepts, but that it has a chancel which has been made unusually wide to accommodate the pageantry of coronations. Beyond the altar, in the Lady Chapel, there is a stunning, bright-blue stained glass window designed by Marc Chagall. In its own way, this modest, three-part window is just as impressive and memorable as the great rose window at the west end of the church.

Much of the cathedral's stained glass was removed for safe keeping during the two World Wars, but the sculptures on the exterior suffered inevitable damage and they have also been seriously eroded by pollution over the years. Many of those on the west front are replicas, but a good number of the original sculptures have been placed in the **Tau Museum**, adjacent to the cathedral, where there is also a display of tapestries and other treasures.

The town

Charles VII is said to have been crowned at Reims Cathedral under a banner held by Joan of Arc, and the great commander is commemorated by an heroic statue in the cathedral square. The square is also the starting point for tours of old Reims. There are five ways to see the core of the medieval city, or rather what is left of it. A Petit Train makes a comprehensive tour of the maze of streets and affords passengers a close-up view of architectural details (and graffiti). There is also the option of a half-hour tour in a horse-drawn carriage. The tourist office organizes regular guided tours and also loans out cassette guides with commentary in English. Some will prefer to make unguided wanderings, but they would be wise to purchase a city map from the tourist information centre.

Anyone visiting Reims between late June and late August is likely to hear the strains of fine music, be it classical, traditional or jazz, because the city plays host to 140 **Promenade Concerts** in a variety of locations. 120 concerts are free.

Another cultural treat awaits visitors at the **Musée des Beaux Arts,** on Rue Chanzy, close to the cathedral. The gallery contains 13 drawings by the Cranachs (Younger and Elder) and 20 landscapes by Corot. (My own favourite is a picture of a windy day with a line of trees which seem to bend in the gale as you look at them. I also love Boucher's picture of a provocative Odalisque and le Nain's painting of peasants consuming a simple meal of bread and wine.) The collection of French paintings covers every

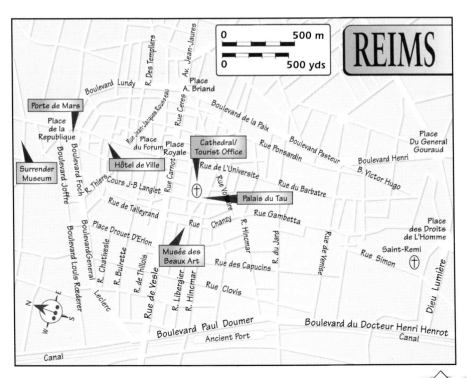

period from the Renaissance to the present day and there are some fine paintings by Dutch masters. The museum is firmly recommended as a delightful art gallery, which can be guaranteed to provide much visual pleasure.

Those who find pleasure in shopping will find much to enjoy in modern Reims, which covers an extensive area to the north-east of the Old Town. There is a large choice of retail outlets offering goods at a wide range of prices and, as always in France, the window displays are imaginative and seductive. Children who become bored on their parents' shopping expeditions are offered respite in the form of two street carousels, both splendidly ornate.

Reims is very well endowed with restaurants, almost all of which offer both indoor and outdoor seating. The choice of cuisine, especially in the area around Place d'Erlon, is so vast that it can almost become bewildering!

Before leaving the shopping and restaurant area, it is worth making a detour to the extreme north-west edge of the city centre, in order to see the **Porte de Mars**, a third-century Roman gate which was one of the few historic buildings to escape unscathed from wartime bomb-ardments, and the nearby **Surrender Museum**, where the Germans signed the surrender on 7 May 1945.

Champagne houses

Retracing the way to the cathedral and then following one of the long boulevards that lead off to the south-east, visitors will find the great **Champagne Houses** of Reims. At least a dozen manufacturers have their cellars here, in a labyrinth of underground caves beneath the old chalk quarries. Most of the producers offer guided tours, with commentary in English, and also free samples to revive visitors at the end of the underground trip. The visits are utterly fascinating and visitors are left feeling that they have ventured into a magical world peopled by alchemists who have discovered the clue to a secret potion. Most visits are on foot, but Piper Heidsieck provides electric trams.

Visitors with time at their disposal can also take a rewarding drive around the vineyards and villages of the **Montagne de Reims**, where the grapes that give the champagne its taste are to be found.

Close to the champagne houses, is Reims' oldest church, the **Basilica of Saint-Rémi**, which was built in the eleventh century, but has been much altered (and damaged) over the centuries. A sound and light show takes place in the church every Saturday evening at 9.30pm. An adjacent museum has a display of tapestries and other treasures.

Bubbly!

According to French law, a drink can only be labelled as champagne if it is made from grapes found in a specified area of 84,000 acres near Reims and if it is produced in a specified manner.

It is said that Dom Pérignon, the cellar-master at the Benedictine abbey of Hautvillers, invented champagne production in the early eighteenth century by blending different grapes and using a double fermentation process that gave the local wine, which was already known for its potency, extra bubble and a fine bouquet. Whether Dom Pérignon actually produced a wine that corresponds to modern champagne is somewhat questionable, because bottles in use at the time would hardly have been strong enough to contain the stuff.

Champagne production is an intricate and painstaking process. Vines in the region are carefully nurtured. They are heated in the spring if there is the slightest hint of frost, and roses are planted at the end of each row to give early warning of any disease that might attack the vine. The grapes are picked entirely by hand, at a time which is strictly specified by local agreement, and they are then pressed as quickly as possible, in order to preserve the quality of the juice, before being fermented for several months.

The wine is then blended. Black grapes from the Montagnes de Reims give the champagne its taste; Meunier grapes give it body and white grapes from Aperney give it freshness. The wine is poured, together with a fermentation agent and a little sugar, into bottles that are then stored upside down in caves. At least a year is allowed for this second fermentation, during which sediment collects. In order to disturb the sediment and allow it to collect in the cork, the bottle is turned through one eighth of a turn every day. Eventually, the cork, sediment and a little wine are removed. The bottle is then topped up with new wine and yeast, re-corked and allowed to settle again for some time.

As a result of all this effort and trouble, we have the gift of a drink that adds extra sparkle to that special occasion.

ACCOMMODATION

LILLE

Lille has a very large number of hotels covering a wide spectrum of prices and facilities. A detailed list can be obtained from the Nord Pas de Calais Hotels brochure available from the tourist office. The following is just a small selection:

****Hotel Alliance**
Seventeenth-century convent incorporated into modern hotel
☎ 0320 306262

****Hotel Carlton**
Luxurious, traditional. On Place du Théâtre
☎ 0320 133313

***Grand Hotel Bellevue**
Traditional hotel on main square
☎ 0320 574564

***Holiday Inn Express**
Modern hotel near Fine Arts Museum
☎ 0320 429090

***Hotel de la Treille**
In the Old Town
☎ 0320 554546

***Hotel Mercure Lille Centre Le Royal**
Mid range prices
☎ 0320 147147

***Novotel Lille Centre**
Mid range prices
☎ 0320 306526

Hotel Breughel
Mid range prices
☎ 0320 060669

Hotel de la Paix
Very moderately priced
☎ 0320 546393

There is a Youth hostel on 12 Rue Malapart
☎ 0320 570894

ST QUENTIN

There is a selection of hotels in the town, but try:

Hotel France Angleterre
Rue Emile Zola
28 rooms, car parking available
☎ 0323 621310

Laon

Visitors wishing to extend their stay in Laon could stay at:

Ibis Georges Pompidou
Avenue Georges Pompidou
41 rooms, all with air-conditioning
☎ 0323 201811

There is a campsite, with 35 emplacements for caravans, which opens from May to September
** Camping la Chenaie**
☎ 0323 202556

Reims

No less than 54 hotels are listed in the Reims Tourist Guide. Visitors who wish to make an extended stay are advised to obtain the booklet from the tourist office.

The following hotels are used by British tour companies:

****L'Assiette Champenoise**
Avenue Paul Vaillant-Coturier
Mansion with indoor pool and sauna
☎ 0326 041560

***Grand Hotel Continental**
Place Drouet d'Erlon
Tapestries, chandeliers, impressive staircase. central
☎ 0326 403935

***Porte Mars**
Place de la République
Central. Modernised rooms
☎ 0326 402835

***Quality Hotel**
Boulevard Paul Doumer
Comfortable, modern, near centre
☎ 0326 400108

ATTRACTIONS

Lille
Belfry of Town Hall
Place Roger Salengro
Open: Monday–Friday 9–11am, 2–4pm. Sundays and Bank Holidays: 9.30am–12noon
☎ 0328 381205

Citadelle
Open: Sunday 3–5pm in June, July, August.
☎ 0320219421

General de Gaulle's Birthplace
9 Rue Princesse
Open:10–12noon. 2–5pm. Closed Mondays, Tuesdays and Bank Holidays.
☎ 0323 81205

Musée de l'Hospice Comtesse
Rue de la Monnaie
Open: 10am–12.30pm, 2–6pm
Closed May 1, July 14. Noveber 1, December 25, January 1 and Monday of Lille Festival
☎ 0320 495090

Palais des Beaux Arts
Rue de Valmy
Open: 2–6pm. Friday: 10am–7pm.
Sunday: 10am–6pm.Closed Tuesdays
☎ 0320 067800

St Quentin
Entomological Museum
Espace St Jacques
Open: Monday, Wednesday, Thursday, Friday, Saturday: 2–6pm. Sunday: 3–6pm. Closed Tuesday.
☎ 0323 069393

Antoine Lécuyer Gallery (pastel portraits by Quentin de la Tour)
Rue Antoine Lécuyer
Open: Monday, Wed, Thur, Friday: 10am–12noon, 2–5pm. Saturday: 10am–12noon, 2–6pm. Sunday: 2–6pm Closed Tuesday.
☎ 0323 640666

Guided Cathedral visits, every afternoon in July and August, and guided tours of the town and walls, every evening and Saturday afternoon. Tickets from the tourist office.
Place de Parvis
☎ 0323 202862

Musée de Laon and Chapelle des Templiers
Rue George Erment
Open: 1 October–31 March: 10am–12noon, 3–5pm. 1 April–30 September: 10am–12noon, 2–6pm. Closed Tuesday.
☎ 0323 201987

Reims
Guided tours of town and loan of cassette guide from tourist office
☎ 0326 774525

Summer Promenade Concerts
Early July to late August
☎ 0326 774525

Music and light show
9.30pm Saturday at Saint-Rémi
☎ 0326 774525

Continued overpage

Tau Palace
Next to cathedral
Open: 15 November–15 March:
10am–12noon, 2–5pm (6pm
Saturday & Sunday); 16 March–30
June and 1 September–14 November:
9.30am–12.30pm. 2–6pm. 1 July–31
August: 9.30am–6.30pm.
☎ 0326 478179

Saint-Rémi Abbey Museum
Rue Simon
Open daily 2–6.30pm. Saturday &
Sunday: 2–7pm.
☎ 0326 852336

Fine Arts Museum
Rue Chanzy
Open: 10am–12noon, 2–6pm. Closed
Tuesdays
☎ 0326 472844

Surrender Museum
Rue Franklin Roosevelt
Open: 10am–12noon, 2–6pm. Closed
1 December– 31 March.
☎ 0326 478419

Tours of Champagne Houses
Most of the champagne houses offer
tours, with English guide, and with
tastings. Visitors could possibly try
one of the following:

Mumm & Co
Rue du Champs de Mars
Open: every day. 1 March–31
October: 9–11am, 2–5pm
☎ 0326 495970

Piper-Heidsieck
Boulevard Henry Vasnier
Tour in electric train. Open every
day: 9–11.45am, 2–5.15pm.
☎ 0326 844344

Taittinger
Place Saint-Nicaise
Open: 1 March–30 November:
weekdays; 9.30am–12noon, 2–
4.30pm. Weekends: 9–11am, 2–5pm
☎ 0326 858433

EATING OUT

Lille

Lille has an enormous choice of
restaurants. The greatest
concentration of eating places is to
be found in and around the central,
interlinked squares and in the Old
Town just to the north of this area.
Two restaurants, in particular, have
very high reputations:

L'Huitriere
Rue Chats Bossus
excellent sea-food
☎ 0320 554341

Le Sebastopol
Place de Sebastopol
☎ 0320 570505

Of the many brasseries, the following
has a high reputation:

Brasserie de la Paix
Place Rihour
Thirties interior
☎ 0320 547041

St Quentin

Try a Portuguese meal at:
Vasco de Gama hotel and restaurant
Place Cordier
☎ 0323 682284

Laon

Try:
Le Petit Auberge
Boulevard P Brossolette
☎ 0323 230238

Les Chenizelles
Rue du Bourg
☎ 0323 230234

Reims

There are very many restaurants, cafés and bars in Reims, especially in the area around Place d'Erlon. Visitors will wish to make their own selection. The tourist office produces a booklet, which lists no less than 140 restaurants, including those in hotels. Acquire the booklet, and enjoy choosing!

SHOPPING

Lille

Euralille, a few blocks east of Place du Général de Gaulle, is a very large modern shopping mall, but the city has a huge range of shops. Look out for furniture, both old and new, household goods, chocolates, cheeses and breads, old books, especially in the Old Stock Exchange, up-to-the-minute fashions, especially in Rue des Chats Bossus and Rue Lepelletier.

St Quentin

The main shopping areas are Rue de L'Isle, Rue St André and the Place de Hotel de Ville

Laon

The main tourist shopping street in the Old Town is the Rue Chatelaine and there are supermarkets in the newer, lower town.

Reims

Reims has an extensive shopping area north-west of the Cathedral. There are street markets every day of the week in various locations. Champagne from the local champagne houses can be purchased from many outlets or obtained directly from the producers.

TOURIST INFORMATION

Lille
Place Rihour
☎ 0320 219420

St Quentin
Rue Victor Bosch
☎ 0323 670500

Laon
Hotel Dieu
Place de Parvis
☎ 0323 202862

Reims
Rue Guillaume de Machault
near the Cathedral
☎ 0326 774525

3.1 BOULOGNE-SUR-MER

INTRODUCTION

The old port of Boulogne, properly known as Boulogne-sur-Mer, has provided thousands of British schoolchildren with their first taste of France. The town serves up just the right ingredients for teachers to provide their pupils with a mixed diet of experiences in a short space of time. The town's shops and street markets allow youngsters to nourish their emerging language skills through direct contact with native French speakers; Boulogne's restaurants and cafés offer menus which include some distinctively French food, and the old part of the town, with its castle, walls and gates, serves up plenty of atmosphere and puts flesh on the bones of school history lessons.

Getting there

Boulogne has now ceased to be a terminal for cross-Channel ferries, but the town is easily reached from the port of Calais or from the Eurotunnel terminal by taking the A16 autoroute. Boulogne is about 21 miles (34km) from Calais and 18 miles (29km) from the Eurotunnel at Coquelles. The town can also be reached in more leisurely fashion from Calais by driving along the D940 coast road (see Chapter 1).

Almost all visiting school children probably gain at least some cultural and linguistic benefits from a trip to Boulogne, even though they may well consider a close-up encounter with sharks at the sea-life centre to be more exciting and less taxing than attempted conversations with French shopkeepers, a game of football on the beach to be more fun than a wander through the cobbled streets of the Haute Ville, and a fast food snack at the nearest branch of McDonald's to be more inviting than a meal at local café.

Boulogne is no longer a destination for cross-Channel ferries – even the Hoverspeed Seacat service has now been discontinued – and many commentators thought that the termination of these services might also signal the end of British school visits to the town, but these fears have proved to be unfounded. The annual invasion of hordes of British youngsters is still taking place.

INVASION POINT

Boulogne has long been a conduit for invasions, both real and imaginary. Julius Caesar's invasion force set sail from here in 55 BC; Napoleon contemplated a repeat performance on a number of occasions between 1801 and 1805; the British used Boulogne to supply men and equipment in World War I and Hitler intended to use the port as a base for an invasion of Britain in World War II.

TOP TIPS FOR BOULOGNE

Not to be missed

- Nausicaa Sea-life Centre
- Boulogne's Old Town – gated and completely surrounded by walls
- Boulogne's Cathedral, especially the view of the dome's interior

Things to do

- Buy fresh fish at the early morning market by the dock
- Hire a boat at the quayside
- Spend half a day in the Nausicaa sea-life Centre and 'enjoy' a close-up view of sharks
- Enjoy Boulogne's golden sands (if you don't mind an industrial backdrop)
- Shop for cheese (especially at the fromagerie of Philippe Olivier), sea-food, bread, cakes, clothes, and more besides, in Boulogne's lower town
- Visit the Wednesday or Saturday market in Place Dalton
- Stop for a drink at the Café de la Mairie in Place Godefroy de Bouillon
- Walk to the top of the old belfry by the Town Hall
- Look at the building where Napoleon stayed with Josephine
- Shop for souvenirs, cheeses, nougats, chocolates or pastries in the Rue de Lille or have a meal at one of its restaurants
- Visit the Cathedral and stare up in awe at the interior of the dome
- Visit the old château and admire Greek vases, Eqyptian mummies and Alaskan masks
- Walk along the top of the town walls and enjoy the spectacular panorama
- Picnic on the Esplanade Auguste Mariette

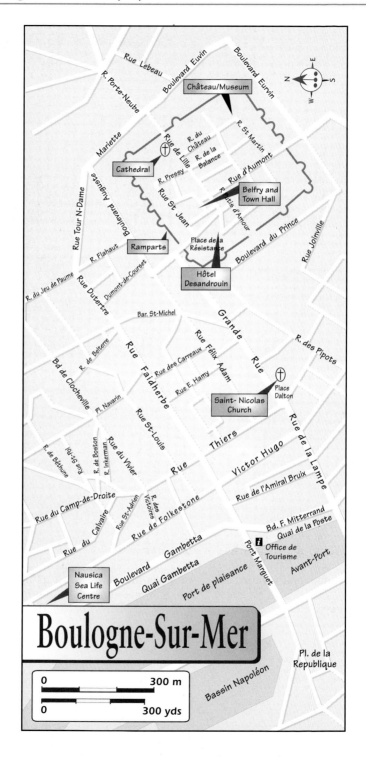

Boulogne-Sur-Mer

Boulogne was damaged by bombing in World War I and suffered widespread devastation in World War II. It has been re-built, of course, but the lower town is not at all attractive because a great deal of the post-war reconstruction involved the hasty erection of characterless concrete slabs, but it does have an excellent street market, a daily fish market and a plethora of good shops, with ample supplies of clothes, antiques, souvenirs, cheeses and sea-food. Fortunately, the old town, up on the hill, escaped the worst of the devastation and has survived more or less intact, complete with a splendid castle, cobbled streets, a complete ring of fort-ifications, a highly unusual, but very distinctive cathedral, and lots and lots of atmosphere.

A WALK AROUND BOULOGNE

The car park near the port offers the best chance of finding a parking place in Boulogne, although visitors who do not relish the prospect of tramping up the long hill from the quayside to the Haute Ville may decide to drive around the ramparts of the higher town until they find a parking place on its perimeter.

The port, which is focused around the Liane river and the Bassin Napoleon, is a busy place and offers opportunities for yachting and speed sailing. Fresh fish is on sale daily on the quayside from 6.30am.

All sea-life is here

The Nausicaa sea-life centre, which opened in 1991 and has been extended since, is the biggest and best aquarium of its kind in the world. Its presence as a major tourist attraction in the town has done much to offset the disappearance of the cross-Channel passenger ferries, which could have had a catastrophic impact on Boulogne's tourist trade.

The French are very good at constructing aquaria that give visitors the feeling of swimming underwater alongside the sea creatures. Nausicaa is no exception: its 50,000ft³ (1415m³) of glass tanks give close-up views of thousands of species of fish. The most popular exhibits include the shark ring, the "touch tank", where giant rays and skates can be touched and fed by hand, and the sea-lion area. Needless to say, this interactive experience is a great hit with children, but there are also cafés and restaurants to keep their parents happy.

Walk along the Quai Gambetta, past the picturesque jumble of boats, to arrive at **Nausicaa**, an inter-active sea-life centre, with its huge array of aquaria and a promise of close-up encounters with thousands of fish, including some rather scary sharks. Beyond Nausicaa, there is a long stretch of popular beach whose splendid sands are somewhat spoilt by a backlcloth of belching industry.

The Grande Rue

Return to the parking area in order to set off up the hill to the Old Town. Start on the Rue de la Lampe, which soon evolves into the **Grande Rue**, one of the main shopping streets of the lower town. The shopping district extends into two streets that run off to the left: the Rue Victor Hugo and the Rue Thiers, where the famous *fromagerie* of Philippe Olivier is situated. Cheeses, chocolates, nougat, seafood, bread, cakes and all manner of other foods are on offer in the area and there are also some good clothes shops. Half way up the hill, on the right, is the Church of St Nicolas, which overlooks the Place Dalton, with its ring of restaurants and bars and its very lively Wednesday and Saturday Street market – occasions not to be missed if you want to buy good local produce and see a snapshot of traditional French life at the same time.

Haute Ville

Eventually, the **Haute Ville** is reached, which is entirely encircled by massive ramparts, first erected in the thirteenth century but modified and extended 400 years later by our old friend Vauban. Enter the Old Town through a fortified gate known as the Porte des Dunes. Immediately through this gate, visitors find themselves in a world of cobbled streets lined with tall, dark-stone town houses. Rather like the old town in Edinburgh, old Boulogne proves that it is possible to be both grey and interesting.

Pass the **Palais de Justice** to arrive in the Place Godefroy de Bouillon, where an archetypal French café, the Café de la Mairie, offers a welcome opportunity for refreshment after the long climb from the lower town. From a pavement table, soak in the atmosphere of old Boulogne. The **Hotel Desandrouins**, where Napoleon stayed with Josephine while he contemplated his next move against England, overlooks the square, which acts as a forecourt for the eighteenth-century, red-brick **Hôtel de ville**, which has a fancy porch, a nice set of window boxes

---

Say cheese

France is the world's largest producer of cheese, making over 400 varieties. Cheese comes in two forms: farm cheeses, which are made with unpasteurised milk direct from farm animals, and pasteurised cheeses, which are made by industrial methods. Camembert, which is made from fermented cow's milk, is sold under 2,000 brand names.

Boulogne has some splendid cheese shops, both in the upper and lower towns, including Philippe Olivier's famous *fromagerie* on Rue Thiers. Hundreds of cheeses can be bought in Boulogne, but visitors might like to try a cheese from northern France called Maroilles, which has a pungent aroma but a surprisingly mild taste.

and a couple of ornate windows in its uppermost floor. But the most striking and unexpected feature is the massive thirteenth-century **Belfry** that emerges incongruously from above and behind the building. Both Town Hall and belfry are open to visitors and the balustrade at the summit of the tower provides a spectacular birds' eye view of the almost perfectly rectangular Old Town and a more distant prospect of the docks and the sea at the foot of the lower town.

The **Rue de Lille**, which runs northwards from the Place Godefroy de Bouillon, is the main street of old Boulogne. It is lined with cafés, restaurants, souvenir shops, *fromageries*, bread shops, nougat and chocolate shops. There are lots of traditional shop frontages and the cobbled street teems with excited British schoolchildren, most of whom are to be found gathered in clusters around street vendors selling cheap souvenirs.

The Cathedral

The Rue de Lille bears more than a passing resemblance to the streets of Montmartre in Paris, not only because its shops and cafés have old-fashioned façades, but also because the streetscape is dominated by a large domed church, much as Montmartre is dominated by Sacré Coeur. Boulogne's hill-top **Cathedral**, built between 1827 and 1866, even matches the Sacré Coeur basilica for eccentricity. It is as if the tower of the church was designed by an architect who could not make up his mind whether to build a tower or a dome, and so ended up by building both, with the dome perched on top of a high cylindrical tower.

The exterior of the cathedral is grey and forbidding and the interior is cold, white and massive. The only visible touches of gaiety are the Corinthian capitals of the columns and the ornate pulpit. However, if a curtain near the chancel is pulled aside, visitors can enter an area of the church whose dazzling decoration contrasts sharply with the sombre appearance of the nave. On the right, there is an altar in brilliant blue. On the left, the interior of the soaring tower rises, tier upon tier, to the great, stunningly-decorated dome.

Walls and Chateau

After leaving the church, carry on to the **Château**, by walking a short distance to the north-east corner of the town walls. The chateau, which dates from the thirteenth century, but was restored (you guessed it!) by Vauban, now contains a huge collection of Greek vases, a set of Egyptian mummies and a batch of Alaskan Eskimo masks.

Now walk back to the Porte Neuve, just behind the Cathedral, and ascend a set of steps to the top of the **Town Walls**, where it is surprising to find that the summit of the ramparts is laid out like a park, with landscaping, trees and a wide path. By following the wall-walk in an anti-clockwise direction, a series of spectacular views can be enjoyed. Along the first stretch of wall, there are excellent glimpses of the cathedral and also some photogenic views over the rooftops of the Old Town. After turning through a right angle at the northern extremity of the ramparts, look down onto a wide esplanade, where there is a large pyramidal **Monument to Auguste Mariette**, the noted archaeologist. Groups of British schoolchildren gather at the foot of the monument for commemorative group photographs; others simply sunbathe by leaning against its sloping wall. The gardens and lawns of the esplanade are ideal for picnics and there is often a large Ferris wheel in the vicinity.

Boulogne's Pasha

Boulogne's stone pyramid, located just outside the ramparts of the Haute Ville, commemorates the archaeologist Gustave Mariette, whose fez-hatted statue crowns the apex of the memorial. Mariette was born in Boulogne and became a schoolteacher, beginning his career in Stratford-upon-Avon, before returning to France. He joined the Egyptology department of the Louvre in 1849 and was sent to Egypt by the museum to collect Coptic manuscripts. While in Sakkara, he spotted some half-submerged ruins in the sand and decided to abandon his official mission and embark on an archaeological dig, whereupon he came across the remains of a building known as the Serapeum.

Unlike many archaeologists of the time, Mariette believed that the Egyptians had a right to retain their own antiquities, and he tried to enlist the support of the Khedive (ruler of Egypt) to set up an Egyptian Service of Antiquities (with Mariette as director) and to impose an exclusive excavation policy (with Mariette as the only permitted excavator).

In 1859, Mariette discovered the burial site of Queen Aahotep near the Valley of the Kings. Before he could remove the queen's gilded coffin and the glittering gems that accompanied it, a local Mudir seized the treasure and ran off with it. Mariette pursued the thief in a fast boat and forced him to hand over the gems, which he then took to the Khedive. The ruler was impressed with Mariette's actions and, having taken some items of jewellery for himself and one of his wives, he allowed the rest of the collection to be placed in a National Museum of Antiquities (with Mariette as director).

The archaeologist, who went on to uncover the sphinx and the great temples of Edfu and Dendera, was showered with honours in both Europe and the Middle East and was even proclaimed a Pasha by the Egyptians.

Upon reaching the south-western corner of the walls, extensive views can be enjoyed over the lower town towards the docks and the sea. By turning around to look back at the Old Town, the architectural features of the old belfry can be appreciated. Descend from the walls at the Porte des Degrés, where there are the remains of an old barbican. It is then but a few strides back to the Place Godefroy de Bouillon, where a pause for further refreshment can be enjoyed, before leaving the Old Town via the Porte des Dunes and commencing the walk down the Grande Rue down to the quayside car park.

3.2 THE BELLE ÉPOQUE TOUR – A ROUND-TRIP VIA LE TOUQUET

INTRODUCTION

This southern excursion from Boulogne is a nice study in contrasts. Travelling along a new stretch of autoroute it goes over a windy plateau and gives a close-up view of a modern wind farm, where up-to-the minute wind turbines harness a low-tech source of energy. Along the coast, there are ample opportunities to hire the very latest equipment and indulge in various water sports, but there is also a choice of excellent courses on which to play the ancient game of golf. The route travels through the carefully manicured pine woods of the elegant and refined Belle Époque resort of Le Touquet-Paris-Plage, where it is a surprise to encounter a promenade and sea-front which has the candy floss, pedal cars, beach clubs and

swimming complexes normally associated with rather more brash resorts. Travel through quieter resorts to the old port of Le Crotoy on the wide estuary of the Somme, but along the way come across a huge modern fun park. Visit the old towns of Rue and Montreuil, before heading back to Boulogne along an arrow-straight, tree-lined stretch of the Route Nationale, which takes many of us back to the days of travelling through France before the construction of autoroutes.

A ROUND-TRIP VIA LE TOUQUET

Leave Boulogne by taking the N41 St Omer road, which climbs past the ramparts of the Haute Ville and heads for the A12 autoroute. At the roundabout complex that gives access to the autoroute there is a commercial complex with a supermarket and fast-food outlets.

The A16 heads south across a windy plateau and there is soon evidence that the prevailing meteorological conditions have been put to good use. A large wind farm, with its tall, white towers and whirring sails, stands close by the autoroute on an exposed summit. The local motorway company has constructed an *aire* (rest area) around the wind farm, and it is worth pulling in for a short break here, not only for a close-up view of the windmills but also for the vast panorama visible from the viewing platform.

Not surprisingly, the windy conditions are also put to good use on the coast, down at **Hardelot**, where it is possible to sail-board, sail-cart, speed-sail or simply fly a kite (see additional information). Anyone taking the slip road to the

TOP TIPS FOR THE
LE TOUQUET ROUND~TRIP

Not to be missed

- The Marine Museum in the Mareis, Étaples
- The Belle Époque villas and hotels, Le Touquet
- Aqualand, Le Touquet
- The old town of Rue
- The walled town of Montreuil
- The porch of St Salve, Montreuil

Things to do

- Pause at the wind farm by the A16 to inspect the machinery and admire the view
- Sail-cart, speed-sail or simply fly a kite at Hardelot
- Play golf at Hardelot or Le Touquet
- See giant sand sculptures at Hardelot
- Go on a short cruise or a 12-hour fishing trip from Étaples
- Take a horse ride by moonlight at Le Touquet
- Shop for fashions, sports clothes, antiques, crystal and leather goods in Rue St-Jean, Le Touquet
- Have a meal in Rue St-Jean
- Buy hand-made chocolates at Au Chat Bleu in Le Touquet
- Buy food in the covered market in Le Touquet
- Enjoy the pools, water shoots etc. in Aqualand
- Enjoy the beach activities at Le Touquet
- See Leveque's paintings in Le Touquet Museum
- Visit the Bagatelle amusement park at Merlimont
- Look across the Somme Bay at Le Crotoy
- Have a drink in the town square in Montreuil
- Visit the Citadelle, Montreuil
- Walk the town walls at Montreuil
- Dine at Hautes de Montreuil
- Shop for lace, antiques, pottery in Montreuil
- Visit Samer's Strawberry Festival if you are in the area in late July

resort will also find two excellent golf courses and opportunities for horse-riding. (see feature box and additional information). From late May to the end of June, Hardelot holds an exhibition of gigantic sand sculptures built by professional artists from all over the world.

A golfer's paradise

Golfing enthusiasts looking for a sporting holiday in France need look no further than the Opal Coast between Boulogne and Le Touquet.

Neufchatel-Hardelot has two 36-hole courses. The Pines has five par-3 holes and five par-5 holes and demands good approach play to the greens. The Dunes, as its name implies, has plenty of sand but also plenty of trees and undulating land. There are 14 tees where it is not possible to see the flag!

Le Touquet has three courses: La Mer, a superb 18-hole course designed by Harry Colt in 1904; La Forêt, a par-71, 18-hole course; and Le Manoir, a par-35, 9-hole course.

All five of these courses are in superb locations on the Opal Coast and, as an added bonus, golfers staying at the Westminster Hotel or the Hotel Red Fox in Le Touquet or at Hautes de Montreuil in the old town of Montreuil can enjoy a ten per cent reduction in green fees on some of the courses.

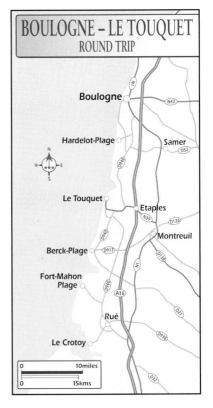

Etaples

Returning to the A16, follow the autoroute until the slip road for the N39 and the road to Etaples and Le Touquet. **Etaples** is an old fishing port, which was once a favourite haunt of painters and was used as a base and training camp by the British in World War I – the conditions in the camp were so harsh that there was a mutiny here in 1917.

The first encounter with Etaples is promising: a nice square is overlooked by a classic French Hôtel de Ville, with a symmetrical façade, a clock tower and a grand entrance way topped by a tricolor-flying flagpole. The Rue de Rosamel, to the right of the town hall, is lined with little whitewashed, tiled-roofed buildings housing local shops, cafés and artists' studios.

The promise of the Rue de Rosamel is short-lived. Approaching the working port, the town becomes rather messy and unattractive, but there is one very imaginative development which gives the impression that the local council is doing its best to attract craftspeople into the town and also market Etaples' maritime past. A long terrace of old, brick fish sheds, known as the **Mareis**, have been superbly renovated and fitted out with good quality craft shops, a remarkable information office, which is shaped like a boat, and a **Musée de la Marine**, in an old rope factory, which uses ingenious devices to give visitors the sensation of being transported to the high seas.

The rest of the town is hardly worth a visit, but the shoreline has much to offer. The tourist office can supply details of boat trips, with the option of a 45-minute cruise or a 12-hour fishing trip, and there are fine opportunities for bird watching along the coast. Look-out posts have been provided for enthusiasts.

Le Touquet

Leave Etaples by crossing the river Canche, and head to the famous resort of **Le Touquet-Paris-Plage**. Driving along the approach road for Le Touquet, visitors catch sight of a succession of villas discretely half-hidden in clearings in the woods. There are mock Swiss chalets, pseudo thatched cottages, Empire-style grand houses and some dwellings that are positively palatial.

Everything that grows, be it in window boxes, gardens, lawns or the woods themselves, is very carefully manicured. Even the advertising hoardings (which mar the entrance to so many French towns) are tasteful, being painted in dark green and neatly lettered.

Le Touquet was developed as a fashionable resort for rich Parisians in the Belle Époque period – hence the name Le Touquet-Paris-Plage – but two Englishmen, John Whitely and Allen Stoneham, were responsible for much of the villa development and sporting clubs which grew up in the early years of the twentieth century. The resort became very popular with well-heeled English francophiles: during the twenties, P G Wodehouse and Noel Coward both bought villas in the pine woods and Somerset Maugham used to socialize here before he was drawn to the sunnier climes of the Riviera.

The elegant surroundings somehow compel visitors to drive slowly and sedately and, as they drive along, there is plenty of time to deduce that the popular sports hereabouts are tennis, golf and horse riding. There are no less than three excellent golf courses, two of 18 holes and one of nine holes (see feature box and additional information). The staff at the equestrian centre at Parc International de la Canche organize horse rides along the coast, at dawn, at dusk and, even more romantically, by moonlight (see additional information).

Entering the heart of the town, there is an area of large Belle Époque and Art Deco hotels. The Rue St-Jean, which links the woods with the seafront, is lined with excellent restaurants, bars and shops. Goods on offer include the very best in golfing, tennis and riding attire, antiques, fashions, shoes, crystal and leather goods. There is also an irresistible opportunity for gluttonous indulgence at Au Chat Bleu, an outlet for hand-made chocolates. A beautiful covered market area, built between the wars to a half-moon plan, houses a Monday, Thursday and Saturday stall market, where there is a splendid selection of cheeses, meat, fish, fruit and vegetables.

After all this Belle Époque elegance, the first view of the sea-front comes as a shocking surprise. Large concrete, box-like hotel and apartment blocks stand in bad-mannered juxtaposition with old, characterful villas. There is even a suggestion that some old buildings from Le Touquet's halcyon days have been swept aside to make way for these new-brutalist monstrosities. The beach area is even more surprising, as it is highly developed even by French standards, with beach-tents and beach-huts, designed to provide protection from the prevailing (often very prevailing!) wind, lots of kids' clubs, volley-ball courts, five-a-side areas, swings, roundabouts, trampolines and all manner of other contraptions. The promenade has snack bars, candy-floss stalls, pedal cars, a petit train and a carousel and, at its very heart, a huge **Aqualand** complex with acres of indoor and outdoor facilities for water-based activities. If the pine woods of Le Touquet are a playground for the rich, the promenade and beach area is a playground for the masses.

Making a splash

The huge Aqualand complex in Le Touquet has 43,010ft² (4,000m²) of indoor water fun under a giant glass pyramid, where the air temperature is a lazy 27°C and the water temperature a comfortable 29 degrees, and another 43,010ft² (4,000m²) of outdoor pool entertainment.

Attractions include a giant toboggan, a "surprise river", a wave pool, cascades, bubble baths, saunas, a "black hole" and a "twister". There is a restaurant with a panoramic view and, weather permitting, the pools stay open until 11pm on Friday and Saturday night in July and August.

A combined ticket can be obtained to gain entry to Nausicaa in Boulogne as well as Aqualand.

Sport and a museum

Having parked on the promenade, where there are plenty of spaces, visitors can choose from a range of energetic or more leisurely pursuits. For example, in addition to the facilities mentioned above, there is the chance to learn sand-yachting from the world champion in the sport, or take the more leisurely option of visiting Le Touquet's one and only museum, **The Le Touquet Museum,** where there is a collection of landscapes and seascapes by Leveque, whose predominantly pink and beige palate reflects the light of the Opal Coast.

The coast to Le Crotoy

The sands stretch for miles in either direction. If the D940 is followed southwards, taking short diversions to the coast along the way, visits can be made to the rather quieter resorts of **Stella-Plage**, with its lawns and fine sands, **Merlimont**, with its **Bagatelle** fun park, which boasts about 50 different attractions, and **Berck-Plage**, with its uncrowded beaches. The D940 bypasses the old town of **Rue**, but it is worth dropping in to have a look at the Flemish belfry and flamboyant church. **Le Crotoy** is soon arrived at, where there are superb views across the huge expanse of the **Somme Bay**. Small wonder that Jules Verne stayed in the port while he wrote *20,000 Leagues under the Sea.*

Montreuil

Return as far as the junction with the D917, and head for Montreuil, an old port, still called **Montreuil-sur-Mer** even though it is now left stranded on a crag some nine miles from the sea as a result of the silting up of the Canche estuary.

Montreuil was fortified in the sixteenth century and it retains a complete two-mile (3.2km) circuit of walls to this day. The large Grande Place (otherwise known as Place Général de Gaulle) is overlooked by a picturesque terrace of cafés and restaurants, and contains a statue to General Haig, reminding visitors that the British made the town their headquarters in the second half of World War I.

A half-timbered sixteenth-century hostelry, known as the **Hautes de Montreuil**, stands on the Rue Pierre Ledent, which runs off the square. The hotel offers a reduction of ten per cent in green fees to golfers who book rooms there and the restaurant has a particularly impressive wine list.

There are lots of old houses in the back streets, squares and alleys of Montreuil. Some buildings are a little shabby but the streetscapes are undeniably picturesque and lots of flowers and ornate lamp holders add brightness to the scene. St-Salve Church, which overlooks the Place Gambetta, is Romanesque in origin, but has been much battered by war and much altered over the centuries. However, the church retains its tall, deep-set and highly ornate, Gothic portal. The interior, by contrast, is disappointing because it is very dimly lit.

Walk down virtually any of the side streets to gain access to the town's ramparts. The two-mile (3.2km) walk along the top of the walls allows a complete circum-navigation of the little town and gives spectacular views over the surrounding countryside. At the north-west corner of the ramparts, there is a seventeenth-century **citadelle**, which was built around the ruins of a thirteenth-century castle – visits are possible.

Montreuil has become a last stopping-point for many British tourists heading back to the Channel ports. It has welcoming cafés and restaurants for a final refreshment halt; the fortified former port affords a last look at an old French town and Montreuil's shops provide a last minute chance to buy souvenirs and gifts, particularly lace, antiques and pottery.

Samer

Return to Boulogne by following the old Route Nationale (N1), which many people remember from travels in France in the days before the A16 autoroute was built. Much of the road is arrow-straight in the Roman manner and tree-lined in true French fashion. The road passes through **Samer**, which has little to offer other than a rather impressive fifteenth-century church and a Strawberry Festival at the end of June, but it is quite nostalgic to drive through a place which is made to look like a piece of ribbon development by the straight path of the Route Nationale as it knifes its way through the town. Before the construction of bypasses and autoroutes, hundreds of French towns and villages along the routes nationales had a similar aspect.

Signs of the times

In the days before billboards and neon signs, advertising slogans were painted directly onto buildings. Painted Dubonnet signs were once commonplace in France and a good many still survive on walls and gable ends, even if some of them are somewhat faded or even truncated.

Today's copywriters engage in a never-ending search for novel catchphrases and new logos, but the artists who painted numerous Dubonnet signs on the buildings of northern France must have been confident that their work would have a long life. Their graphic art is a reminder of days when tastes were much less fickle than they are today.

Driving along to Boulogne, another nostalgic touch is added by occasional glimpses of faded Dubonnet advertisements painted on the gable ends of roadside buildings. All in all, the return trip along the N1 has provided a nice contrast to the outward journey along one of France's newest autoroutes.

3.3 THE SOMME BATTLEFIELDS

INTRODUCTION

This tour takes visitors from a haven of peace and tranquillity in the Somme Bay to the battlefields of World War I, where thousands of young men lost their lives in the bloodiest of wars.

Sightseeing begins in the most unlikely location: a motorway service station whose landscaped grounds have been carefully designed to recreate the Somme marshlands, with their rich diversity of bird life. The horrors of war are far from the mind in this peaceful place, but all the subsequent places of interest on the tour cannot fail to remind everyone of the devastating effects of twentieth-century conflicts. Three urban centres which have risen from the ashes after suffering enormous destruction are visited: Abbeville, three-quarters of which was destroyed by air raids in 1940; Amiens, where 5,000 houses were destroyed and a further 17,000 suffered damage during World War II; and Arras, whose wonderful squares and superb Hôtel de Ville were reduced to ruins in 1914. All of these places are worthy of visits, because their great arch-

Top tips for the Battlefields tour

Not to be missed

- The Aire de la Baie de la Somme (motorway service station)
- The sculptural representation of Mary Tudor's marriage to Louis XII, Abbeville
- Museum of pre-history, Abbeville
- St Riquier Abbey (Flamboyant Gothic)
- Amiens Cathedral (fabulous from within and without)
- The tower topped by the Golden Virgin, Albert
- The 1916 Museum at Albert (for a representation of life in the trenches)
- The British War Memorial, Thiepval
- Newfoundland Park
- Scottish Memorial, Beaumont-Hamel
- Delville Wood
- The Ulster tower
- War Museum at Péronne
- Arras' two great squares

Things to do

- Indulge in a spot of bird-watching and amateur electricity production at Aire de la Baie de la Somme
- Inspect sculpture on the church at Abbeville
- Admire the great west facade of Amiens Cathedral
- Experience the west facade of the Cathedral illuminated by the Son et Lumière
- Take a close look at the 4,000 carved figures on the choir stalls at Amiens
- Visit the floating market at St Leu
- Take a boat trip around the Hortillonnages
- Eat macaroons and pancakes in Amiens
- Visit at least one of the many war graves in the Somme
- Follow the Battlefields Tour (and visit the memorials listed under 'Not to be Missed')
- Visit the Welsh memorial at Mammetz
- See a mine crater at La Boiselle
- Learn about the impact of the war on all participating nations at Péronne
- Have a drink under the arcades in one of Arras' great squares
- Visit one of the stall markets in Arras
- Tour the underground tunnels of Arras
- Dine in a restaurant in the Grand' Place, Arras
- Shop in Arras for Arras d'Bleu china, heart-shaped chocolates, cheeses, spiced bread and sausages
- Drink the local beer
- Visit Vimy Ridge and the Canadian Memorial

itectural treasures, which are among the finest in France, have now been rebuilt and restored to their full glory.

At the heart of the tour is a notorious patch of countryside between Albert and Bapaume, where almost half a million British servicemen lost their lives fighting for a stretch of land no more than 7.5 miles (12km) in length. A succession of cemeteries, with row upon row of simple crosses and white headstones, is a poignant reminder of five appalling months in 1916 when the great nations of Europe almost wiped out a whole generation.

The combination of natural beauty, magnificent architecture and moving memorials makes this tour an unforgettable journey.

THE SOMME BATTLEFIELDS TOUR

The A16 autoroute has brought the Somme valley within easy reach of Boulogne, but this particular autoroute is also a tourist attraction

in itself. British motorways seem designed to offer minimum distraction to drivers and journeys along them can be very boring, but French motorways are full of distractions. The A16 makes valley crossings over some spectacular viaducts and, as seen earlier (Le Touquet tour) one of its rest areas is set in a wind farm, but the entire autoroute is distinctive because it is designed around an environmental theme. The carriageway runs between a series of green embankments and passes under a succession of quaint, but newly-constructed, double-arched bridges clothed in vegetation. Entrance to the Somme valley, just north of Abbeville, is marked by a most unusual service station, where the environmental theme is picked up in a most imaginative way.

Aire de la Baie de Somme

The award-winning **Aire de la Baie de Somme service station**, which was designed by architect Bruno Mader and land-scape designer Pascal Hannetel, is powered by energy generated from a 131ft (40m) high wind turbine. There is an imaginatively-designed play area at the foot of the mast and lots of hands-on displays inside the exhibition hall, where children can produce electricity in a variety of novel ways. Some other exhibits are devoted to Jules Verne, who divided his time between Le Crotoy, where he had a writer's house and a yacht, and Amiens.

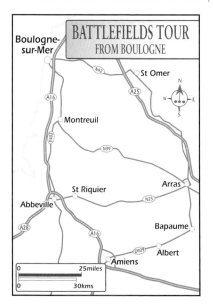

BATTLEFIELDS TOUR
FROM BOULOGNE

Boulogne-sur-Mer

N42
St Omer
A25
A16
Montreuil
E402
N39
St Riquier
Arras
Abbeville
N25
A28
Bapaume
A16
D929
Albert
Amiens

0   25miles
0   30kms

Science fiction or science prediction?

Jules Verne was born in Nantes in 1828. He studied Law in Paris and, from 1848 until 1863, wrote a succession of librettos and plays.

In 1856, he came to Amiens to attend the wedding of one of his friends, but ended up falling in love with the bride's sister, Honorine, whom he subsequently married. The couple, who were married for 50 years, lived in Amiens from 1871, although he also had a writer's house in Le Crotoy. Verne became heavily involved in the city life of Amiens, as a councillor and as founder of the Circus Hall. He must have been something of a workaholic, because he also found time to write three books every year.

Verne's imagination was captured by the plethora of inventions and scientific discoveries of the nineteenth century, and he began to write fantasies which had a good scientific foundation. His first success came in 1849 with *Five Weeks in a Balloon*. His later books included: *Journey to the Centre of the Earth; From the Earth to the Moon; 20,000 Leagues under the Sea* and *Around the World in 80 Days*.

Verne's writings anticipated space travel, submarines, helicopters, air-conditioning, guided missiles and even movies. Fittingly, many of his stories have been made into films.

This area of the Somme is home to a wide variety of bird life, and many species, such as grey geese, shelducks, black and white oyster-catchers, avocets and white storks, can be spotted from the circular observation tower and from the wooden promenades which criss-cross a series of lakes in the grounds of the service station. The information point has an excellent selection of high quality books on natural history and ornithology.

Abbeville

At **Abbeville**, the motorway swings east and heads for Amiens. Motorists who have negative recollections of Abbeville from their days of driving to Paris down the N1 are unlikely to be tempted off the autoroute. Their memories will be of a town of dull, red-brick houses and textile factories, which was slowly recovering from appalling devastation. But Abbeville is much brighter these days and it does have a couple of worthwhile tourist attractions in the form of its collegiate church and its museum.

The **Collegiate Church of St Vulfran** is an eclectic mix of architectural styles. There is a Flamboyant west front, a Renaissance doorway, a couple of western towers with watch turrets and even a leaning tower next to one of the transepts, but the most interesting features are the decorations on the west front, which include sculptural forms depicting the marriage of Louis XII and Mary Tudor.

The **Musée Boucher-de-Perthes** is an important museum of prehistory, thanks, at least in part, to Jacques Boucher de Perthes, a local archaeologist who was one of the pioneers of the study of pre-history. The museum also contains portraits by Largilliere and some other works of art.

Abbeville has experienced a violent recent past, but in former, better times it was an artistic centre of some importance and famous for its tapestries. The town was originally known as Abbatis Villa and was part of a rural estate belonging to the **Abbey of St Riquier**, which was built in flamboyant Gothic style and is located five miles (8km) north-east of Abbeville on the D925.

Amiens

Leave the A16 autoroute 20 miles (32km) east of Abbeville at the exit for **Amiens**, another place that has suffered massively from the ravages of war. Fortunately, its great **Cathedral of Notre Dame**, the last of the early Gothic churches to be built in northern France, escaped the worst of the damage. A huge paved concourse provides an ideal platform from which to admire the west front, a towering work of art, with three deeply-set, highly ornate portals and a façade with row upon row of statues. There are some 3,000 figures in all, including representations of 22 French kings. The façade is topped by two asymmetric towers, each with delicate tracery, and is further embellished with a huge rose window added in the fifteenth century. The west front was soot-blackened for many years, but all of its wonderful features have now been revealed in fine detail by a revolutionary laser cleaning process. The detail is also highlighted in the most dramatic fashion every evening when coloured lights are beamed onto the façade in a spectacular **Son et Lumière**.

The church occupies a larger area than any church in France and was big enough to accommodate the entire population of Amiens when it was completed in the thirteenth century. The cathedral is well over 400ft (122m) long and the nave reaches a height of 140ft (43m), making it the highest in the country. Although the dimensions are awesome, the interior looks rather stark when compared with the sumptuously decorated façade. This is largely because most of the nave's stained glass was destroyed in World War I.

Ruskin's Rapture

In the second half of the nineteenth century, John Ruskin became the dominant arbiter of taste. He reacted against the depressing effects of industrialisation, by suggesting that artists and architects should produce work with a spiritual foundation and turn for their inspiration to the Gothic art of the late Middle Ages.

Ruskin said of the carved choir stalls at Amiens: "There is nothing else so beautiful cut out of the Godly trees of this world. Under the carver's hand, it seems to cut like clay, fold like silk, grow like branches, and leap like a living flame."

But Ruskin was equally impressed by the cathedral's aisles, porches, lancets and rose windows, and glorious carved and decorated stonework. In fact, he regarded Amiens as the most perfect manifestation of religious art in northern Europe.

As at Laon, the tall, clear windows allow light to flood in and illuminate the finely-proportioned interior and, also as at Laon, stunning stained-glass rose windows in the transepts provide compensation for the lack of glass in the nave. Most of the interior decoration is found in and around the choir, which contains 110 medieval choir stalls with 4,000 carved figures representing local trades and Biblical scenes. The aisles surrounding the choir contain fabulous murals and sculptures.

Other sights

The cathedral alone is, of course, sufficient reason for visiting Amiens, but the **Musée de Picardie**, a few streets to the south, contains Classical sculptures and a good collection of paintings, principally by eighteenth-century French artists. There are also works by Bonnard and Matisse, two of my favourite French artists of the twentieth century.

The heart of Amiens, which was all but destroyed in the two world wars, has been rebuilt. A fair amount of the more recent post-war architecture is really rather good, but some of the earlier attempts at reconstruction are rather bland, especially the stark, 25-floor skyscraper known as the **Tour Perret**. However, the central streets, which contain splendid shops and bars, have been pedestrianised with the usual French flair. Amiens offers plenty of opportunities for eating out. Local specialities include macaroons, pancakes and duck pie.

On the banks of the Somme, there is a surprisingly picturesque old quarter of small, gabled houses, known as **Quartier St Leu**, where a "floating market" takes place every Thursday and Saturday. The foodstuff on sale here is produced in small market gardens and allotments, known as **Hortillonnages**, which are linked and irrigated by a network of streams and canals. Between April and October, visitors can take boat trips around this fascinating area.

During World War I, Amiens was the site for temporary hospitals, war factories and bases for military staff. The city has some good hotels and is an ideal base for exploring the Somme battlefields, just 20 miles (32km) to the east.

Albert

The D929 links Amiens to **Albert**, now a neat, reconstructed town of brick houses, but a place that was utterly shattered by persistent bombardment in World War I. In the middle of Albert there is a very tall basilica, **Notre Dame de Brebieres**. In January 1915 a German shell hit the base of the statue of the Golden Virgin on the top of the basilica; the figure was tilted over until it was almost horizontal and, for the next three years, the virgin was left leaning over the town with her child. The "Leaning Virgin" came to symbolize the suffering of Albert.

The town has two other belfries, one on the Flemish-style Town Hall, built in the thirties, and the other on the railway station, which has nice stepped gables. The rest of Albert consists of brick houses, largely built after the destruction of World War I in a vernacular Art-Deco style.

The **Musée des Arbris (Somme 1916)** is housed in a former underground air-raid shelter. Fifteen niches along the tunnel contain tableaux depicting daily life for the soldiers in the trenches, which stretched along a 15-mile (24km) front immediately east of Albert.

The battlefields

The Battle of the Somme began on 24 June 1916 with a non-stop Allied artillery barrage designed to weaken the German defences. On 1 July, the British and French infantry advanced from their trenches, only to find that the German networks had not been significantly weakened by the preliminary bombardment. On that day alone, there were 58,000 British casualties. Trench warfare continued for another four and a half months, often on ground that had been turned into a morass by torrential rain. During that period, the British advanced just seven and a half miles (12km) but lost 418,000 men. To make matters worse, the modest advance was made almost meaningless in March 1917 when the Germans decided to make a tactical retreat behind the powerful Hindenberg Line, in order to shorten their lines by 43.5 miles (70km).

The Battlefields Tour

M aps and guidebooks available from the information offices in Albert and Péronne describe a tour of the Somme battlefields, which encompasses war graves, memorials, battlefields, mine craters, trenches and every other possible evocation of the Great War.

Taken from Albert, the tour follows the D929 to **La Boiselle**, where there is the huge Lochnager crater from one of the mine explosions which marked the opening of the four and a half months of conflict in the Somme. The route runs west from La Boiselle to **Beaumont-Hamel**, where Newfoundland Park marks the place where every officer of the Newfoundland Regiment was killed or wounded within half an hour of battle commencing on July 1 1916. There is also a memorial here to Scottish soldiers. The route heads back to the D929 via the **Ulster Tower**, a memorial to Irish soldiers who were caught between British artillery fire and German machine gun fire. The tower is a copy of a tower near an army training camp in Belfast. The road then passes the huge British memorial at Thiepval (see main text).

The route runs past a tank memorial at **Pozières**, the spot where tanks were first introduced into the battle on 15 September 1916. Look closely at the village's main street – it was totally reduced to rubble in the battle. The route now turns off to the right to **Longueval**, where there are memorials to soldiers from New Zealand and Canada at Delville Wood. Only 143 out of 4,000 South African troops survived a six-day battle in the woods. At **Rancourt**, the tour visits the chapel that was erected by the De Bos family in memory of their son and his comrades who were killed on 25 September 1916. Here also are French, British and German cemeteries. The route now follows the N17 to the Museum of the History of the Great War at Péronne (see text), before tracking back to Albert via **Mammetz**, where there is a Welsh Memorial topped by a red Welsh dragon.

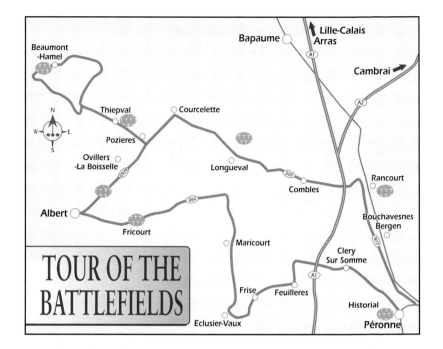

TOUR OF THE BATTLEFIELDS

Poppies in Flanders' fields

Poppy seeds often lie dormant in the soil for many years, but they begin to germinate, grow and flower when the ground is disturbed. When the warm weather came to the fields of the Somme, which had been heavily disturbed in the ferocious battles of the Great War, the poppies began to bloom and were seen as a symbol of new life and hope.

John McCrae, a doctor serving with the Canadian forces, wrote a poem, which ended with the words:

'If ye break faith with us who die
We shall not sleep, though poppies grow
In Flanders' fields.'

On reading this poem, Moina Michael, an American war secretary with the YMCA, decided to buy red poppies and sell them to her friends to raise money for servicemen in need. One of her French colleagues, Madame Guerin, then hit upon the idea of making and selling artificial poppies to help ex-servicemen.

The first Poppy Day was held in Britain on 11 November 1921, to mark the ending of the Great War on the eleventh hour of the eleventh day of the eleventh month. The tradition continues to this day and has widened into a remembrance for all those who have died in conflict.

Thiepval memorial

The story of this dreadful carnage can be traced in detail by following the **Battlefield Tour**, which takes in battle sites, cemeteries and memorials along both the German and Allied fronts, and includes a visit to the **Historal de la Grand Guerre** at **Péronne**, which covers the sociological and human aspects of conflict and the wartime experiences of soldiers and civilians from France, Germany and Britain.

Those with more limited time at their disposal can gain an insight into the futility of the conflict and the appalling loss of life by following the D929 from Albert to Bapaume. The road passes huge expanses of war graves, including a large French cemetery, just outside Albert, and the **British War Cemetery** at Pozières, where a colonnade of Doric columns fronts row upon row of war graves, including many to unknown soldiers.

A short diversion to the left at Pozières leads to **Thiepval** and the 148 ft (45 m) high memorial, designed by Sir Edwin Lutyens, to 72,085 British and South African soldiers who fell between July 1915 and March 1918. The gargantuan brick structure, which is visible for miles around, is an inescapable reminder of the dreadful carnage that took place in these French fields.

The Albert–Bapaume road has other poignant reminders of the Battle of the Somme. Roadside signs indicate the position of the front on different dates, and the huge cemeteries between the signs reveal the cost in human life of gains of just a few kilometres. The Café du Souvenir has a doorway that is flanked by life-size models of two soldiers and topped by a sign bearing the name "Le Tommy."

The Battle of the Somme ended in November 1916, but the war continued for another two years. When the Armistice was finally signed 1918, on the eleventh hour of the eleventh day of the eleventh month, most people thought they had witnessed the end of the "war to end all wars." As we all know, they were wrong!

Arras

A further 12 miles (19km) north of Bapaume, along the N17, lies **Arras**, the capital of Pas-de-Calais. The outskirts are far from inviting, but after entering the city centre and parking in the cobbled **Grand' Place**, visitors find themselves in one of the largest and most beautiful squares in Europe. The Grand' Place is entirely surrounded by elegant town houses, all with Flemish-style scroll gables and ground floor arcades. Some buildings are in stone, others in brick, some in a combination of the two, and every gable is different, but there is a marvellous unity because of the consistency of period styling and height. Also, because all the buildings are just four floors high, the horizontal dimensions of the Grand' Place are exaggerated, giving the square an apparent area even greater than its actual area.

As if this architectural and visual feast were not enough, a short street, known as the Rue de la Taillerie, leads into another cobbled square, the **Place des Héros**, or Petit Place, which is equally impressive. Gabled, arcaded houses again line much of the perimeter, but one side is dominated by the flamboyant Gothic **Hôtel de Ville**, with its 246ft (75m) high belfry. Sit at a table under the arcades of one of the cafés in the Place Des Héros, survey the scene and step back over two centuries in your imagination to a time when Arras was one of the great trading and artistic centres of Europe.

The two squares, which are masterpieces of seventeenth and eighteenth-century town planning, were very badly damaged in the wars of the twentieth-century, but their painstaking renovation is also a triumph of twentieth-century reconstruction.

The 155 gabled façades around the squares are remarkable enough, but Arras has another outstanding, but hidden tourist attraction with highly impressive dimensions. Underneath the city, there are 20 miles (32km) of **Les Boves**, or Les Souterrains, underground passages, which have often been used as refuges over the centuries, not least in times of war. The British Army used the tunnels as a headquarters in World War I and greatly extended them. Guided visits to this underground world are available to tourists.

Arras was famous for its tapestries in the fifteenth century, when the Pope had his tapestries made here to the designs of Raphael. The town also became well known for its porcelain in the eighteenth century. Today, it is noted for its Bleu d'Arras china, and for locally-produced beer, heart-shaped chocolates, cheeses, spiced bread and white sausages. Huge stall markets are held in the Place des Héros on Wednesday and Saturday and there are markets in other locations on Sunday, Wednesday, Thursday and Saturday.

Just behind the Hôtel de Ville, is the eighteenth-century **Abbey of St Vaast**, which contains the **Musée des Beaux Arts**, whose galleries house a good collection of French, Dutch and Flemish art and, of course, porcelain.

Vimy Ridge

There are three possible routes for the return to Boulogne. Follow the N39 to Montreuil and then take the N1 or A12; use the A26 to St Omer and then take the N42; or take the N25 to Abbeville and then take the A25.

Those who have the stomach for yet more memorials to a horrendous war, might wish to make a short detour to **Vimy Ridge** by following the N17 towards Lens. On 9 and 10 April 1917, 60,000 Canadians died here in a battle for command of the ridge, then known as Hill 145. A memorial has been erected to those who were killed, including 11,000 whose bodies were never found. Trenches and tunnels have been preserved as a reminder of the circumstances in which the soldiers died.

Boulogne

ACCOMMODATION

Boulogne

Boulogne has a 3-star hotel in the middle of the shopping district:

***Hotel le Metropole**
Rue Thiers
☎ 0321 315430

There are no less than three Ibis hotels, all offering good accommodation at modest prices:

Ibis Vieille Ville
Rue Porte Neuve, in the Old Town
☎ 0321 312101

Ibis Centre Ville
Boulevard Diderot
☎ 0321 312101

Ibis Plage
on Boulevard Sainte-Beuve, near Nausicaa
☎ 0321 321515

Even cheaper, but perfectly acceptable accommodation can be obtained at:

*Hotel au Sleeping**
Boulevard Daunau
☎ 0321 806279

For those wanting a romantic stay in an eighteenth-century chateau, just 6 miles (9km) from Boulogne, try:

***Chateau Clery**
at Hesdau l'Abbe
☎ 0321 831983

There is a Youth Hostel at Place Rouget de Lisle, near the station
☎ 0321 991530

Le Touquet round-trip

Neufchatel-Hardelot

Golfers may wish to stay close to the courses at one of the following:

***Hotel du Parc**
Avenue Francois 1
☎ 0321 332211

Hotel le Regina
Avenue Francois 1
☎ 0321 838188

Le Touquet

Le Touquet has almost twenty hotels graded 2-star or above. A selection follows:

****Westminster Hotel**
Avenue de Verger
The premier hotel in Le Touquet. Reductions on some green fees.
☎ 0321 054848

****Hotel Holiday Inn Resort Le Touquet**
Avenue de Maréchal Foch
Glass roofed public area, indoor pool.
☎ 0321 068585

****Park Plaza Grand Hotel**
Boulevard de la Canche
Good standard, reasonable prices, indoor pool.
☎ 0321 068888

**Hotel le Nouveau Caddy
Rue de Metz
Central, reasonable prices
☎ 0321 058395

**Hotel Blue Cottage
Rue Jean Monnet
Central, popular restaurant
☎ 0321 051333

**Hotel Red Fox
Rue Saint-Jean
Modern. near shops, some
reductions on green fees.
☎ 0321 052758

Montreuil

****Hotel Chateau de Montreuil
Rue Pierre Ledent
The height of luxury
☎ 0321 815304

***Hautes de Montreuil
Rue Pierre Ledent
Sixteenth-century hostelry, superb
wine list
☎ 0321 819592

*Hotel Bellevue
Avenue 11 Novembre
Just outside walls, good value for
money
☎ 0321 060419

Camping
There is a camp site, with swimming
pool at:.

Camping du Blanc Pignon
on N39 2 miles NW of Montreuil
☎ 0321 869812

The battlefields of the Somme

Abbeville

Abbeville has 230 hotel rooms. A
sample follows:

***Hotel de France
Place du Pilori
Rooms have been renovated recently
☎ 0322 240042

**Le Relais Vauban
Boulevard Vauban
22 rooms
☎ 0322 317597

**Hotel Ibis
Route d'Amiens
60 rooms
☎ 0322 248080

Formula 1
Route d'Amiens
For cheap, basic, clean
accommodation
☎ 0322 240750

There is a campsite at:
Airotel Chateau des Tilleuils
Rue Amiral-Coubet, on D40
☎ 0322 241528

Amiens

Amiens is an excellent base for those
who wish to spend time exploring
the Somme battlefields. Hotels
include:

***Hotel Carlton
Rue de Noyon
Air-conditioned rooms, traditional
dishes
☎ 0322 977722

***Novotel**
Rue Michel Strogoff
Swimming pool, fenced parking
☎ 0322 504242

****Holiday Inn Express**
Boulevard Alsace Lorraine
Free Continental breakfast
☎ 0322 223850

****Hotel Campanile**
On RN29
Terrace in the summer
☎ 0322 538989

****Ibis Centre**
Rue de Mal de Lattre de Tassigny
☎ 0322 520404

Kyriad Vidéotel
Rue Le Gréco in St Ladre
☎ 0322 520404

La Prieuré
Rue Porion
Attractive location by cathedral
☎ 0322 922767

Arras

There are a number of good hotels in
Arras. The larger ones include:

***L'Atria Mercure**
Boulevard Carnot
80 rooms, all well-equipped.
☎ 0321 238888

***Le Moderne**
Boulevard Faidherbe
55 rooms
☎ 0321 233957

***L'Univers de la Providence**
Place de la Croix rouge
37 rooms in a converted monastery
☎ 0321 713401

****Astoria Carnot**
31 rooms
Place Foch
☎ 0321 710814

**** Hotel Ibis**
Place Ipswich
63 rooms
☎ 0321 236161

ATTRACTIONS

Boulogne

Nausicaa Sea-Life Centre
Boulevard Sainte-Beuve
Open: every day: 9.30am–8pm in July
and August. 9.30am–6.30pm at other
times of year.
☎ 0321 309999

**Chateau and Museum
(Antiquities and Eskimo masks)**
Rue de Bernet
Open: every day, except Tues.: 10am–
12.30pm, 2–5.30pm
☎ 0321 100220

Belfry and Hotel de Ville
Place Godefroy Bouillon
Open: Monday–Friday 8am–12noon,
2–6pm. Sat: 8am–12noon
☎ 0321 878080

Sail-karting, speed sailing
Char a Voile Club
Boulevard Sainte-Beuve
☎ 0321 832548

Yachting
Yacht Club Boulonnais
Boulevard Sainte-Beuve
☎ 0321 318067

Le Touquet round-trip

Etaples

Musée de la Marine
In the Mareis
Open: 10am–12noon. 3–6pm (7pm in high season. Closed Sunday am)
☎ 0321097721

Fishing trips
(45mins or 12 hours)
apply tourist office, Mareis
☎ 0321 095694

Bird watching
apply tourist office, Mareis
☎ 0321 095694

Hardelot

Golf
Golf des Dunes (2 courses)
☎ 0321 837310

Sail-karting
Les Drakkars
☎ 0321 832793

Horse riding
Ecole d'Equitation Pony Club
☎ 0321 918377

Le Touquet

Aqualand
Every day: 10am–6pm (late night Friday, Saturday in July and August)
☎ 0321 056359

Le Touquet Museum
Leveque paintings
Open: Wednesday–Saturday: 10am–12noon, 2–6pm. Sunday: 10am–12noon, 2.30–6pm
☎ 0321 056262

Sand-yachting
Bertrand Lambert
☎ 0321 053351

Golfing
Golf Club Group
3 courses
☎ 0321 062800

Riding
Parc International de la Canche
Avenue de la Dune aux Loups
☎ 0321 051525

Montreuil

Citadelle
Esplanade de la Citadelle
☎ 0321 061083

Battlefields of the Somme

Abbeville
Musée Boucher-de-Perthes
Rue Gontier-Patin
☎ 0322 240849

Amiens

**Guided boat trips
around Hortillonnages**
Boulevard Beauville
Every day: April–October
☎ 0322 921218

Jules Verne Centre
Rue Charles Dubois
Open: Tuesday–Saturday: 9.30am–12noon, 2–6pm.
Includes tours of the writer's favourite haunts
☎ 0322 453784

Musée de Picardie
Rue de la République
Open: Tuesday–Sunday 10am–12.30pm, 2–6pm.
☎ 0322 913644

Albert

Musée des Arbres (Somme 1916)
Rue Gambetta
Open: 9.30am–12noon, 2–6pm
☎ 0322 751617

Péronne
Historal de la Grand Guerre
Place du Chateau
Tuesday–Sunday: 10am–6pm out of
high season. In high season, open daily.
☎ 0322 831418

Arras
Tour of underground passages
ask at the tourist office
Place des Héros
☎ 0321 12643

Musée des Beaux Arts
Rue Paul Douner
Open: Out of season: 10am–12noon,
2–6pm. Closed Tuesday. In high
season: daily: 10am–6pm.
☎ 0321 712613

EATING OUT

Boulogne
The many restaurants and cafés in
Boulogne are located in four main
areas: the quayside; the lower town
shopping area; Place Dalton and Rue
de Lille in the Haute Ville.

La Matelote
Boulevard Sainte-Beuve
Has a high reputation for fish dishes
☎ 0321 301797

Mimi d'Anvers
On the same street as La Matelote
offers good fish dishes at much more
reasonable prices.
☎ 0321 999090

Au Bon Accueil
Rue de Lille
Offers a good vegetarian choice, as
well as fish dishes
☎ 0321 803741

Le Touquet round-trip

Le Touquet
There are plenty of good restaurants
and bars in the town, including
those that are located in hotels. A
small selection of restaurants
follows:

Café des Sports
Rue Saint-Jean
Good brasserie in the main shopping
street
☎ 0321 505022

Le Village Suisse
Rue Saint-Jean
Traditional food in traditional
surroundings
☎ 0321 056993

Café des Arts
Rue de Paris
Good vegetables, good sea food
☎ 0321 052155

La Dune aux Loups
Avenue de la Dune aux Loups
Olde world atmosphere, near
equestrian centre.
☎ 0321 054254

Montreuil
Chateau de Montreuil
Chef trained by the Roux Brothers
☎ 0321 815304

Hauts de Montreuil
Superb restaurant, superb wine
☎ 0321 819592

Battlefields of the Somme
Abbeville
Visitors might like to try:
La Picardiere
Route de Paris
Picardy specialities
☎ 0322 241528

Amiens

There is lots of choice, including:
La Couronne
Rue St Leu
One of the best restaurants in the
old quarter
☎ 0322 918857

La Mangeoire
Rue des Sergents
Good vegetarian options
☎ 0322 911128

La Dent Creuse
Rue Cormont
Near the cathedral, good local
specialities.
☎ 0322 910699

Arras

Lots of options. Visitors may wish
to try:
La Faisanderie
Grand' Place
High reputation
☎ 0321 482076

La Rapiere
Grand' Place
☎ 0321 550992

La Coupole
Boulevard de Strasbourg
☎ 0321 718844

Le Viviani
Rue Housse
☎ 0321 513692

SHOPPING

Boulogne

The Rue de Lille, in the Haute Ville
(upper town) is good for souvenirs,
cheeses, nougats, bread, pastries and
chocolate.

Place Dalton, half way down the hill,
which leads to the quayside, has a
famous Wednesday and Saturday
market.
There is an extensive range of shops
in the area around the Grande Rue,
Rue Victor Hugo and Rue Thiers –
the famous *fromagerie* of Philippe
Olivier is on Rue Thiers.
The fish market, on the quayside,
operates from 6.30am every
morning, except Sunday.

Le Touquet round-trip

Etaples

The new Mareis centre has a good
selection of crafts, especially those
with a seafaring theme.

Le Touquet

The main shopping street in Le
Touquet is Rue Saint-Jean –
particularly good for sports clothes,
fashions, antiques, crystal, leather
goods, hand-made chocolate.
Montreuil shops have a good
selection of lace, antiques and
pottery.

Market days:

Etaples:	Tuesday, Friday. Daily fish market.
Le Crotoy:	Friday. Sunday fish market.
Le Touquet:	Monday (summer only), Thursday, Saturday.
Montreuil:	Saturday.

Battlefields of the Somme

Amiens

Amiens is good for shopping. Locally
produced vegetables are on sale in
the water-side market in the Saint-
Leu quarter on Thursday and

Saturday mornings. There is a flea market on the second Sunday in each month in Saint-Leu, which is always good for bargains and antiques.

Amiens has all the usual chain stores and a wide range of shops. Look out for macaroons and almonds, especially in Les Halles market area.

Arras

The central markets on Sunday, Wednesday, Thursday, Saturday are very extensive. There are good shops throughout the city. Look out for Bleu d'Arras china, heart-shaped chocolates, cheeses, spice bread, white sausage and local beer.

TOURIST INFORMATION

Boulogne
Quai de la Poste
☎ 0321 316838

Le Touquet round-trip

Berck-sur-Mer
Avenue Francis Tattegrain
☎ 0321 095000

Etaples
In the Mareis
☎ 0321 095694

Le Touquet
Place de l'Hermitage
☎ 0321 067200

Merlimont
Rue de la Station
☎ 0321 943290

Montreuil
Rue Carnot
☎ 0321 060427

Neufchatel-Hardelot
Avenue de la Concorde
☎ 0321 830265

Samer
Rue de Desvres
☎ 0321 871042

Battlefields of the Somme

Abbeville
Place Courbet
☎ 0322 242792

Amiens
Rue Duseval
☎ 0322 716050

Albert
Rue Gambetta
☎ 0322 751642

Péronne
Rue St Fursy
☎ 0322 844238

Arras
Place des Héros
☎ 0321 512695

4.1 A TOUR OF DIEPPE

The place-name Dieppe means "deep", a reference to the deep inshore waters that helped to establish this 1,000-year-old town as France's oldest port. Seafarers who have set sail from Dieppe include: Jehan Ango, who was born here in 1480 and has been variously described as pirate, shipbuilder, naval adviser to François I, Governor of Dieppe, entrepreneur and politician; Admiral Duquesne, who was denied promotion after his famous naval victories because he refused to give up his Calvinist faith; and Samuel de Champlain, a Dieppe shipbuilder who was one of the founders of Quebec.

A Personal view of Dieppe

Dieppe has always had a special place in my imagination. At secondary school, I was taught French by a teacher who had a habit of telling the class just before each half-term holiday that he was "planning to pop over to Dieppe for a few days". Whenever he made this announcement, a picture would come into my mind of a panama-hatted, French-speaking Englishman sitting at a pavement café with a copy of Le Monde. After leaving school, I became a fan of the paintings of Walter Sickert, who was also fond of popping over to the old Normandy port and even lived there for a time with his French mistress and her children. His painting of Bathers, Dieppe formed a definitive image in my mind of the French seaside.

Many years later, on my first trip to Dieppe, I searched in vain for a panama-hatted Englishman and I was disappointed to find that the sea temperature on the particular day of my visit was far too low for bathers. Despite these disappointments, I quickly became entranced by the old French port.

When I parked my car on Quay Henri IV on that first visit, in the early morning of a crisp, clear October day, yachts were bobbing gently in the harbour, causing their rigging to clink out a dawn chorus; fishermen were selling their fresh catch from quayside stalls; cafés were opening up for their first customers and dog-walkers were taking their pets for an early morning constitutional. So began a magical first day in Dieppe, which ended, many hours later, with my joining the late evening strollers on the town's long seaside promenade.

Getting there

Hoverspeed operates high-speed Seacat crossings from Newhaven to Dieppe. The 60-mile (97km) journey takes about 2 hours. Until recently, Hoverspeed only ran a summer service, but all-year-round services have now been reinstated.

Dieppe can be reached by car from Calais by taking the A16 autoroute to Abbeville and then the D925 via Treport. The journey, of about 120 miles (193km), takes roughly two and a half hours.

TOP TIPS FOR DIEPPE

Not to be missed

- Dieppe Quayside
- Church of St Jacques, Dieppe
- Café des Tribunaux, once a meeting place for the Impressionists
- The Chateau, Dieppe

Things to do

- Buy fresh fish from a quayside stall
- Have a drink in a window seat at a café on the Quai Henri IV
- Shop for chocolates, cheeses, wines, coffee and fashionable clothes on the pedestrianised Grande Rue
- Watch the world go by in the Place du Puits Sale
- See the seventeenth-century organ at St Rémy church
- Visit Dieppe's castle-museum and see ivory carvings and Impressionist paintings
- Visit the memorial to the Canadians killed in the disastrous Dieppe Raid of 1942
- See the castle by floodlight
- Join the strollers on Dieppe's long promenade
- Have a drink in a glass-fronted café overlooking the beach
- Fly a kite, play tennis or play mini-golf on the esplanade
- Visit the fishermen's quarter
- Fish from the quayside or hire a boat to go sea-fishing
- Play golf at Pourville
- See the sights on a petit train
- Have a meal in a restaurant on Quai Henri IV

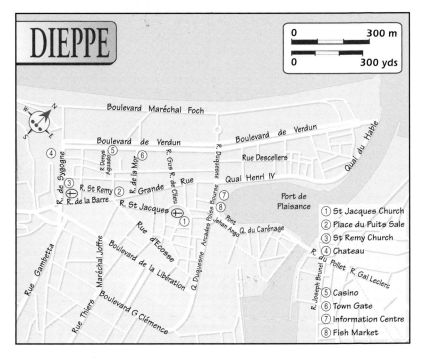

By the seventeenth century, Dieppe had become a major focus for the carving of ivory, which was brought here from the west coast of Africa, and the town had evolved into France's largest fishing port. Fishing is still an important local industry and the super-fresh catch is still sold each morning at the fish market next to the tourist office, but the basin at the heart of Dieppe has been converted into a marina and is now home to a large number of pleasure craft.

Dieppe has much to recommend it, for it is not only an attractive port and watering place, but also the gateway to the Alabaster Coast: a succession of hanging valleys, spectacular cliffs and pleasant seaside resorts with fantastical villa architecture. Rouen, one of the most fascinating historic cities in France, is but a short journey to the south,

Monet's wonderful garden at Giverny is reached by taking the road from Rouen to Paris; the great cathedral of Beauvais and the pretty villages of Clères and Gerberoy are all within easy reach of Dieppe.

A WALKING TOUR OF DIEPPE

Motorists entering Dieppe soon find themselves caught up in a relentless one-way system that loops around the town in an anti-clockwise direction. There are some parking places at the beginning of the loop, on the Quai Henry IV, and there are further parking lots at the seaward end of Quai du Hable, where there is a wide area between Boulevard de Verdun and Boulevard Maréchal Foch. Motorists have a final chance to find a parking place at the western end of the promenade, just below the castle, but anyone who misses this third opportunity has little option but to carry on around the loop and start the search all over again.

After looping-the-loop in search of a parking spot, enjoy a change of pace by taking a stroll around the town. Dieppe has a compact central area and is ideal for an on-foot exploration. A rectangular walking route, followed in a clockwise direction from the Tourist Information Centre, takes in no less than seven attractive and contrasting features: the harbour; the Saint Jacques market area; the main shopping street; a famous inn; St Rémy Church; an impressive castle and the long seaside promenade.

Begin at the tourist office, which is located by the Jehan Ango Bridge overlooking the busy port with its backcloth of picturesque quayside buildings. If it is early enough in the morning, fishermen will be selling their fresh catch at stalls near the tourist office. Along the quay, there are attractive bars, cafés and restaurants, all of which provide seats with a fine view over the colourful harbour. It will be hard to resist the opportunity for an early morning coffee at a window seat, before setting off on a walk around the town.

With regard to meals, there are menus to suit all tastes, but seafood, not surprisingly, is a speciality. The name of one café, the New Haven, emphasizes Dieppe's considerable economic dependence on the daily influx of English tourists who come over on the Newhaven-Dieppe Seacat. Councillors in the French port have even suggested that they might have to consider purchasing the ferry terminal at Newhaven as a means of ensuring the continuing flow of the town's life blood along this vital tourist artery.

Dieppe's tallest structure, the **Church of Saint Jacques**, is situated close to the quayside, just a few strides west of the Tourist Office. The building, which dates from the fourteenth century, is characterized by prominent flying buttresses, lacework-like tracery in the west window and a plethora of gargoyles. The church is depicted in many paintings by Pissarro, who had a particularly fine view of the building from the Hotel du Commerce where he took up residence.

Saint Jacques overlooks the Place National, which contains a monument to Admiral Duquesne and is the location for Dieppe's excellent Saturday open-air market, which often spills over into nearby streets to accommodate the wide range of produce from the region's farmers, as well as goods from many other areas of the country.

Grande Rue

Now enter the pedestrianised **Grande Rue**, Dieppe's main shopping street, which runs, arrow-straight, from the Place National to the Place du Puits Sale. The Grande Rue is a treat for shoppers, because it is fully pedestrianised and contains a splendid variety of retail outlets, including chocolate shops with mouth-watering displays, boutiques with chic fashions for both adults and children, épiceries with a fine selection of wines and cheeses, and coffee shops which diffuse their rich aroma into the street. The French flair for display is evident in every window.

The Grande Rue ends at the **Place du Puits Sale**, where six streets radiate from a saltwater well topped by an ornate wrought-iron canopy. There is a pleasant seating area by the well, where visitors can rest for a while and take in the street scene. The square is overlooked by the famous **Café du Tribunaux**, a picturesque, half-timbered inn that rivals the Parisian cafés at Montparnasse and St Germain des Pres as a historic mecca for artists and writers. Oscar Wilde is said to have written *The Ballad of Reading Gaol* here; Walter Sickert famously met Gauguin here (see feature box) and Pissarro, Renoir, Monet and Whistler were all in the habit pausing at the inn for refreshment, as visitors will surely wish to do too.

After pausing for a drink, carry on walking along the street, which evolves into the Rue de la Barre after the Place du Puits Sale. Streets lead off to the right into a square dominated by the **Church of St Rémy**. This fine structure, which was largely built in the sixteenth and seventeenth centuries, was used as an arms dump by the Germans in World War II and partially destroyed in 1944. The restored building contains a very impressive seventeenth-century organ.

Château

Roads run westwards from St Rémy to the foot of a hill topped by Dieppe's flint and sandstone **Château**. This large pepperpot-towered building looks out to the sea and also commands impressive views over the town and surrounding countryside.

The **Musée du Château** contains many interesting exhibits, including maritime artefacts, a collection of locally-carved ivory and paintings by

Don't give up the day job

Time spent in Tahiti proved to be the making of the artist **Paul Gauguin**, but his experiences in Dieppe at the beginning of his artistic career were far less encouraging. In his biography of Gauguin, David Sweetman explains how the artist was out walking in Dieppe one day when he came across Degas, who promptly invited Gauguin to visit him in his studio. When Gauguin took up the offer and arrived at Degas' studio two days later, he clearly saw Degas at work through the window, but was told by the maid who answered the door that Degas was not in.

After this snub, Gauguin felt rejected as an artist and became a very solitary, but his friend Mélicourt, who was a local painter, tried to cheer him up by promising to arrange a meeting between Gauguin and the English artist Walter Sickert, who was a frequent visitor to Dieppe.

It is said that the two duly met at the Café du Tribunaux, whereupon Sickert told Gauguin that it would be unwise to give up his job as a bank clerk in order to devote himself to painting. Sickert recalled in his memoirs that he had felt at the time that Gauguin was little more than a Sunday painter. A sketch of Gauguin's, which he had seen, had "left no very distinct impression."

After these snubs by fellow artists, it is surprising that Gauguin not only gave up the day job, but also gave up living in France to go off and paint in the South Seas.

masters such as Renoir, Braque, Boudin and Pissarro. The nearby **Square du Canada** is a reminder that sailors from Dieppe played a major role in the exploration of Canada and it also acts as a memorial to the Canadian soldiers who lost their lives in the raid on Dieppe in 1942.

A SUICIDAL RAID

On 19 august 1942, Dieppe was the scene of a suicidal raid on German-occupied France. Six thousand Allied troops, including 4,961 Canadians, made landings at Dieppe, supposedly to test whether it would be possible to launch an invasion of the Continent from a Channel port.

If this was the purpose of the attack, the mission produced a very emphatic answer. The German defences were far too strong for the raiders. Very heavy casualties were sustained; 3,363 Canadians were killed, wounded, captured or went missing in the attack. Some were even shot down before they had chance to disembark.

Some historians suggest that the raid was carried out to make the Germans think that information was being sought in preparation for an imminent invasion. Others suggest that the Canadian forces in Britain were sent on this ill-fated mission because they had become bored through inactivity.

The raid was justified to the public as an assignment that had taught the Allies invaluable lessons. As the historian Mark Arnold-Foster has said, "the only real lesson learned from the Dieppe Raid was that it should never have been launched."

Dieppe's seaside

The castle, which looks especially impressive when floodlit, stands above the town at the western end of Dieppe's long, straight, seaside promenade. Two roads, Boulevard Maréchal Foch and Boulevard de Verdun, which run parallel with the promenade, are separated by a large expanse of lawn, somewhat reminiscent of that at Southsea in England. A line of large hotels, including two rather incongruous modern structures, is interrupted by an impressive, sensitively-restored, fortified town gate (**Les Tourelles**).

Dieppe is France's oldest seaside resort. The Duchesse de Berry is said to have started the craze for sea-bathing on these very shores in the early nineteenth century and the town subsequently became especially popular with Parisians, as it is the nearest seaside resort to the French capital. In the 1920s and 1930s, the town also became a favoured destination for trippers from England (including my old French teacher!). It has to be said that the beach is somewhat pebbly and the climate is generally bracing rather than warm, but Dieppe remains a very popular resort, not only with Channel-hoppers, but also with French families.

There is a casino on the Boulevard de Verdun and, at the western end of the promenade, there are a swimming pool and facilities for tennis and mini-golf. Thanks to the frequently windy conditions, wind-surfing in the sea and kite-flying on the lawns are especially popular activities – a kite-flying festival is held in Dieppe in September in even numbered years. But the most popular activity of all seems to be an evening promenade along the 1.2 mile (2km) length of the **Boulevard Maréchal Foch**. Having joined the

---

Footnote!

Early morning in Dieppe is dog-walking time, especially for fashionably-dressed ladies and their dogs. The British painter Adrian George, who lives in France, has said, "French women dress from the back and, like turned playing cards, the face value is often a surprise." This is certainly the case in Dieppe, where there seems to be a high concentration of mature lady dog-walkers who manage to look like young women when viewed from the rear, largely because they have the means to dress well and keep their figures in trim.

As required fashion accessories for these ladies, the dogs are often dressed in the very latest line in dog-coats and they often have to endure cute little bows in their fur. Watching the dog-walkers can be entertaining, but there is a downside to this daily fashion parade by humans and their canine companions, because very few French dog-walkers take the trouble to clear up after their pets. Consequently the pavements of Dieppe show plenty of evidence of dog fouling. Be careful where you tread!

---

throng of strollers for a slow perambulation by the sea, pause for a drink at one of the many beach-side cafes, where patrons are suitably protected from the chill Channel breezes by glass wind-breaks. For visitors who wish to snack while walking along, there are plenty of food and drink stalls to cater for their needs.

The town trail can now be completed by returning to the Port de Plaisance Jehan Ango and the Tourist Information Office via the Quai du Hable. Those with enough energy left, might wish to cross the Jehan Ango bridge and then the Pont Colbert, in order to gain access to **Le Quartier du Pollet,** the old fishermen's quarter. This part of the town is marketed as a quaint, picturesque area. Perhaps I have made an insufficient exploration of the quarter, but I have to report that I do not find it particularly attractive.

Apart from the usual beach fun and the wide choice of sporting facilities encountered on the promenade, Dieppe has much to offer in the way of other diversions. Anglers can fish from the quayside or hire boats for sea-fishing. Horse riding and golf are available nearby and both children and adults can enjoy a petit train ride from the Information Office.

In common with almost all French towns, Dieppe has a large out-of-town commercial complex. The Belvedere Shopping Centre, on the Rouen road, includes an Auchun hyper-market, many retail outlets and a number of fast food restaurants.

102

4.2 A JOURNEY ALONG THE ALABASTER COAST

INTRODUCTION

The **Alabaster Coast**, between Dieppe and Étretat, is one of the most spectacular stretches of coastline in France. Sheer cliffs of white chalk form a dramatic, but vulnerable interface between the pounding sea and the rich Normandy farmlands. Erosion of the soft chalk has created some fantastic needles and rock arches and punctuated the line of cliffs with a succession of remark-able hanging valleys (*valleuses*). Not surprisingly, every single indentation in the wall of chalk is occupied by a holiday resort, whose size is dictated by the width of the dip in which it stands.

Some of the resorts along the coast are quite small, but very well equipped with paddling pools and play areas and therefore much frequented by families with small children, while Étretat and Fécamp are large, well-developed holiday resorts with all the usual amuse-ments and entertainments, but every one of these places is within easy reach of wonderful cliff walks and superb coastal scenery, which takes its most spectacular form at Étretat, whose alabaster stacks and rock arches are some of Europe's finest and most memorable rock formations.

Some of the man-made structures of the Alabaster Coast are equally memorable, especially the Art Nouveau mansion at Bois des Moutiers and the seaside architecture of the region, which is a highly eccentric and highly entertaining interpretation of the traditional Normandy half-timbered style. Many of the seaside villas are top-heavy concoctions of deep-set gables and mock half-timbering. A concoction of a different sort is produced at Fécamp, where the monks developed a new liqueur, which came to be known as Bénédictine.

With the coming of a fast and frequent rail link between Paris and Dieppe, the Alabaster Coast became very popular, not only with holiday-makers from the capital, but also with the many artists based in Paris. Monet was greatly inspired by the cliffs at Varengeville, a village whose church-yard contains the grave of Georges Braque, the great Cubist painter. It is hardly surprising that artists were drawn to this coast, because it is one of the most visually impressive stretches of coast in a country that rightly boasts that it has some of the finest coastal scenery in the world.

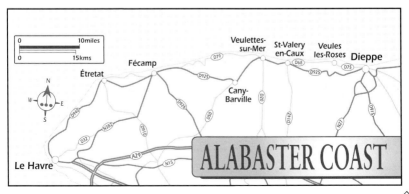

Top tips for the Alabaster Coast

Not to be missed
- The British-designed house and garden at Bois des Moutiers
- The cliff-top church of St Valéry. Varengeville
- The Benedictine Museum at Fécamp
- St Trinité, Fécamp
- The rock arches and stack rocks at Étretat
- The sea-farers' chapel and aviators' museum at Étretat

Things to do
- Spot top-heavy villas at Pourville-sur-Mer
- Picnic in the grounds of Manoir d'Ango
- See the Jesse window in the church of St Valéry, Varengeville
- See the grave of George's Braque in the churchyard of St Valéry
- Admire the cliff scenery at Varengeville
- Spend time on the sands at St Marguerite or Quiberville or St Aubin
- Walk to the edge of the cliffs at Sotteville
- Give the children time on the play area or the paddling pool at Veules-les-Roses or St Valéry-en-Caux
- Have morning coffee at the Hotel de Mer in Fécamp
- Buy a bottle of liqueur at the Benedictine Museum, Fécamp
- In the church of St Trinité, Fécamp, see the casket that is supposed to contain droplets of Christ's blood
- Check out the phases of the moon and the times of the tides on St Trinité's astronomical clock
- Trace the history of babies' bottles in the museum at Fécamp
- See reminders of deep-sea fishing in the North Atlantic at the Museum of the Newfoundland Fishermen, Fécamp
- Walk the Sailors' Path to Notre Dame du Salut
- Hire a sail-board or sail-scooter at Fécamp
- Watch the sun set under the 'Elephant rock', Étretat
- Walk on the cliff tops at Étretat for magnificent views of rock arches and stacks
- Have a meal in a glass-fronted restaurant overlooking the sea at Étretat
- Marvel at the fantastical Manoir de Salamandre, Étretat
- Shop for wooden gifts in the market hall at Étretat
- Look out for references to the 51st Highlanders
- Visit the aquarium built into the cliff at Étretat
- Visit an Étretat house dedicated to the 'Gentleman Burglar'
- Ride in a steam train from Étretat to Les Loges

A JOURNEY ALONG THE ALABASTER COAST

For a memorable trip along this fine coast, take the D75 westwards from Dieppe. After a short rise, the road descends to a brief dip in the cliffs at **Pourville-sur-Mer**, for a first encounter with those top-heavy, mock half-timbered, seaside villas which are so characteristic of the Normandy coast. The nearby Pourville-Dieppe golf course, which also has a good restaurant, is a popular attraction (see Additional Information).

Varengeville

After Pourville, the road twists and turns back to the cliff tops through a richly wooded area known as **Varengeville-sur-Mer**. Here there are glimpses through the beech trees of some highly desirable residences, not least the celebrated **Bois des Moutiers**, which was designed by Sir Edwin Lutyens in a style that is clearly based on the revolutionary Art Nouveau buildings of Charles Rennie Mackintosh. The mansion is set in a splendid landscaped garden designed by Gertrude Jekyll and has been developed over the years by the occupants of the house, the Mallet family. The garden, which can be visited in the summer months, is famed for its rhododendrons, azaleas and roses.

Bois des moutiers

The Bois des Moutiers is a remarkable piece of English house and garden design. In 1898, a French banker called Guilliaume Mallet asked the up-and-coming young English architect Edwin Lutyens to re-design and extend his house at Varengeville, near Dieppe. Lutyens, who was influenced by William Morris and the Arts and Crafts movement, had already designed a number of private houses in southern England. The house he built at Varengeville has something of the Home Counties about it, but Lutyens was also influenced by the revolutionary Art Nouveau buildings of the Scottish architect Charles Rennie Mackintosh and he duly inserted Mackintosh-style "ladder" windows in Guilliaume Mallet's house.

The interior of the house was also carefully designed by Lutyens, who was known for his creative use of materials, be they stone, marble, wood or plaster. The Music Room, with its double-height window is the most striking of the rooms, but high-backed Mackintosh chairs and a Burne-Jones tapestry also add to the period splendour of the interior. The Mallet family, who still live at Bois des Moutiers, have proudly and carefully conserved the house and its contents, and they often show visitors around the house themselves.

When he was just beginning to establish his own architectural practice, Lutyens was introduced to Gertrude Jekyll, a landscape gardener with a growing reputation (pun intended!). From that moment, Lutyens and Jekyll, who was also much influenced by William Morris, worked together on many projects, including Bois des Moutiers.

Jekyll believed that "there is no spot of ground, however arid, bare or ugly, that cannot be tamed into such a state as may give an impression of beauty and delight." The 45 acres (18 hectares) of land at Bois des Moutiers gave Jekyll plenty of scope. The acid soil of the locality allowed her to introduce rhododendrons and azaleas and the sloping site, which runs down to the sea, was ideal for her artistry.

Lutyens went on to achieve great fame with his designs for the Viceroy's House in India, the Cenotaph in London and many other war memorials, including Thiepval (see the Battlefields of the Somme tour). He was knighted in 1918.

Jekyll and Lutyens continued to work together and were two of the designers involved in the construction of Queen Mary's Doll's House. Gertrude Jekyll died in 1932; Lutyens designed her tombstone, which bears the words, "Artist, Gardener, Craftswoman."

Jehan Ango's sixteenth-century residence, the **Manoir d'Ango**, is close to Bois des Moutiers. It is designed in an Italian Renaissance style and has a distinctive round dovecote, which is said to have spaces for no less than 1,600 pairs of birds! The grounds make a good spot for a picnic.

St Valéry

The road finally opens up at the cliff top, where there is a small, isolated flint and brick church, beautifully sited in a slight dip on the edge of the cliffs. The church, known as **St Valéry**, is surrounded by a very extensive graveyard, which is very reminiscent of that at St Tudno's Church, on the Great Orme, above the Welsh resort of Llandudno.

Georges Braque, one of the founders of Cubism, is buried here. His tombstone is a very plain, flat, grey slab with a simple inscription, but it is backed by a wide headstone with a beautiful mosaic depiction of a dove. Braque spent his last years at Varengeville and designed a stunning, stained-glass **Tree of Jesse**

window in the church. Before proceeding to the next resort, visitors will almost certainly wish to linger in this peaceful place – I always find on my visits to St Valéry that I am drawn back into the church time and time again for further glimpses of that marvellous Braque window which almost seems to radiate its own brilliant blue light.

The artists' church

The thirteenth-century church of St Valéry , near Varengeville, was embellished in the sixteenth century by Jehan Ango, who lived at nearby Manoir d'Ango. The result is a nave roof that looks like an upturned boat and columns with carved shells, suns and scallops, supposedly to represent his voyages around the world.

However, the finest addition to the church came four hundred years later with the insertion of stained-glass windows designed by the Cubist artist Georges Braque. Braque lived in Varengeville from World War II until his death in 1963. His Jesse window, which depicts Christ's line of descent from Jesse's son King David, is a brilliant composition in blue, which seems to bring both the sun and the sea right into the church.

The church, which almost seems in danger of slipping into the sea, also attracted the attention of Claude Monet, who painted the building on one of his many painting trips from nearby Pourville.

More resorts

The road from Varengeville drops down to St Marguerite-sur-Mer, where there is a nice promenade and good little beach with a very neat line of brightly-painted, cloned beach huts. Half way along the sea front, the place-name suddenly changes to Quiberville-sur-Mer..

After another up-and-over, the road drops to yet another small inlet. This indentation contains the hamlet of St Aubin, where there is a very striking Art Deco house right by the sea.

The route now climbs out of St Aubin to Sotteville-sur-Mer, which, contrary to its name, is not by the sea at all, but occupies high ground half a mile or so from the cliff-edge. This unspoilt village, which seems to have been bypassed by the modern age, has a nice church with a typical Normandy-style, layered tower, a busy Tabac and a scattering of farms, all set around a very wide open space.

A short drive to the cliff-top provides splendid views over the sea and an encounter with some friendly cows. The seashore can be accessed from this bracing cliff-top via 250 rock steps. Anyone contemplating the descent should bear in mind the prospect of the tiring return journey!

The D75 now heads for another dip in the cliffs at Veules-les-Roses, a pleasant little resort with a beach-side play area and a paddling pool to keep the children happy, and a casino to give the adults a sporting chance of happiness. The little wooden promenade is a miniature version of Deauville's famous *planches* and there are some splendid wooden benches for sea-watching. Veules-les-Roses' attractions do not end with its seaside facilities. Just behind the seafront, in the valley of the Veules (France's shortest river, at just over half a mile [1km]) there is a pretty hamlet of half-timbered houses.

St Valéry-en-Caux

After the next summit, the D75 descends below two large, cliff-top residences, whose architecture is totally outlandish, even by Normandy standards, and then runs past a richly timbered quayside house (Maison Henri IV), which now houses the local tourist office, into St Valéry-en-Caux.

St Valéry is a much bigger version of Veules. Here too, there are a children's play area, a paddling pool and a casino, but also a lighthouse and the jetties of a working port. The cliffs are impressive and, judged on their numbers, seagulls absolutely love the place, but it is not nearly as pretty as Veules.

Now take the D925, which runs past a large Mercure hotel and through the unattractive bottleneck town of Cany-Barville, before it crosses a broad plateau of agricultural land and then plunges into Fécamp.

Fécamp

First impressions, dropping down the hill into Fécamp, are of a rather unattractive working port, but visitors finally arrive at a seafront promenade stretched along a wide gap between high cliffs. Fécamp is indeed a working port, with deep-sea trawlers leaving at regular intervals for northern Atlantic waters, but there are hotels, restaurants and all the usual facilities for holidaymakers.

Although the Hôtel de Mer has a rather uninviting, slab-like exterior, it is a good place to stop for a morning coffee, not least because it has immaculate toilet facilities and an adjacent children's play area, which has good climbing frames. Scuba-diving is a popular activity in the sea, which seems a little rougher at Fécamp than in the more easterly resorts. The cliff scenery is impressive, the promenade is partially surfaced in Deauville-style planks, and a restaurant and casino complex has rather pretentiously adopted the name La Croisette from the Riviera resort of Cannes.

Fécamp may have pretensions to be a northern version of the Côte d'Azur but, to many eyes, the beach and promenade are rather bleak and strangely uninviting, and the juxtaposition of holiday resort and working town, which could be a positive feature, strikes a rather discordant note here.

However anyone who enjoys water-based activities is unlikely to be disappointed at Fécamp. Sail boards and "sail-scooters" are available for hire by energetic visitors and there are one-hour boat trips along the spectacular coast for those who enjoy more leisurely pursuits. But, be warned – the sea can be rough along this shore!

Bénédictine

Fécamp does have a unique claim to fame. A short walk into the town from the promenade takes visitors to an elaborate set of wrought-iron gates which open onto the grandest, most sweeping stairway you are ever likely to see. The steps lead to the **Bénédictine Museum**, housed in a building that is covered in a bewildering riot of decoration. The museum, which has a plant and spice hall, cellars and a distillery, tells the story of Bénédictine liqueur, which was first concocted by monks in the former Bénédictine monastery at Fécamp (see feature box). Guided tours of the distillery (available in English) end, as one would expect, with a tasting of this very special liquid.

The monk's concoction

As already seen with the story of champagne, France is full of tales of monks concocting new drinks from novel combinations of ingredients. The story of Benedictine is no exception, but it contains the added twist of a recipe lost and found.

It is said that Benedictine was first produced by Dom Bernado Vincelli, a Venetian monk who was staying at the Benedictine monastory in Fécamp. Apparently, he created the elixir in the early sixteenth century by mixing no less than 27 aromatic herbs.

The recipe, which includes the mixing of myrrh with juniper oil, saffron and lemon peel, was lost when the monastery was destroyed in the French Revolution, but was supposedly re-discovered in 1863 by Alexandre Le Grand when he was rifling through some old papers. This chance discovery allowed Le Grand, who was also a great publicist, to set up his own distillery, make the most of the lost-and-found story and market his product all over the world.

The first production of Bénédictine by the monks of Fécamp is depicted on a stained-glass window in Fécamp's huge church of St Trinité. However, the church is chiefly famous for its possession of liquid of a very different nature. Behind the altar, there is a special casket, which supposedly contains a sample of blood said to be that of Christ. Local legend has it that the blood was delivered to Fécamp in a mysterious boat which came ashore in the first century. The church also has a seventeenth-century clock in the north transept that shows the phases of the moon and the times of the tides as well as the hours. The church is celebrated for its cathedral-like dimensions but its architecture, which is a strange juxtaposition of Gothic and eighteenth-century Classical, is not particularly attractive.

There is no shortage of museums in Fécamp. In addition to the church's relic and the Bénédictine Museum, there is the **Musée des Arts et de l'Enfance** (on Rue Alexandre-Legros), with an eclectic range of exhibits, including ceramics, carved ivory, paintings, furniture and even a collection which traces the history of babies' bottles, and a **Museum of Newfoundland Fishermen** (on Boulevard. Albert I), which tells the story of Fécamp's relationship with the sea from the time of the Viking invasions, through its development as a port for deep-sea fishing in the north Atlantic to its evolution as a holiday resort.

The north cliff is floodlit at night and there is a splendid walk up the old Sailors' Path to the little cliff-top chapel of **Notre Dame de Salut**, which is traditionally hailed by the sirens of fishing boats as they pass by.

Étretat

Take the D940 for the short journey to **Étretat**, the most impressive location on the Alabaster Coast. The resort is very popular with trippers, but parking in this busy place is surprisingly easy, because the irregularly-shaped "square", just behind the promenade, has plenty of pay-and-display spaces.

The cliffs

Étretat occupies a deep gash in a spectacular line of cliffs. The town seems to have developed in a rather higgledy-piggledy fashion, but the geometry of the sea front is very appealing. The promenade, which curves gently alongside a sloping, pebbly beach, is framed to both north and south by magnificent chalk cliffs.

To the north, the cliffs of the **Falaise d'Amont** rise almost vertically from the shore, but one cliff extends a long alabaster arm into the sea and seems to embrace the bay. The northern summit is reached by a path that winds up a wide grass incline. The skyline is pierced by two contrasting, yet complementary structures: the vertical, slender, pointed spire of the seafarers' chapel, **Notre-Dame-de-la-Garde**, and the tilted, but even more slender and pointed **Aviators' Monument** to Charles Nungasser and François Coli, whose plane was last seen over Étretat on 8 May 1927, just before their attempt to cross the Atlantic from east to west ended in disaster. A museum near the monument tells their story.

The southern cliff, the **Falaise d'Aval**, is even more spectacular than the northern cliff, because it has been fashioned by the sea into a series of immense stacks and rock arches. The **Pont d'Aval Arch**, located just a few yards beyond the southern edge of the shore, extends a limb into the sea, which looks, for all the world, like an elephant's trunk searching for water. A splendidly pointed stack rock, which is visible through the arch, looks as if it has been placed there deliberately for maximum photographic effect, and the boats which are moored on the sloping beach also seem to have been strategically placed as suitable items of foreground interest for the many photographers who stand on the promenade to take snaps of the Pont d'Aval.

A walk to the summit of the southern cliffs is just as rewarding as that to the top of the northern cliffs, because the southern summit affords a superb view to the southwest of a second great rock-arch, the **Manneporte**, which was a popular subject for the Impressionists.

The town

A walk along the promenade and into the town also brings its rewards. An eight-sided pavilion, housing the l'Huitière restaurant, stands at the southern end of the shore, and a line of four more restaurants extends northwards along the promenade. All have outdoor seating, which is sheltered from the persistent westerly winds by large glass panels.

Just one block from the seashore, are a pair of pizzerias, separated by a bar called The Highlanders (see feature box). Turning right along the Boulevard President René Coty, visitors are confronted by a pair of fantastical, half-timbered villas, the

second of which, **Manoir de Salamandre**, has a rather crumbling façade, which is decorated by an amazing profusion of timbers and jetties. The building houses a hotel and Le Tricorne bar and restaurant.

Homage to the liberators

In 1940, during the evacuation from Dunkirk, the 51st Highlanders were ordered to pull back to Le Havre, where they fought a last ditch battle which occupied a number of German divisions. Eventually, thousands of Scottish soldiers had to surrender. Four years later, on 2 September 1944, the 51st Highlanders returned as liberators when they landed at Étretat.

Étretat's old-fashioned, timbered market hall, which was actually built in 1926, now contains a plaque that not only makes reference to the heroics of the Highlanders, but also mentions the British and American hospitals that existed in the area in World War I, the 549 British soldiers who died at Étretat, and the American Pall Mall Camp that was established in the town in 1945.

The plaque, which was unveiled on 2 September 1946, two years to the day after the liberation of Étretat by the Highlanders, expresses "gratitude and friendship" to Great Britain and the United States.

Nearby is the market place where there is yet another pizzeria – this one with a take-away hatch – and a restored wooden market hall filled with craft shops, some of which sell carved wooden goods carrying motifs in English. A plaque on the market hall is dedicated to the 51st Highlanders (It's them again!)

Other attractions in Étretat include: the **Aquarium Marin**, a home for tropical fish which is built into the cliff; a chateau (**Chateau des Aygues**) which was home to the Queens of Spain, and **Le Clos Lupin**, which was home to Maurice Leblanc, who wrote popular thrillers about Arsene Lupin, the "Gentleman Burglar". To complete the list of attractions, there is a casino, a night club and a miniature steam train which runs to **Les Loges**.

After leaving Étretat, travel over a wide, exposed landscape of open fields until the port of Le Havre is reached (see next chapter). Return to Dieppe from Le Havre by driving along the A29 autoroute and finally following the N21.

4.3 THE ROUTE OF RECONSTRUCTION – CLÈRES, ROUEN, VERNON, GIVERNY, BEAUVAIS, GERBEROY

INTRODUCTION

The final tour from Dieppe visits Rouen, a city with an outstanding legacy of ecclesiastical and vernacular architecture, and to Beauvais, a city with the most audacious Gothic cathedral in France. The route also takes in Giverny, where Claude Monet created a garden, which was to become the subject of some of his greatest paintings, and to Gerberoy, a hamlet that can justifiably claim to be the prettiest village in northern France.

All four of these places have one characteristic in common: they have been restored to their former glory after periods of destruction or deterioration. Rouen and Beauvais have risen phoenix-like from the ashes of war. Monet's garden was lovingly and faithfully replanted after a period of shameful neglect. The village of Gerberoy, which had been allowed to fall into decay, was splendidly restored after it was discovered by Henri Le Sidaner. He was another artist who planted a garden, which he then depicted in his paintings.

During this journey, visitors will also discover the attractive village of Clères and the old town of Vernon, two places which are not so well known as the other places on the tour, but are certainly worthy of attention.

All the attractions described in this itinerary are within easy reach of Dieppe, but it would be difficult to do justice to them in a single car journey. Rouen alone demands at least a day, and Channel hoppers who have an artistic pilgrimage to Giverny as their prime objective will probably choose to stay in Rouen or Vernon, rather than in Dieppe.

Clères

Begin the journey by taking the N27 for Rouen. Shortly after crossing the intersection with the A29 autoroute, keep a careful eye open for a left turn to **Clères**. This side road enters an area of pleasant rolling countryside, dotted with half-timbered farm houses. Clères is a pleasant country

Top tips for the Route of Reconstruction

Not to be missed

- The picturesque village of Clères
- Rouen Cathedral
- Rue St Romain and Rue Martainville, Rouen (half-timbered houses)
- Rue du Gros Horloge, Rouen (great clock)
- The enormous church of St Ouen, Rouen
- Rouen's museums with paintings, ceramics and ironwork
- The modern church in Rouen's old market square
- The church at Vernon
- Monet's house and garden at Giverny
- Beauvais Cathedral
- The beautiful village of Gerberoy

Things to do

- Visit the zoological park and motor museum at Clères
- Play golf on Rouen's new golf course
- Tour the tax collector's house in Rouen
- Admire the façade of Rouen Cathedral for Café le Centre
- Admire the interior proportions of Rouen Cathedral
- Take photographs of Rouen's greatest concentration of half-timbered houses in Rue St-Romain and Rue Martainville
- Visit St Maclou, Rouen's Flamboyant church
- Join the tourist throng in the Rue du Gros Horloge
- Climb the belfry next to Rouen's famous clock for a great view over the city
- See the tower where Joan of Arc was interrogated
- Visit the spot where Joan of Arc was burned at the stake
- See Flaubert's parrot and discover the relationship between the writer and medicine
- Take a boat trip on the Seine from Rouen
- Take a ride on a Ferris wheel at Rouen's fair
- Visit the 'House of Time Gone By' at Vernon
- Pay a visit to the chateau and grounds at Bizy
- Walk straight into an Impressionist painting by walking around Monet's garden
- Visit Monet's house and studio
- See the work of American Impressionists at Giverny's American Art Museum
- Shop in Beauvais' pleasant shopping area
- Marvel at the preposterous height of Beauvais Cathedral
- See the world's first chiming clock in Beauvais Cathedral
- See the famous Beauvais tapestries
- Wander around the beautiful village of Gerberoy
- Buy cheese from the Saturday market at Neufchâtel-en-Bray

village with some timber-framed houses and a splendid timbered market hall, which bears a plaque to Edmund Spalikowski. Although his Polish-sounding name would suggest otherwise, Spalikowski was born in Rouen in 1874 and died in Clères in 1951. He wrote and illustrated a number of books about Normandy and was President of the Normandy group of writers.

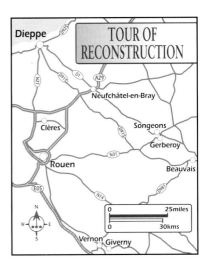

All the local shops seem to be alive and well in Clères, as in so many other French villages, despite the building of an enormous number of out-of-town supermarkets over the last twenty years. This state of affairs is in marked contrast to the situation in Britain, where so many local shops are struggling to survive in the era of one-stop weekly shopping. It is also noticeable that the signs on small French shops indicate the function of the shop, be it grocer, butcher, pharmacist or optician, rather than the name of the proprietor or the particular trading name. Perhaps there is a lesson here for British shop keepers.

On the perimeter of the market place, there is a small **Museum of Automobiles and Military Vehicles** and in the grounds of the old chateau, just outside Clères, there is an extensive **Zoological Park**, with well over 1,000 birds representing some 180 species. For anyone interested in exotic birds, a visit to this attraction is a must, although some enthusiasts got decidedly too enthusiastic in the millennium year when 28 flamingos were stolen from the park. The countryside between Clères and Rouen contains yet another attraction in the form of a golf club, called **La Forêt Verte**. The club, which opened in 1990 and is a member of the Nouveaux Golfs de France Group, welcomes visitors on its 18-hole and 9-hole courses (see additional information).

From Clères, follow the D6 back to the Dieppe-Rouen road which evolves at this point into the A13 autoroute.

Rouen

Rouen was built at the first point where the river Seine could be spanned by a bridge and it has long been an important industrial, trading and cultural focus for the area. The city is also a treasure house of ecclesiastical and vernacular architecture, but it suffered badly in the last war, as a result of German bombing in 1940 and Allied bombing (especially by the RAF) in 1944. The worst damage was inflicted on an old area of the city between the cathedral and the river, but industrial installations on an island in the Seine were badly hit as were many buildings of architectural importance in other parts of the city.

Rouen has been fully rebuilt, but some of the new buildings which have sprung up leave a great deal to be desired from an architectural point of view, especially a dreadful piece of New Brutalism on the northern perimeter of the Cathedral Square. However, three aspects of the restoration are very laudable. Firstly, districts that used to contain an unhealthy mix of factories and housing have now been replaced by distinct and separate industrial and residential zones. Secondly, the island in the Seine has been given over to recreational use and, thirdly, the reconstruction of the old quarter east of the cathedral, where there is one of the greatest concentrations of half timbered town houses in the world, has been carried out so well that it is virtually impossible to distinguish between original buildings and reconstructions.

Parking in Rouen is surprisingly easy. There is considerable on-street parking outside the confines of the old quarter and there are multi-storey car parks. Head first for the tourist office to begin an exploration of this fascinating city. The information office is housed in the **Maison des Finances**, a former tax office which has a magnificent Renaissance façade with emphasized stone ribs, deep-set windows and playful detailing. The half-timbered inner courtyard is equally fascinating. Tours of the building take place on a regular basis.

The cathedral

It is said that an upper room in the Maison des Finances was one of the lodgings used by Claude Monet when he was painting his series of depictions of the west front of the **Cathédrale Notre-Dame**, which faces the tourist office from across the Cathedral Square.

Different impressions

Claude Monet was so impressed by the play of light on the stonework of Rouen Cathedral that he completed over thirty paintings of the church's western façade. His pictures depict the cathedral in a variety of weather and light conditions and from all manner of viewpoints. In some of the paintings the stonework is shown in high relief; in other works the sculptural decoration of the facade fades into shadow. In some depictions, the cathedral is dazzling white; in others it is a mere grey silhouette. The whole series looks like different exposures of the same photographic shot. This sort of playful multiplication and variation can be achieved so easily by photographers using modern technology, but Monet could only achieve variation by repeating the painstaking process of artistic depiction over thirty times!

The Café Le Centre, on the south side of the Cathedral Square enjoys a fine view of the cathedral's west front, although the view has been somewhat spoilt by the enormous flower displays that have been created on a large mound of earth in front of the cathedral by local authority gardeners. Perhaps their aim is to partially mask and soften the impact of the scaffolding, which currently covers much of the façade, but the juxtaposition of rampant vegetation and rampant sculpture is an unhappy one.

Rouen Cathedral was built over a 300-year period from the thirteenth to the sixteenth century. A cast-iron spire was added in the nineteenth century and considerable rebuilding was necessary after damage inflicted in World War II. A great deal of renovation work is still being carried out and the reason for this is revealed by taking a look at the crumbling stonework and the headless sculptures on the western façade.

The west front is an eclectic mix of styles. The central porch is a soaring flamboyant Gothic affair, whose riot of sculpture culminates in a Jesse Tree. The porch reaches a climax in an apex, which is so tall that it occludes the base of the deep-set rose window set high up on the façade. The two flanking porches are thirteenth-century in geometry but much later in decoration. The central porch is flanked by two towers. The northern tower, known as the **Tour St-Romain**, stands on a thirteenth-century base, which is a surviving remnant of the church that previously occupied the site. The southern tower, which is more ornate and dates from the flamboyant Gothic period, is known as the **Tour du Buerre** (the Butter Tower) because its construction is said to have been financed by taxes from people who paid for a special dispensation that allowed them to eat butter during Lent.

The soaring central porch and the sculptural detail of the west front are both undeniably magnificent, but the mix of architectural styles makes for a rather disjointed and unsatisfactory whole. In fact, the façade of the south transept is much more satisfactory as a unified work of art than the west front and the entrance to the north transept is utterly stunning.

The interior of the cathedral is unusually light and bright, because clear glass in the very tall clèrestory (clear storey) allows in massive amounts of daylight to highlight the splendid proportions. The three sections of the nave wall (nave arches, triforium and clèrestory) are in the classic 3:1:3 ratio which is so typical of the grandest French churches; the aisles are thin and high, and lined with side chapels containing fine religious paintings and excellent stained glass. The north transept of the church has a magnificent Renaissance staircase.

Old Rouen

Many people who visit Rouen Cathedral enter and leave by the west door and then walk down the Rue du Gros Horloge. But, by taking this route, they miss the finest half-timbered streets in the city, which can be entered by leaving the cathedral via the north transept.

After emerging from the transept, do not fail to turn around and look at the wonderful gateway to the so-called Booksellers' Court. From here enter the Rue St-Romain, which is lined with the most superb half-timbered town houses. Walking eastwards along the street, visitors pass a number of interesting court-yards, one of which contains an inviting salon de thé.

Rue St-Romain terminates at the intersection with the Rue de la République, which runs across the front of the courtyard of **St-Maclou**, where there is a fountain, which looks like Rouen's answer to the Mannekin Pis in Brussels. St-Maclou is a highly decorative example of flamboyant Gothic, entered through sixteenth-century carved doors.

Walk now along the Rue Martainville. Here are yet more

half-timbered houses and court-
yards, before the road opens out
onto the Place Aitre, which has a
half-timbered book shop, worthy of
a visit both for its appearance and
its contents. Return to the Place de
la République and then turn right,
to head for the nineteenth-century
Hôtel de Ville and the church of **St-
Ouen**, another Gothic church with
a huge, plain interior and some good
stained glass.

Rue du Gros Horloge

Carry on westwards to the Rue
Beavoisine, then head southwards,
via the Rue des Carmes, to return
to the cathedral square. Rouen's most
famous tourist street, the Rue du
Gros Horloge, runs westwards from
here. The street is given over to
tourism. Venerable half-timbered
buildings are incongruously occupied
by a succession of fast food outlets,
souvenir shops and bargain stores.
There are lots of street vendors
selling giant posters, with Ché
Guevara vying for prominence with
the Mona Lisa. Visitors will pass a
number of odd-looking statues,
which turn out to be street enter-
tainers playing at not moving for
long periods.

The piece de resistance of the
street is the **Gros Horloge**, a highly
decorative clock built over the
street. Visitors can climb the adjacent
Belfroi du Gros Horloge for a
magnificent view over the city.

The old market square

The Rue du Gros Horloge terminates in the Place du Vieux Marché,
where Joan of Arc is said to have
been burnt at the stake in 1431. The
square is lined with restaurants and
tourist shops, including a pizzeria
with a *trompe l'oeil* painting on its

The story of Joan of Arc

Joan of Arc was born in 1412 to peasant parents. At the age of 13
she began seeing visions and hearing voices. Four years later,
she claimed that the voices had called upon her to help the Dauphin
(later Charles VII) to save France from the English, who were about to
take Orléans.

Charles agreed to give Joan some troops to command and she duly led
them to victory. As a reward, Joan was given a place alongside the King at
his coronation at Reims, but she lost favour when she set out on another
operation against the English without the consent of Charles. Joan was
captured by Burgundian soldiers, who handed her over to their allies, the
English. The "Maid of Orléans" was then passed to an ecclesiastical court
at Rouen to be tried for heresy, on the grounds that she had listened
directly to God rather than the Catholic Church.

Joan was interrogated for 14 months and then condemned to death.
Her sentence was reduced to life imprisonment after she had confessed to
her errors, but she was condemned to death again when she insisted on
wearing men's clothes on her return to prison. Joan was burned at the
stake in Rouen's market place on 30 May 1431 for being a relapsed
heretic. She was just 19 years old.

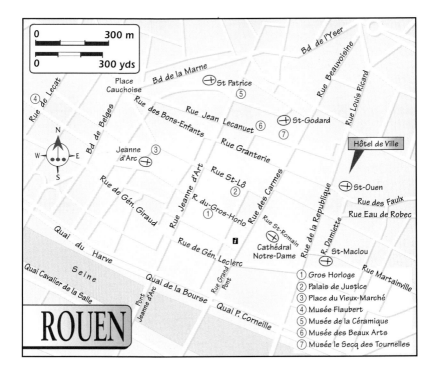

exterior wall and a postcard shop with a profusion of flags. There is a statue of Joan of Arc in the square, as well as a modern church and a reconstructed market. Whether by accident or design, the modern buildings have darting contours that suggest flames gathering around the stake. The theatricality of the interior of the church is accentuated by its ceiling which looks rather like two drawn curtains. The stained glass windows are oddly shaped, with unusual semi-circular bases, but with traditional tracery super-imposed on them.

The area immediately north of the Rue du Gros Horloge contains Rouen's excellent shopping area. The department stores and shops even have sales in August. The huge, reconstructed **Palais de Justice** is to be found in this vicinity. Its flamboyant Gothic façade becomes ever more elaborate as the floors rise. The profusion of flamboyant Gothic structures in the city is clear evidence that Rouen had a period of considerable prosperity in the sixteenth century.

Museums

The city's extensive museum area lies to the north of the shopping district and is focused on Square Verderel. The **Musée des Beaux Arts** has a large collection of paintings, which includes Caravaggio's *Flagellation of Christ*, one of Monet's depictions of Rouen Cathedral, a typically attenuated portrait by Modigliani and Ingres' portrait of Madame Aynion.

The nearby **Musée de la Ceramique** contains a fine collection of porcelain, not only from Rouen, but also from Delft and Italy, and the

Musée de la Ferronerie is home to the greatest collection of decorative ironwork in the world, including some amazing seventeenth-century ironwork trees. The **Tour Jeanne d'Arc,** a little further to the north, is said to be the place where Joan of Arc was imprisoned and tortured before being put to death.

In the far west of the city centre, is the **Musée Flaubert et d'Histoire de Médecine.** The apparent strangeness of this mix of themes is explained by the fact that Flaubert was the son of a Rouen doctor and often consulted medical books when researching his novels. The author's stuffed parrot, made famous by Julian Barnes' novel *Flaubert's Parrot,* is exhibited in its authentic location on the writer's desk.

Flaubert's Parrot

Gustave Flaubert borrowed a stuffed parrot from Rouen's Museum and placed it on his writing desk as a source of inspiration when he was writing *Un Coeur Simple*. His novel tells the story of Felicité, a servant girl who sacrifices her own life in supporting others. When she finds herself alone, she becomes attached to a stuffed parrot called Loulou and even kneels in front of the bird to pray.

In 1984, Julian Barnes wrote *Flaubert's Parrot,* a novel that tells the story of Flaubert's life and loves and, more especially, his obsessions.

As would be expected of France's fourth city, Rouen has a good range of hotels and some splendid restaurants, many of which serve up the local speciality of duck.

Visitors can take boat trips on the river or perhaps enjoy the thrills of the massive fair with its giant Ferris wheel and its shamrock. The city also hosts many festivals, including a Bugatti festival and an international fair in April, 24 hours of speedboats in early May and a Joan of Arc festival in late May.

Vernon

Leaving Rouen behind, drive towards Paris on the Route de Normandie (the A13 autoroute). At junction 16, leave the autoroute and head for **Vernon,** whose hotels are often used a base for tourists visiting Monet's garden at Giverny. Vernon is not the prettiest town in France, partially because it too was badly damaged in the war, but it does have a very photogenic set-piece at its heart, where the **Église Notre Dame** and the **Maison du Temps Jadis** (House of Time Gone By) stand side-by-side.

The church has an elaborate, fifteenth-century façade, an impressive rose window, some good stained glass and a sixteenth-century sculptured organ loft. The fifteenth-century, half-timbered House of Time Gone By now accommodates the tourist office, where information can be obtained about the nearby **Chateau de Bizy,** an eighteenth-century mansion in an extensive park.

Giverny

Now cross the river, and head for **Giverny,** one of the most visited and most magical places in France. Claude Monet lived in the village from 1883 until his death in 1926. His pink-washed house is open to the public and contains striking interior decor designed by the artist to complement his large collection of Japanese prints, which are hung throughout the house. Some rooms have a light blue ceiling and light blue walls, while others have a yellow ceiling and yellow walls. The unexpected air of modernity and the quality of the reflective light are both very evident.

Monet's huge studio is also open to the public, as are the wonderful gardens, now replanted according to Monet's original designs after a period of neglect. It is hard to think of this garden as a reconstruction, but that is what it is. However, the work has been carried out with such care that the whole place has a wonderfully authentic feel to it. **Monet's garden** is in two parts: the section nearest the house, which is planted around a very long tunnel of ironwork rose arches, and a section that is accessed through an underpass, which runs under the road. This second section of the garden contains the famous lily ponds and the Japanese bridge, which were the subject of some of Monet's grea test paintings. Anyone strolling through the colourful profusion of plants experiences the uncanny sensation of walking into a painting.

The artist becomes a gardener

Monet first spotted the village of Giverny from a railway carriage and took up residence there in 1883 with Alice Hoschedé, a friend of his first wife. The artist soon set about remodelling the orchard that occupied the slope between his house and a roadway. He cut down a whole avenue of pines in order to create a spectacular tunnel of rose arches, but retained two of the pines in deference to the feelings of Alice, who became Monet's wife. The artist loved to let flowers grow freely, but he deliberately created a kaleidoscope of colour by a careful mixing of plant species.

Ten years after moving in, he acquired an area of land beyond the roadway with the aim of converting it into a Japanese garden on the lines of the images he had seen in Japanese prints. The locals were not too happy with Monet because they thought his plants would poison the tributary of the river Epte, which ran through his garden, but the artist pressed ahead and created a superb combination of Japanese bridges, lily ponds and colourful plants. Many artists before him had made deliberate arrangements of objects for still life compositions, but Monet was the first artist to rearrange a natural landscape for the purposes of painting.

Monet died at Giverny in 1926 and left the house and gardens to his son, Michel, who did little to maintain the property. However, Michel left the house and garden to the Académie des Beaux Arts, on his death in 1966 and, with the generous help of American benefactors, restoration work began in 1977.

The road between the two gardens is still there, but American diplomat Walter Annenberg paid for the construction of an underpass (painted in an appropriate "environmental green") to form a seamless link between the gardens.

The shimmering surface of the lily ponds and the reflections in the water are the very essence of Impressionist subject matter. In fact, the reflections are so intense that it is often difficult to differentiate between the real and the reflected image.

The village of Giverny itself has a very pretty main street of creeper-covered cottages. At the far end of the village there is an **American Art Museum**, full of work by American artists who admired Monet's work to such an extent that they felt compelled to copy it.

Beauvais

Travel on now for **Beauvais**, either by following the D181 northwards from Giverny and then the D981, or by heading back to Rouen and then taking the N31.

Beauvais suffered appalling destruction in 1940. 2,000 houses, including 75 that were listed as architecturally important, were destroyed. Post-war reconstruction has produced a townscape with an architecturally characterless monotony, but all has been saved by an imaginative and sensitive pedestrianisation scheme, which has brought life and character to the shopping area. The scheme is an object lesson in the enormous benefits resulting from a few nice fountains, some good street furniture and neat paving.

There is parking on the Square Jeanne Hachette. Even this space, which is largely given over to car parking, has a welcoming feel because it has a good modern fountain and a children's roundabout.

The cathedral

The centrepiece of Beauvais is the enormous, partially complete **Cathedral of St Pierre**, which

mercifully escaped damage in the bombing of 1940. If the church had been finished, it would have been the largest Gothic church in the world. However, the nave was never built, so the building consists of a choir and two transepts, with a would-be nave chopped off by a blank wall, which is now largely screened by a modern organ. The absence of a west front is compensated by the façade of the south transept, which is just as impressive as many west fronts. The other striking feature of the exterior is the structurally and aesthetically impressive set of double flying buttresses that support the choir.

The builders of the cathedral were hugely ambitious – too ambitious, in fact, because the church over-reached its limits of structural stability and suffered collapses on three different occasions. There were roof collapses in 1247 and 1284 and the tower and spire came tumbling down in 1573. Every architectural detail in the interior seems to have been designed to emphasize the height of the building. There are narrow gaps between the pillars, the clèrestory windows are lofty and the east end looks narrow and tall because it is sharply curved. The choir, which is reached by a flight of steps, is the highest in the world.

The absence of a nave means that the congregation has to be fitted into the choir and the transepts. The soaring transepts are held up by unsightly wooden beams, but there are superb rose windows, and the rose in the northern transept has modern stained glass by Max Ingrand. In the north-west corner of the choir, there is a fourteenth-century clock, which is the oldest chiming timepiece in the world.

The **Galerie Nationale de Tapisserie** is located next to the cathedral in a modern building which has replaced a structure destroyed by incendiaries in 1940 – Beauvais has long been famous for its tapestries. The pepper-pot towered **Palais de Justice**, on the other flank of the cathedral, survived the bombing. It also contains a museum, but its exhibits are mainly ceramics, sculpture and archaeological finds. The modest height of both museum buildings emphasizes the dimensions of the cathedral. Although it is incomplete, this preposterously tall structure will prove to be one of the highlights of any channel-hopping tour, even in an area of France that is rich in great cathedrals.

Gerberoy

From Beauvais, follow the D133 to **Songeons**, a picturesque village of half-timbered houses and something of a surprise in northern France but, as it turns out, only the warm-up act for the show village of **Gerberoy**, just down the road.

Parking is available in Gerberoy on the tree-lined Boulevard Guillaume Conquerant, which defines the perimeter of the settlement. Having parked, visitors can pause for refreshment at a half-timbered restaurant which has a mouthful of a name – Ambassade de la République de Montmartre en Picardie. The galleried interior of the building is wonderfully "olde worlde."

Gerberoy is an old frontier town between the Duchy of Normandy and the Kingdom of France. Thanks to the promptings of Henri Le Sidaner, an artist who lived here for a long period in the first half of the twentieth century, the village has been renovated and generally smartened up after a period of neglect and partial destruction, but the restoration is not overdone. Gerberoy is a delightful place: unspoilt, tranquil, and festooned with roses – a Rose Festival takes place on the third Sunday in June. Most old French villages are characterized by a unity of style and material, but Gerberoy is more like an English village in having a varied, but harmonious mix of brick, stone and timber-framed buildings.

The Monet of Gerberoy

Henri Le Sidaner was born in Mauritius in 1862. He became an accomplished artist, beginning as a Symbolist but then converting to neo-Impressionism. He moved to Gerberoy in 1900, 17 years after Monet had moved to Giverny. Like Monet, he developed an exotic garden in the grounds of his house. Le Sidaner cleverly used the village's ruined castle as a setting for his creation.

The artist also initiated the planting of roses throughout Gerberoy. They now form one of the village's most memorable features and have led to the establishing of an annual Rose Festival.

Le Sidaner prompted the restoration of the village and inspired other artists to settle and work in Gerberoy, which soon became the host for a consid-erable artists' colony. Le Sidaner died in 1939, after spending the last 39 years of his life as a resident of this splendid village.

Walking into the village from the Avenue of William the Conqueror, the visitor will come to a split in the road. The left fork leads to the Market Hall, which was restored in 1999 and has an upper floor supported by timber beams. The road twists right to the **Church of St Pierre**. The church has a wide interior with walls that are very plain except for the Stations of the Cross, which are in blue relief. The congregation is seated in four blocks of very squat box pews; there are nice chandeliers, some stained glass windows at the east and west ends and fifteenth-century choir stalls. A little balcony completes the picture.

A stone archway at the side of the church leads to the castle ruins, which were used as a set by Henri Le Sidaner for his rather theatrical garden. Walk back to the car park by meandering slowly along the lower road through the village. Mellow, rose-covered cottages line the route.

Le Sidaner's watercolours can be seen in the Hôtel de Ville, but his greatest work of art is the village itself, the most surprising and most picturesque settlement in northern France.

After leaving Gerberoy, follow the D135 to **Neufchâtel-en-Bray**, where one can pause to buy Neufchâtel

Above: Gerberoy.

cheese, particularly if passing through on Saturday when the stall market takes over the town. As elsewhere on this trip, much of the town, including the Church of Notre Dame, had to be reconstructed after wartime damage.

Return to Dieppe along the D1.

> Dieppe, the Alabaster Coast, Rouen,
> Giverny, Beavais and Gerberoy

ACCOMMODATION

DIEPPE

With a long history of welcoming visitors from across the Channel, Dieppe has some excellent hotels, especially along the fine esplanade. A selection follows:

***Hotel Aguado
Boulevard de Verdun
On sea front, all rooms with bath and shower
℅ 0235 842700

***Hotel la Présidence
Boulevard de Verdun
Just below castle, secure car park.
℅ 0235 848670

**Hotel de Europe
Boulevard de Verdun
All rooms with sea view. Some large family rooms
℅ 0232 901919

**Hotel de la Plage
Boulevard de Verdun
Family run hotel
℅ 0235 061010

**Ibis
ZAC du Val Druel
Near Belvedere shopping centre
℅ 0235 826530

**Hotel Windsor
Boulevard de Verdun
Includes family rooms. Restaurant has panoramic views.
℅ 0235 841523

*Tourist Hotel
Rue de Halle au Blé
32 rooms, all with shower, toilets. 2 mins, from beach.
℅ 0235 061010

There is an excellent campsite at:

Les Goelands
In St Martin-en-Compagne, 8 miles (13km) north-east of Dieppe
Situated close to the sea, above a characteristic hanging valley, but do not arrive at lunchtime – the warden leaves the site for a mid-day siesta.
℅ 0235 838290

There is a Youth Hostel at:
Rue Louis Fromger, in an old college building.
℅ 0235 848573

Alabaster Coast

Visitors wishing to tour the Alabaster Coast will probably wish to use Dieppe as a base, but they may wish to stay nearer the dramatic cliff scenery at Fécamp or Étretat:

Étretat
**Hotel d'Angleterre
Avenue Georges V
℅ 0235 270165

Fécamp
**Hotel d'Angleterre
Rue de la Plage
℅ 0235 280160

Tour of reconstruction

Rouen

Rouen has a very large choice of hotels. A small selection follows:

***Hotel de Dieppe
Place Bernard Tissot
Now in Best Western chain
℅ 0235 719600

***Tulip Hotel**
Near market square
48 rooms, well-equipped
℅ 0235 710088

****Hotel des Carmes**
Place des Carmes
Central location
℅ 0235 719231

****Dandy Hotel**
Near Vieux Marché
Well-equipped, period-style rooms
℅ 0235 073200

Camping
Municipal site on N27,
north-west of Rouen
℅ 0235 740759

Vernon
***Hotel Normandy**
In Vernon
Modern, comfortable
℅ 0232 519797

Giverny
****La Musardiere**
Rue Claude Monet
10 rooms, 100yd (100m) from
Monet's house
℅ 0232 210319

Beauvais
***Hotel Chenal**
Boulevard Géneral de Gaulle
℅ 0344 060460

****Hotel du Palais**
Rue St Nicolaus
℅ 0344 451258

****Hotel Formule 1**
Avenue Montaigne
℅ 0344 847084

ATTRACTIONS

Dieppe
Chateau-Musée
Rue de Chastes
Open: June–September: Daily from:
10am–12noon, 2–6pm. October–May:
10am–12noon, 2–5pm (not Tuesday)
℅ 0235841976

Golf
Dieppe-Pourville Golf Course
Route de Pouville
Has a restaurant
℅ 0235 842505

Alabaster Coast

Varengeville
Bois des Moutiers
Open: March–November: 10am–
12noon, 2–4pm
℅ 0235 851002

Fécamp
Benedictine Museum
Rue Alexandre Le Grand
Open: February–March, Noveber–
December: 10–11.15am, 2–5pm.
March–June, September–November:
10am–12noon, 2–5.30pm. July,
August: 9.30am–6pm
℅ 0235 102610

Musée des Arts et de l'Enfance
Rue A Legros
Open: September–June: 10am–
12noon, 2–5,30pm (closed Tuesday).
July and August: 10am–12noon, 2–
5.30pm daily
℅ 0235 283199
Same ticket admits to Museum of
Newfoundland Fishermen

Étretat

Aquarium
Rue Offenbach
Open: July, August: 2–6pm
℅ 0325 289277

**Chateau des Aygues
(home of Queens of Spain)**
Rue Offenbach.
Open: July and August: 2–6pm
℅ 0235289277

Le Clos Lupin (Gentleman Burglar)
April–September: Daily: 10am–7pm
(7–10pm night visits) October–
March: Monday, Friday–Sunday:
11am–5pm
℅ 0235 270823

Tourist Train
Étretat to Les Loges
℅ 0235 270521

Route of reconstruction

Clères

Golf
Golf du Rouen La Fôret Verte
18- & 9-hole courses
℅ 0235 336294

Car museum
Open: April–October (except
Tuesday): 1–6pm
℅ 0235 331351

Zoological park
Open: May–September: 9am–6pm;
March, April, October, November:
9am–12noon, 1.30–6pm
℅ 0235 332308

Rouen

Boat trips, ascent of belfry, guided
tours of tax collector's house – ask at
Information Office
℅ 0235 714177

Musée des Beaux Arts
Square Verdrel
Open: Monday, Wednesday–Saturday:
10am–12noon, 2 – 6pm. Sunday:
10am–12noon
℅ 0235 712840

Ceramics Museum
Rue Faucun
Open: Thursday–Monday: 10am–
1pm. 2–6pm
℅ 0235 073174

Ironwork museum
Open: Thursday–Monday: 10am–
12noon, 2–6pm
℅ 0235 712840

**Flaubert & History of
Medicine Museum**
Rue de Lecat
Open: Tuesday–Saturday 10am–
12noon, 2–6pm

Vernon

Chateau de Bizy
Open: April–October: daily except
Monday: 10am–12noon, 2–6pm
November–March: 2–5pm
℅ 0232 510082

Giverny

American Art Museum
Open: April–October: Tuesday–
Sunday: 10am–6pm
℅ 0232 519465

Monet's House & Garden
Open: April–October: Tuesday–
Sunday: 10am–6pm
℅ 0232 512821

Beauvais

Tapestry Museum
Open: April–September (not
Monday) 9.30–11.30am, 2–6pm.
October–March: 10–11.30am, 2.30–
4.30pm

Town Museum
Open: 10am-12, 2pm-6pm
Information on both above from
information office
℅ 0344 153030

EATING OUT

Dieppe

Lots of options, particularly along
the Quai Henri IV. Visitors might
like to try:

Le Newhaven
Quai Henri IV
English spoken. Vegetarian dishes on
request
℅ 0235 848972

à la Marmite Dieppoise
Rue Saint-Jean
Creative fish stew a speciality
℅ 0235 842426

Les Ecamias
Quai Henri IV
Sea food a speciality
℅ 0235 846767

Alabaster Coast

Try:

Auberge d'Etang
at Manneville-es-Plains
between St Valéry-en-Caux and
Veules-les-Roses
℅ 0235 970377

Les Embriens
at Sotteville-sur-Mer
℅ 0235 977799

Tour of reconstruction

Rouen

Rouen has a huge choice of excellent
bars and restaurants. You could try:

Le Beffroi
Rue du Beffroi
Dine in a half-timbered restaurant
℅ 0235 715527

Le Queen Mary
Rue du Cercle
Dine in a mock ocean liner
℅ 0235 215209

Vernon
Hotel d'Evreux
Place d'Evreux
Dine on duck and apple
℅ 0232 211612

Giverny
Les Jardins de Giverny
Dine in a Belle époque mansion
℅ 0232 216080

Auberge du Vieux Moulin
Rue de la Falaise
Dine in the presence of
Impressionist paintings
℅ 0232 514615

SHOPPING

Dieppe

A fish market operates on the
quayside in the early morning and
there is an extensive Saturday stall
market in the St Jacques area. The
pedestrianised Grande Rue is a
superb shopping street, especially for
excellent chocolate shops, fashion

boutiques, épiceries and coffee shops. The Belvedere commercial complex, on the road to Rouen, has a large Auchan hypermarket. There is a Decathlon just further along the road. and an Intermarché nearby.

Alabaster Coast

You will probably wish to buy Benedictine in Fécamp and perhaps cider in Étretat. There are some good stall markets along the coast, as follows:

Étretat:	Thursday
Fécamp:	Saturday
St Valéry-en-Caux:	Friday
Veules-les-Roses:	Wednesday

Route of reconstruction

Rouen is excellent for fashion, food, wines, porcelain and cheese.
Vernon is also good for wine and cheese and there is a flea market on Sundays.
The Saturday market at Neufchâtel-en-Bray is good for cheese.

TOURIST INFORMATION

Dieppe
Pont Jehan-Ango
℅ 0235 841177

Alabaster coast

Étretat
Place Maurice Guillard
℅ 0235 270521

Fécamp
Rue Alexandre Legros
℅ 0235 285101

Tour of reconstruction

Beauvais
Rue Beauregard
℅ 0344 445821

Clères
In village centre
℅ 0235 393864

Rouen
Place Cathédrale
℅ 0235 714177

5 Le Havre, the Côte Fleurie and Chartres

5.1 LE HAVRE AND THE CÔTE FLEURIE

INTRODUCTION

The Portsmouth-Le Havre ferry is popular with those visitors to France who prefer to opt for a lengthy sea-crossing rather than a lengthy drive from the more northerly Channel ports. It takes about 5 hours 30 minutes by day and about 8 hours by night (P&O Portsmouth ☎ 08702 424999). Le Havre is often used as a convenient jumping-off point by tourists heading to the chateaux of the Loire, or the great cathedral at Chartres, or the spectacular river scenery of the Dordogne and the Lot. Closer to hand, it can be used as an alternative to Dieppe as a base for visits to the Alabaster Coast, Rouen and Monet's garden, but it is also the gateway to the Côte Fleurie, where the four superb seaside towns of Honfleur, Trouville, Deauville and Cabourg are strung out like pearls along a coast that has attracted the rich and famous ever since the railway line from Paris was completed.

LE HAVRE

The Channel ports that have been covered in the earlier chapters of this guide have all been described by means of detailed walking tours. Le Havre will not be described in this way, simply because it does not merit such treatment. A drive through the city is depressing enough!

Modern Le Havre is a grey, soulless place of grid-like streets and monotonous concrete blocks, which have resulted from a well-intentioned, but misguided re-construction after the destruction of the city in World War II. RAF carpet-bombing in September 1944 reduced the business and administrative area to rubble and made Le Havre the most severely damaged place in France. Over 4,000 people were killed, 12,500 buildings were destroyed and 80,000 people were made homeless. Adding insult to injury, the Germans systematically destroyed all the port facilities be-fore they made their final departure.

The reconstruction of the town, which began after a whole year of rubble clearing, was masterminded

TOP TIPS FOR LE HAVRE AND THE CÔTE FLEURIE

Not to be missed

- The interior of St Joseph's Church, Le Havre
- A visit to Cap Le Hève
- The Musée des Beaux Arts, Le Havre
- A drive over the Pont de Normandie
- The quayside at Honfleur
- The wooden church at Honfleur
- The grand villas on the corniche at Trouville
- Les Planches and the beach at Deauville
- Les Halles at Dives
- William the Conqueror's Inn at Dives
- The Grand Hotel, Cabourg
- Promenade Marcel Proust, Cabourg

Things to do

- Windsurf at Le Havre
- Stop and stare at Niemeyer's 'Volcano,' Le Havre
- Shop in the Coty centre, Le Havre
- Shop at the commercial centre at Montvilliers
- Admire the view from the orientation table on the road to Ste-Adresse
- Observe artists at work in Honfleur
- Purchase cider in Honfleur
- Sketch or take photographs in Honfleur
- Visit the Boudin Museum in Honfleur
- Enjoy the beach in Trouville
- Visit the aquarium at Trouville
- Shop in Trouville's open-air market
- Buy fresh fish in Trouville
- Swim in Deauville's swimming pool
- Photograph the lines of beach tents at Deauville
- People-watch from a café alongside Les Planches, Deauville
- Gamble at Deauville's casino, even if it is only on the slot machines
- Search for fossils on the beach at Houlgate
- Buy crafts at Dives
- Stare at Cabourg's eccentrically-styled villas
- Walk the full length of the Promenade Marcel Proust at Cabourg
- Copy Marcel Proust, if you have the cheek, by observing the diners in the restaurant of the Grand Hotel
- Make the most of the beach and the sea at Cabourg

CÔTE FLEURIE
FROM LE HARVE

Concrete proposals

by the architect Auguste Perret, whose efforts were much praised at the time as a model of enlightened town planning. His intentions were certainly good and even ground-breaking in the 1940s; the streets of his new town were made suitably wide and his apartment blocks were constructed so that their housing units could catch the maximum amount of sunlight. Balconies ran the whole length of many of the blocks and shops were constructed in the ground floor units, below the tiers of living quarters. Unfortunately, Perret had an unshakable passion for reinforced concrete, a material which made his huge apartment blocks dull, grey, soulless and repetitive. The blocks, with their strict rectangular lines, were constructed alongside avenues arranged in the most boring grid pattern imaginable. Modern Le Havre may well be of interest to students of architecture, but it is certainly not a place to uplift the soul!

Auguste Perret was born in a suburb of Brussels in 1874. His father, who was a builder, had fled to Belgium after participating in the Paris Commune. On their father's death, Auguste and his brother Gustave, inherited the family firm and pioneered the use of reinforced concrete in their construction work. Auguste developed a style known as Structural Classicism, with the concrete frames of his buildings exposed as pilasters, and was praised by Le Corbusier as 'the architect who paved the way for modern architecture.' In 1911, he won the commission to build the Théatre des Champs-Elysées in Paris and his reputation as an innovative architect grew rapidly.

In 1945, when he was 71 years old, Perret was appointed to plan and design the reconstruction of Le Havre, which had been all but destroyed by RAF bombing. His work was much praised at the time as an imaginative example of enlightened town planning, but his concrete apartment blocks now look drab and repetitive. Perret also had a fondness for constructing very tall concrete towers. It was noted in an earlier chapter how his high, stark tower in Amiens looks completely out of place. His two towers in Le Havre, which were both completed after his death in 1954, are also monstrously tall, but have a somewhat better design.

A wide, tree-lined avenue, known as Avenue Foch, runs arrow-straight across the full width of the city centre. The path of the road is interrupted, in the middle, by a huge square, which is said to be the largest in Europe and was designed as a setting for Perret's new **Hôtel de Ville**. The preposterously tall tower of the Hôtel de Ville is 236ft (72m) high and is constructed, as one would expect, in reinforced concrete. This central square, which should be the pumping heart of a vibrant city, has about as much life as one of those eerily-still urban scenes in a surrealist painting by Utrillo.

Is there anything worth seeing in this urban nightmare? Am I being unfair to modern Le Havre which, let's face it, is a repercussion of relentless British bombing? I have to admit that there are good shopping facilities in the centre and on the outskirts of Le Havre, there is a very attractive and spectacularly-located suburb on the cliff to the north-west, and there are three buildings of interest in the area sandwiched between the Avenue Foch and the port.

Between Avenue Foch and the port

Perret's **Church of St Joseph** is situated to the north-west of the main business quarter. With its grey concrete exterior and its 275ft (84m) high concrete tower, the church looks remarkably like a clone of the Town Hall, but it has to be said that the interior, which is symmetrically arranged around the central tower, is really quite magical. A high, octagonal lantern sends beams of light down into the body of the church and long windows, decorated with coloured panes of glass, add to the stunning optical effect.

Another architect who has been let loose on Le Havre in recent years has an approach that is very different from that of Perret. Oscar Niemeyer, who is well known for his spectacular work in Brasilia, won the commission for a new cultural centre on the Place Gambetta, just south of the Town Hall. The commission was for a theatre, two cinemas, a restaurant and an exhibition space. Ignoring the strict rectilinear geometry of Perret's city, Niemeyer has come up with a curved, all-white, giant mound of a building, which is known to the people of Le Havre as **Le Volcan** (The Volcano), but has also been likened to a huge ship's funnel. To my eyes, it looks rather more like the cooling tower of a power station. Unfortunately for Le Havre, it would be difficult to claim that it is any more beautiful than Perret's buildings.

A volcanic eruption

Oscar Niemeyer, Brazil's most famous modern architect, was born in Rio de Janeiro in 1907. He is responsible for many of the spectacular buildings in the city of Brasilia, some of which stand as isolated monuments in vast spaces. His work has been variously described as 'sensuous,' 'abstract.' 'uncompromising.' and even 'poetry from concrete.' Beauty, of course, is in the eye of the beholder and visitors might like to judge whether Niemeyer's Volcan cultural centre in Le Havre , which exploded on the scene in 1982, fits any of these descriptions.

However, beauty is to be found in the collection of paintings in the **Musée des Beaux Arts**, situated on Boulevard John Kennedy, close to the dock. The museum was the first reconstructed art gallery to be opened in France after the war; it contains impressionist and fauvist pictures from the likes of Monet, Pissarro and especially Dufy and Boudin, painted in a period when the port and beach at Le Havre were magnets for artists.

Shopping

Le Havre has a good selection of shops, although the shopping district could benefit from being more concentrated. However, the new multi-storey Coty shopping precinct has a high concentration of good retail outlets, together with a large Monoprix. At Montvilliers, on the outskirts of Le Havre, there is a massive commercial centre, which includes an Auchan hypermarket. A word of warning for drivers travelling between districts: *Priorité a Droite* operates throughout Le Havre's grid system of roads. Beware!

Ste-Adresse

Before leaving Le Havre for the Côte Fleurie, visitors would be well advised to take a short detour by driving along the Boulevard Albert, which runs alongside the long beach to the north-west of the town. Le Havre's beach is a mixture of sand and shale, but it has all the usual beach-side bars and cafés, and meteorological conditions have helped to make it one of the main centres of windsurfing in France. The boulevard rises up Le Havre's northern cliff and is lined all along the way with cafés, grand villas and apartment blocks, culminating in the massive Nice Havrais building, which houses the Eden Roc Hotel. This is the posh suburb of **Ste-Adresse**, which was the seat of the exiled Belgian government during World War I and was also home to Monet for a time.

At the summit, which is known as **Cap de la Hève**, there is a radar station, a lighthouse and a Table d'Orientation, from which there is a most spectacular view, which encompasses the city of Le Havre, its port and docks, with their huge twin chimneys, and takes the eye across the wide Seine estuary to Honfleur and the Côte Fleurie.

The port

The port of Le Havre, which was first established in 1509 by Francois I to replace the silted-up basins at nearby ports, eventually became a sort of French Liverpool. Colonial imports, such as cotton, coffee, timber and tobacco, were brought into France through Le Havre; there was also considerable trade with America and the great transatlantic liners used the port. Post-war reconstruction has restored Le Havre to its rightful place as France's second port (second only to Marseille). The port is also the nearest deep-sea yachting basin to Paris.

CÔTE FLEURIE

Until 1995, it was necessary to make a 37-mile (60km) detour in order to reach the Côte Fleurie from Le Havre. Thanks to the completion of the **Pont de Normandie**, this journey has been cut to 15 miles (24km).

After leaving Le Havre, head for the A29, and then take the southbound entrance to the autoroute. After a short distance, the A29 crosses the Seine via the Pont de Normandie toll bridge. The huge bridge looks dauntingly humped when it is approached along the road, but this is deceptive. The bridge is, in fact, a superbly elegant structure and one of the longest bridges of its type in the world. Although it may look like a suspension bridge, it is actually a cable-stayed bridge and very light, but very strong.

After crossing the bridge, leave the autoroute on the D513 for Honfleur.

Honfleur

The word 'picturesque' is heavily over-used in guide books, but **Honfleur** is one of the most undeniably picturesque places to be found anywhere in the world. Its Vieux Basin (Old Dock) is crammed with pleasure boats and fishing craft and the quayside is lined with tall, narrow, grey-slate and timber buildings. Many of these seventeenth century 'mini-skyscrapers' are seven floors high and some are jettied. A raised street runs behind this terrace, with the result that most of the buildings have entrances at two levels: a quayside entrance at ground floor level and a back entrance at first or second floor level.

It is hardly surprising to find that many well-known artists have painted the quayside scene. Lesser-known painters cannot resist the temptation either: many of the quayside buildings are occupied by artists' studios and painters are often to be seen on the quayside at work at their easels.

Aside from artists' studios, Honfleur has shops selling local cider and plenty of cafés whose seats offer splendid views of the Old Dock

and its picturesque buildings. **Église Ste-Catherine** is a most unusual dock-side church, in that it was constructed almost entirely in wood by local shipwrights. It has sloping aisles, two unequal naves and some interesting wooden carvings. Its detached belfry, **Clocher de Ste-Catherine**, which is built of oak and picturesquely (There I go again!) supported by wooden stays, houses part of the **Musée Eugene Boudin**, which contains paintings by Boudin and other artists, as well as costumes and head-dresses. Boudin's father was a local fisherman.

Samuel de Champlain sailed from Honfleur in 1608 to establish Quebec as a French colony.

Trouville

After leaving Honfleur, the D513 road, which is not very well surfaced in places, twists and turns through wooded country. The route passes through **Villerville**, a little resort with a terrace above the beach, before it heads for **Trouville**.

On the approach to Trouville, there is a succession of large, elegant, individually-styled villas sandwiched between the corniche and the beach. These sumptuous houses are a reminder that Trouville was the first holiday resort to be developed along this coast. The earliest resort facilities were built in the days of Louis-Philippe and by the mid-nineteenth century, well-to-do Parisians were coming here in numbers in order to take the sea air, indulge in a spot of gambling and be seen on the wooden-plank promenade in their fashionable attire.

After 1860, Trouville was eclipsed as a resort for the aristocratic set by nearby Deauville, but it survived by re-inventing itself as a family resort. The casino and the thalassotherapy centre (sea-water treatment) are still there in a large and elegant building; the wooden-plank promenade has also survived to remind us that this is a resort of some class, but the superb sandy beach now teems with happy families. The **Musée Villa Montebello** has works of art celebrating the history of Trouville and the rise of sea-bathing as a fashionable recreation, and there is an **Aquarium** with reptiles as well as fish.

An open-air market is held on Wednesdays and Sundays and there is a fish market everyday.

Deauville

Trouville is linked to **Deauville** by the Touques bridge, which runs alongside a very busy marina.

Deauville was developed in the 1860s by Napoleon III's half-brother, the Duc de Morny, and soon became the chosen resort of rich aristocrats and society figures. In the 1920s and 1930s, it also became the haunt of film stars and the nouveaux riches.

Whereas Trouville has become a homely place, where it is easy to settle in and relax, Deauville has remained exclusive and elitist. To enter the resort is like walking into one of those houses where everything

Silver ladies and ugly ducklings

Anyone who has visited France will testify that French motorists differ from their British counterparts in showing a distinct preference for cars made in their own country: the streets of France are full of Renaults, Peugeots and Citroens. Very few British-made cars are to be found, except in Deauville, where the possession of a Rolls-Royce is as much a recognised status symbol as strolling along Les Planches in the latest fashions. The Silver Lady on the bonnet of a Rolls-Royce represents the wealth, elegance, good manners and style which the French visitors to Deauville are keen to project.

In fact, the Rolls-Royce has French origins. Henry Royce began manufacturing cars in 1904 after making modifications to his second-hand French light car, a two-cylinder Decauville.

If Rolls-Royce is still seen as the 'Best of British', the idiosyncratic Citroen 2CV is still regarded as quintessentially French, even though it is a rapidly dying breed on the roads of France. The car's canvas roof, corrugated-metal body, detachable panels and removable rear seats make it an easy target for derision, but these self-same characteristics have also made the 'Deux Chevaux' a wonderful work-horse. Those Frenchmen who still possess a 2CV testify that it is a flexible load-carrier which is easy to maintain, economical to run and just as much at home on the cart tracks of French farms as on the roads. In fact, the 2CV meets to perfection one of Henry Royce's mission statements: 'Whatever is done rightly, however humble, is noble.'

is so immaculately arranged that it seems to carry a 'Do Not Touch' label. It is the British who have a reputation for snobbishness, but the French can be very, very pretentious too, and Deauville represents them at their snobbish worst.

Deauville was designed to bring all the comforts of aristocratic Paris to the seaside. Its boulevards are wide and splendid; its villas and grand hotels are exuberant, 'look-at-me' fantasies; its lawns and gardens are spacious and carefully manicured; and its tennis courts and menages have that 'Members Only' look about them. Events in the 'season' include horse races, including the Deauville Grand Prix, polo world championships, golf tournaments, regattas and an American film festival.

There is a swimming pool and a large casino in a most elegantly styled building, where it is possible to gamble at the tables between 10pm and 3am and enjoy a late-night cabaret to soften the blow of losing money. Plebeians can play on the slot machines from 10 o'clock in the morning.

Even the beach is manicured at Deauville and made into a huge, flat desert, which looks unbelievably desolate out of season, but is transformed in summer into a giant landscape sculpture, when it is decorated with neat row, upon neat row of bright beach tents, seen at their best in the early mornings before the red, blue, green and yellow canvasses are unravelled from their supporting poles.

Costume change

The French have led the world in the fashion for minimal beachwear. The craze for topless sunbathing began on the very beaches at St Tropez where Brigitte Bardot had first popularised the bikini. In no time at all, the fashion had spread to most French beaches, including those on the Côte Fleurie. It is now the norm in France for young women, and even the not so young, to sunbathe topless. The habit has even survived a recent comeback for the one-piece bathing costume.

The mile and a half-long (3km) beach is backed by a long promenade of wooden planks, known as **Les Planches**, which acts like a catwalk for the daily fashion parade of well-heeled Parisians of a certain age and much younger wannabes. Running alongside Les Planches, there is a succession of cafés offering drinks at exorbitant prices and a line of changing huts, each of which is labelled with the name of a film star – although how Buzz Aldrin's name came to be included is something of a mystery.

Deauville to Dives

Deauville seems to be fossilised in an age before tourism became affordable to the masses, but real fossils are a feature of the next stretch of coast. As well as possessing an extensive beach, a long promenade and a casino, Villers-sur-Mer has a **Musée Paléontologique**, which is crammed with fossils, seashells and stuffed birds. **Houlgate**, a little to the south, is approached from Falaise des Vaches Noires (Black Cows Cliff), an eroded cliff face, below which there is an extensive deposit of fossils. The resort has a fine beach.

Dives-sur-Mer

Dives is famous as the departure point for William the Conqueror when he set out to invade England in 1066. The west wall of the fifteenth-century **Church of Notre Dame** is engraved with the names of the Norman lords who accompanied William and there is a sixteenth-century timbered inn called **Guillaume le Conquérant**. Its old stable yard now contains art and craft shops.

The most notable feature of Dives is the sixteenth-century, timber-framed covered market (**Les Halles**), whose stalls have wrought iron signs.

Dives is built on the estuary of the river Dives and there is a fine view across the water of the resort of Cabourg.

Cabourg

Cabourg is easily my favourite Normandy resort. It was developed after Trouville and Deauville, at the end of the Second Empire. The villas of Trouville and Deauville are exuberant enough, but the villas of Cabourg are the most outlandish architectural fantasies imaginable. Most are top-heavy with turrets, balustrades, balconies and overhanging gables, and their walls are decorated with mad mosaics of stone, brick and timber. Anyone who remembers the house that featured in the film *What's New Pussycat* will be familiar with this kind of wild, neo-Gothic, debased Norman structure. Imagine this one house multiplied one hundred times, and you will have a pretty accurate picture of Cabourg.

The part of Cabourg that I love most is the very long, arrow-straight, aggregate-covered promenade, which is separated from the golden-yellow beach by a balustrade and is flanked on its landward side by large hotels and mad villas. At its heart, there is the preposterously opulent **Grand Hotel**, a monument to Belle Époque extravagance, where Marcel Proust often stayed to muse over his past life and observe his fellow guests. The Grand has its own casino and its own collection of distinctive beach umbrellas on the sands beyond its forecourt. The hotel is literally the focus of the town, because a series of avenues fan out from the rear of the hotel to form a semi-circular, planned resort.

Past and present

The long promenade at Cabourg is known as Promenade Marcel Proust and the Grand Hotel makes much of its Proustian associations.

Marcel Proust was born to a well-to-do Parisian family in 1871. His schooling and his law studies at the Sorbonne were both interrupted by distressing bouts of chronic asthma. Although he became a semi-invalid and something of a hypochondriac on reaching adulthood, Proust was a well-respected member of fashionable society until his mother's death in 1905. At this point, he largely retreated to his room and devoted his life to writing his multi-volume masterpiece *A la Recherche du Temps*

Perdu, which traces the life of Proust's hero (essentially himself) from childhood through adolescence to adulthood. In this novel, memories of the past share equal reality with activities of the present. Proust was often reminded of the past by a smell, a noise or the sight of a small object, and he was a meticulous observer of the present.

Young Marcel first came to Cabourg in 1891 in an attempt to find fresh air to help remedy his asthmatic condition. He returned in 1907 and then came every summer until 1914, always staying at the Grand Hotel, where he indulged in detailed observation of other guests, but also spent long periods in his room musing over the past. He used the town of Cabourg as a model for Balbec, a town in his novel.

Ironically, the road which runs arrow-straight from the Grand Hotel, and so forms a line of symmetry for the town's fan of streets, is the one and only tacky street in the whole place. Whereas the rest of Cabourg is a monument to the Belle Époque, this street is a monument to the age of mass tourism. There are snack bars, pizzerias, trinket shops, bars, ice cream stalls, and lots of bargain shops, but this incongruous intrusion in the town highlights the very quality of Cabourg that I admire. Whereas Deauville tries to hang on to its exclusivity, Cabourg does not take its high society past too seriously. It is now popular with people of all ages and all classes, who come to enjoy its golden beach and its safe seas (when the jelly fish are not around), and who are often to be seen smiling fondly at its crazy villas.

At the western extremity of the sea-front, beyond the semi-circular fan of grand old Cabourg, the promenade peters out and sand permeates the parallel roads which lead to campsites, caravan parks and holiday villas. This area of the town is very popular as a location with French film-makers who make those movies in which nubile girls have daily assignations on the beach with teenage boys and nightly assignations in their holiday villas with older men.

After this evocative trip along the Côte Fleurie, the return journey to Le Havre is a simple matter of taking the A13 autoroute, which then merges with the A29 before crossing the Pont de Normandie and returning to base.

5.2 A VISIT TO CHARTRES

INTRODUCTION

The trip from Le Havre to Chartres is a fairly lengthy one (about 120 miles/193km), but it is a journey that would be worthwhile even if the distance were twice as long.

Chartres Cathedral is one of the greatest architectural treasures in Europe. The church is particularly celebrated for its sculptured portals, its superb interior proportions and its utterly stunning stained glass, but it is a fabulous building in every respect.

Because the reputation of the cathedral is so high, the qualities of the town tend to be overlooked, but Chartres is one of the most charming towns in France. Its gabled houses cluster in picturesque fashion on the hillside below the cathedral and there are very good examples of vernacular architecture from many periods. This is a visit not to be missed.

Top Tips, Chartres

Not to be missed

- Cathedral of Notre Dame, Evreux
- The Reliquary of St Taurinius, Evreux
- The organ case in Dreux Cathedral
- The first view of Chartres Cathedral across the wheatfields
- Chartres Cathedral – west front, portals, stained glass etc, etc
- The Musée des Beaux Arts, Chartres
- The Old Town Chartres
- The house with a timbered turret, in the Old Town, Chartres

Things to do

- Spot architecture from many different periods in the Cathedral of Evreux
- Relax in the gardens by the river Iton, Evreux
- See the Soulages abstracts in Evreux Museum
- Take a long, lingering look at both the exterior and interior of Chartres Cathedral
- Sit at a pavement café in Chartres and follow the example of Rodin by staring at the external sculpture on the cathedral
- Listen to organ music in the cathedral
- Shop for works of art and antiques in the Old Town, Chartres

THE JOURNEY TO CHARTRES

Chartres is reached from Le Havre by taking the A131 to the A13, following the autoroute in an easterly direction and then turning off at the N151 Evreux junction. Thereafter, the route is fairly straightforward, although the road numbers change at Evreux and Dreux. The N12 runs from Evreux to Dreux and the N154 links Dreux with Chartres.

If time permits, the two main towns along the way are worthy of inspection.

Evreux

The town of **Evreux**, which is built at a point where the river Iton splits into three streams, is a busy industrial centre and the chief agricultural

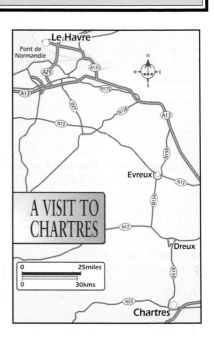

market for the Eure region. Its mixture of old and new architecture suggests that it is a place that has been knocked about rather a lot, and this is certainly the case. It was bombed by the Germans in June 1940 and by the Allies in June 1944.

During the bombing, the **Cathedral of Notre Dame** was quite badly damaged, but extensive restoration work has been carried out. The church will appeal to anyone who likes spotting and dating architectural elements from different periods. The façade is largely sixteenth-century; the nave is clearly Romanesque at its lower levels; but has later additions in its higher reaches; some of the stained glass in the main body of the church looks very old, but the superb stained glass in the Lady Chapel is fifteenth- or sixteenth-century; much of the north transept, especially its wonderful doorway, is very clearly fashioned in the sixteenth-century Flamboyant style and the altar railings are elaborate ironwork from the eighteenth-century.

It seems particularly apt that the adjacent **Museum** should also contain an eclectic mix, with archaeological finds keeping company with medieval exhibits and even with twentieth-century abstract paintings by Soulages.

The **Église St-Taurin**, west of the cathedral, contains the noted thirteenth-century **Reliquary of St Taurinius**. The shrine is covered in ornate enamel and silver guilt. Evreux has some nice gardens by the river, ideal for those who wish to spend a relaxing few moments after an exhausting bout of architecture spotting in the cathedral.

Dreux

The next town on the journey to Chartres also contains a church that was built over a long period. Dreux's church of **Saint-Pierre** was begun in the thirteenth century, but not finished until four centuries later. It has good stained glass and a wonderful seventeenth-century organ case in the south transept.

The town also contains an elaborate sixteenth-century **Belfry** and the **Royal Chapel of St Louis**, a domed nineteenth-century edifice which contains the tomb of Louis-Philippe. The chapel contains a great deal of stained glass and a lot of elaborate sculptures, and is altogether very ornate. Worth a visit if you like that sort of thing!

The approach to Chartres

The little architectural detours into Evreux and Dreux pale into insignificance when compared with the wonderful sight that greets motorists as they approach **Chartres**. The silhouette of the town's great **cathedral** suddenly looms up on the horizon. This magnificent first view of the church is strangely deceptive, because the cathedral appears to stand in splendid isolation in the heart of vast wheat fields, even though it is actually located in the heart of the town.

As the town draws closer, the cathedral looms ever larger and some of the architectural details start to come into focus, with tall asymmetric towers and great flying buttresses beginning to take shape. Anyone approaching Chartres cannot fail to experience of a feeling of great anticipation.

THE TOWN OF CHARTRES

In Chartres, all roads seem to lead to the cathedral, but motorists entering the town have two alternative starting points for their pilgrimage to the great church. Visitors who park in the lower town by the river Eure are treated to a view of the cathedral standing majestically above a jumble of gabled houses. However, there are better opportunities for parking near the Place des Epars, in the upper town, so it probably makes good practical sense to begin an exploration of Chartres from that point.

The cathedral is best approached along the Rue Noel Balley, where there is a good selection of shops, including some nice clothes shops. Although this is the newer part of the town, there are some interesting buildings along the way, including a superb iron-framed market hall and a modern pharmacy, whose upper floors are composed of an eclectic mix of geometric shapes. This eccentric riot of modernist detail is housed, rather surprisingly, below a conventional gable.

The cathedral

Any visit to Chartres Cathedral is an experience never to be forgotten, but maximum benefit is obtained by taking the tour slowly and methodically. I would recommend that visitors start their inspection by walking around the outside of the building beginning at the west end. The west front comes as something of a surprise to first-time visitors and I have to admit that I felt some sense of disappointment when I first encountered it, simply because the façade is made decidedly lopsided by its twin towers, which were not only built in different architectural periods, but also have different heights. However, as soon as I began to study the individual elements that make up the façade, I became

transfixed by their beauty. As I discovered, a 'bit-by-bit' inspection pays great dividends.

Pilgrims' Progress

The Cathedral of Chartres has been a place of pilgrimage ever since 876 AD, when Charles the Bald presented the town with a 16ft-long (5m) piece of silk, said to have been a chemise worn by the Virgin. The relic is still kept in a special case behind the altar. When the cathedral was rebuilt after a disastrous fire in 1194, pilgrims actually helped to construct the new church and help float stone from the quarries of the Seine and Oise down the river Eure to Chartres. The new church was built on a very large scale in order to accommodate pilgrims as well as townspeople.

As with all relics, much doubt has been cast on the authenticity of the Virgin's chemise. One analysis carried out in 1927 supposedly showed the remnant to be very old indeed – but not quite old enough! Pilgrims are still drawn to the church, not only by the Chemise of the Virgin, but also by the sixteenth-century wooden statue of the Virgin of the Pillar and by the supposedly miraculous well in the crypt, where martyrs were once thrown.

In truth, most modern pilgrims who visit Chartres are tourists, most of whom are able to appreciate fine architecture and sculpture, but have little, or no religious faith.

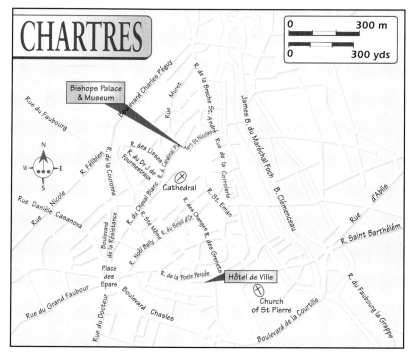

The lower part of the west front and the southern tower are the only exterior features of the cathedral to survive the disastrous fire of 1194. The southern tower begins as a square structure but evolves into a very tall, very plain, octagonal spire, which rises to a height of 349ft (106m) and is the highest Romanesque steeple to be found anywhere. The northern tower, which was added in the early sixteenth century by Jehan Tixier, is a much more elaborate, Flamboyant structure. French Gothic architecture, which had inspired architects throughout western Europe, rather lost its way in the Flamboyant period, just at the moment when English architecture was coming into its own with the development of the Perpendicular style. However, this particular tower is French Flamboyant at its most tasteful.

Between the towers there are four stages, beginning at the base with the fabulous Royal Portal, three sculptured doorways illustrating the life of Christ in beautiful twelfth-century stonework. Many of the figures are attenuated, most have realistic faces and some even smile enigmatically. Above the Royal Porch, there are three lancet windows, topped by a rose window, which was added in the thirteenth century. The rose is a superb composition, which thankfully, is not crowded out by a riot of surrounding decoration, as is so often the case in French cathedrals. Above the rose, there is a thirteenth-century frieze comprising sixteen splendid statues of the Kings of Judah.

After inspecting the west front, visitors should take a walk around the outside of the building, in order to admire the flying buttresses, which were the first to be used anywhere in the world, and the portals on the north and south transepts. These portals differ from the Royal Portal in that they are housed, rather splendidly, under projecting Gothic canopies, but their sculptural detail is equally impressive. The figures on the north portal represent the Virgin and Old Testament figures; the ones on the south portal illustrate the Last Judgment. Above both the transept portals, there are further rose windows.

The interior

In contrast to the lopsided exterior, the interior, which was finished in 1260, is wonderfully unified, largely because it was completed in just seventy years, except for some later additions of sculpture and stained glass. Aside from its wonderful proportions, the great glory of the interior is the magnificent stained glass. Chartres has the largest concentration of stained glass in the world and much of it is at least 700 years old. When the sun shines, the thirteenth-century reds and the twelfth-century blues shine out like jewels.

The choir has a fine screen with sculptured Biblical scenes by Jehan Texier, who was also responsible for the northern tower. The wooden sculpture adjacent to the choir of the Virgin of the Pillar is much venerated.

Half a million people, two-thirds of them from overseas, visit Chartres every year, and the cathedral is always crammed with parties and their tour guides. Malcolm Miller, an Englishman who has lived in Chartres for many years, has long specialised in taking English tour groups around the great church. The large number of visitors and the rows of church seats both succeed in partially obliterating the maze on the nave floor, which pilgrims were once required to follow on their knees.

Musée des Beaux Arts

Just behind the north transept, in the old Bishop's Palace, there is a **Musée des Beaux Arts**, which contains an interesting, if somewhat odd mix of tapestries, enamels. alabasters, military implements and paintings, including works by Watteau, Fragonard, Chardin and Philippe de Champaigne.

After exiting the museum, visitors would be well advised to relax over a drink at the pavement café opposite the south portal, where visitors might well become as entranced as Rodin, who was so transfixed by the external sculpture on the cathedral that he refused an umbrella that was offered to him when it began to rain.

The Old Town

Rodin christened Chartres the 'Acropolis of France,' and the church certainly stands like the Acropolis when it is viewed from the foot of the **Old Town**, which tumbles down to the river Eure in a series of 'hillocks.' A walk down to the river is very rewarding, because the Old Town is crammed with picturesque gabled houses, some of which are half-timbered. One house has a timbered turret that encases a spiral staircase. Because the external timbers of the tower follow the line of the spiral, the whole edifice looks like a wooden version of the famous Renaissance staircase at the Chateau of Blois.

The sound of music

Throughout the summer months, Chartres is alive to the sound of music.

A festival of dance and a harpsichord festival are both held in May. There is a European accordion forum in June and an international organ festival is held from June to September, when concerts are performed every Sunday on the organ of the cathedral.

Free concerts and street events, some of which are very spectacular, are held throughout June, July and August.

At the foot of the Old Town, there are humped-back bridges, plus some old wash-houses and tanneries, and a church with yet more stained glass. This is the church of **St Pierre**, which has a fat twelfth-century tower, a thirteenth-century nave and a nice choir. Its glass is mainly thirteenth- and fourteenth-century.

After pausing to look back up the hill at one of the greatest buildings in western Europe, visitors can return to their vehicle by walking up the fairly gentle slope of the inner ring road or they can climb back up the streets and alleys of the Old Town, perhaps pausing to browse around the art and antique shops along the way.

The easiest way to return to Le Havre is simply to reverse the outward journey.

ACCOMMODATION

Le Havre

Visitors wishing to book a hotel in Le Havre could try:

*** Best Western Hotel de Bordeaux
Rue Louis Brindeau
☎ 0235 226944

** Hotel Celtic
Rue du 129e Régiment d'Infanterie
☎ 0235 226944

There is a camp site at:

Camping de la Forêt de Montegeon
Cours de la République
Open: Easter to September
☎ 0235 465239

Côte Fleurie

There are many hotels along the Côte Fleurie, some of which are outlandishly expensive. Some possible hotels follow:

Honfleur
** Hotel du Dauphin
On the quayside
Place Pierre Berthelot
☎ 0231 891553

Trouville

A reasonable option might be:

** Hotel Flaubert
Rue Gustave Flaubert
☎ 0231 883723

Deauville

The Normandy, Royal and Golf are Deauville's premier hotels, but tourists looking for a less expensive option might like to try:

** Hotel le Chantilly
Avenue de la République
☎ 0231 887975

Cabourg

Those wishing to splash out and re-live the Marcel Proust experience will want to stay at:

**** Grand Hotel
Belle Époque elegance
Promenade Marcel Proust
☎ 0231 910179

Another possible option:

*** Le Cabourg
All rooms are identified by the names of flowers
Avenue de la République
☎ 0231 244893

ATTRACTIONS

Le Havre
Musée des Beaux Arts
Boulevard John Kennedy
Closed Tuesday. Open: 11am–6pm.
Weekends: 11am–7pm.
☎ 0235 423397

Côte Fleurie
Honfleur
Musée Eugene Boudin
Open: March–September: daily, except Tuesday 10am–12 noon, 2–6pm. October–March: 2.30–5pm, weekends: 10am–12 noon.
☎ 0231 895400

Trouville
Aquarium
Rue de Paris
Open: July, August: 10am–7.30pm. Easter–June and September, October: 10am–12noon, 2–7pm. November–Easter: 2–6.30pm.
☎ 0231 884604

Musée Villa Montebello
Rue du Général Leclerc
Open: April–September, except
Tuesday: 2–6pm. Free on
Wednesdays.
☎ 0231 881626

Deauville
Casino de Deauville
Rue Edmond Blanc
Slot machines from 10am. Casino:
3.30pm–3am.
☎ 0231 143114

EATING OUT

Le Havre
There are lots of restaurants in Le
Havre, but the restaurants with the
best locations are situated on the
road up to Ste-Adresse. Visitors may
like to try:

La Petite Auberge
In a half-timbered building
Rue Ste-Adresse
☎ 0235 482732

Côte Fleurie
There are very many restaurants and
cafés along the Cote Fleurie. A small
selection follows:

Honfleur
L'Assiette Gourmande
Good sea food
Quai des Passages
☎ 0231 892488

Restaurant l'Absinthe
Traditional surroundings
Quai de la Quarantine
☎ 0231 881810

Deauville
If you really want to splash out and
join high society for a meal, book at:

Ciro's
Promenade de la Planche
☎ 0231 881810

Dives
For a pleasant meal in Art Deco
surroundings, try:

Les Vapeurs
Boulevard Fernand Moureaux
☎ 0231 881524

SHOPPING

Le Havre
The new Coty indoor shopping area
is a multi-storey shopping precinct.
There is a large commercial centre,
including an Auchan hypermarket,
at Montvilliers, on the perimeter of
the city.

Côte Fleurie
Buy paintings, pottery and cider in
Honfleur.
Shop at the outdoor market in
Trouville (Wednesday, Sunday),
where there is also a daily fish
market.
Look at, and possibly buy, expensive
goods in Deauville.
Buy souvenirs, possibly with
Proustian connections, in Cabourg.

TOURIST INFORMATION
Le Havre
Boulevard Clémenceau
☎ 0235 740404

Côte Fleurie
Honfleur
Place Arthur Boudin
☎ 0231 892330

Le Harve and the Cote Fleurie

Trouville
Boulevard F Moureaux
☎ 0231 883619

Deauville
Place de la Mairie
☎ 0231 144000

Cabourg
Jardins de Casino
☎ 0231 912000

VISIT TO CHARTRES

ACCOMMODATION

Chartres
Many visitors will wish to spend more than one day in Chartres. Hotel choices include:

*** Hotel du Grand Monarque
Place des Epars
Chartres' main hotel
☎ 0137 210072

** Hotel de la Poste
A cheaper alternative and member of the Logis de France chain
Place du Général Koenig
☎ 0137 210427

ATTRACTIONS

Evreux
Musée d'Evreux
Rue Charles Corbeau
Open: Tuesday–Sunday: 10am–12 noon, 2–6pm.
☎ 0232 315229

Chartres
Musée des Beaux Arts
Cloître Notre Dame
Open: April–October: Wednesday–Monday: 10am–1pm, 2–6pm.
November–March: Wednesday–Monday: 10am–12 noon, 2–5pm.
☎ 0137 364139

SHOPPING

Chartres has a good range of general shops and also art, antique and book shops.

TOURIST INFORMATION

Evreux
Place de Gaulle
☎ 0232 240443

Dreux
Rue Port Charbraine
☎ 0237 460173

Chartres
Place de la Cathédrale
☎ 0137 215000

Above: Half-timbered houses, Rouen. *Below:* Beach umbrellas, Deauville.

Above left: seaside villa, Trouville. *Above right:* cider, Honfleur.
Below: The Royal Portals, Chartres.

Above: Lafayette Store, Paris. *Below left:* The Pyramid at the Louvre.
Below right: Paris rooftops from the Samaritaine store.

Paris is within easy reach of four of the Channel ports featured in this guide. Dieppe, at just over 100 miles (160km) distance, is the port which is closest to the French capital, but there are good autoroute links to Paris from Le Havre (about 135 miles/217km) and from Calais and Boulogne (about 180 miles/289km).

The French capital, which is endlessly fascinating, surprising, exciting and romantic, deserves a whole guide book to itself. It is beyond the scope of this book to give detailed coverage to the city's many tourist attractions, shopping opportunities, entertainment possibilities and its huge range of eating, drinking and accommodation options. How-ever, an entirely personal selection of 'dos' and 'don'ts,' gathered from many years of visiting and enjoying Paris, may help to whet the appetite of Channel hoppers for a trip to one of the world's most beautiful cities.

A day in Paris need not be an expensive affair. So much of the joy of visiting the French capital comes simply from looking.

- Shop in Boulevard Saint-Michel – great for fashions.

- Visit the Place Vendome and admire the (unpriced) jewellery in the windows – but do not think too seriously of buying any pieces!

- Enjoy a similar experience at the Dior shop in Avenue Montaigne.

- Shop in Les Halles. There was great criticism when the old market halls were replaced by this largely subterranean glass-topped precinct, but shopping here is a pleasant experience.

- Browse among the bookstalls of the bouquinistes on the banks of the Seine.

- Visit the Village Voice bookshop on Boulevard St Germain.

- Visit W H Smith's English bookshop on the Rue de Rivoli.

- Visit the Musée d'Orsay. Admire the wonderful conversion of a great railway station into a great art gallery and then drool over the impressionist paintings. Renoir's *Two Girls at the Piano* and Degas' paintings and sculptures of ballet dancers are among my own favourites.

- Enter the Louvre through the glass pyramid (a wonderful focal point, which not only draws people into this great museum, but also provides stunning views of the old Louvre Palace through the glass panes of the pyramid). If you must, join the crowds who watch the Mona Lisa's eyes follow them around the room, but also seek out works by Ingres – in my view, the world's greatest painter of human flesh.

- Visit the Musée Rodin and see copies of *The Kiss, The Thinker,* and *The Burghers of Calais*, as well as Rodin's own collection of paintings, sculptures and furniture.

- See the twentieth-century Picassos in the seventeenth-century Hotel Salé.

- Have a ride on the ghost train in the summer fairground in the Tuileries gardens. I am convinced that the hand which comes across your face in one of the pitch-black spaces is human!

- Watch the human statues who perform (by standing perfectly still) in streets all over the city.

- Visit a cinema on the Champs-Élysées. The French are great cinemagoers.

- Drive out to Versailles and admire the grand, cobbled approach, the statue of Louis XIV in *L'État, C'est Moi* pose, the gardens and, of course, the house.

- Drive out to Fontainebleau. The view of the great curved external staircase alone makes the drive worthwhile.

- Have a day at Disneyland Paris. You'll be surprised how much you enjoy yourself, despite the nauseating fixed smiles of all the assistants, the long queues and short rides, and the incessant music that still plays in your head long after you have left the complex. The electric procession each evening is hugely enjoyable, despite being over-the-top, American kitsch.

6.2 A few don'ts

- Don't patronize the pet shops near Notre Dame. The birds and animals are kept in appallingly cramped conditions.

- Don't park your car in a tight spot – the driver of the adjacent car will almost shunt your vehicle when he or she leaves.

- Don't drive around the traffic island at the Arc de Triomphe unless you are prepared to risk life and limb by cutting across the traffic that is circulating the island – it is the correct way to proceed here!

- Don't park anywhere where there are small, very solid stone bollards – they cannot be seen from your windscreen or rear window and they do lots of damage to your bumper!

- Don't try to change lanes quickly (or even at all!) on the Périphérique.

- Don't try to cross the road as a pedestrian in Place de la Concorde, if you want to live to see the rest of Paris.

- Don't walk the streets of the Bois de Boulogne at night, unless you are prepared to risk being mistaken for a professional street-walker!

- Don't stay at a hotel without its own parking provision, unless you are prepared to spend hours circling the nearby streets for a spare meter space. There is one consolation: the meters can be fed at night in order to pay for parking time the following morning.

- Don't buy a drink in the Place du Tertre in Montmartre – the prices are exorbitant!

- Don't agree too readily to have your portrait drawn by a street artist in the Place du Tertre – many of the artists are not capable of achieving a likeness and some even have a pair of eyes drawn on the paper before the sitter arrives!

- Don't ascend the glass-encased, external escalators at the Pompidou Centre on a hot day. The greenhouse effect is unbearable!

- Don't attend a live show in Pigalle unless you are prepared to pay astronomical prices for drinks and risk the attentions of the bouncers if you refuse to pay.

- Don't go to the new Opera House in Bastille Square, unless you intend to see a production there. The building is the worst of Mitterand's Grands Travaux.

- Don't waste much time admiring Napoleon's Tomb in Les Invalides. The tomb is very large and very ugly (like a giant piano stool). Admire the building instead.

Left: Art Nouveau architecture on the Avenue Rapp, Paris.

Below: Versailles.

Above: Pegasus Bridge.

Above: The beach, St Malo. *Below left:* Mont St Michel. *Below right:* Dinan.

INTRODUCTION

This chapter takes the form of a semi-circular tour from Bayeux to Caen, via the beaches along the Calvados Coast where the D-Day landings took place. Caen is a terminal for ferries from Portsmouth and can be reached from England in about six hours. Bayeux is some 16 miles (26km) north-west of Caen along the N13.

The port of Cherbourg, which is a terminal for ferries from Poole and Portsmouth, and can be reached in a shorter time of under three hours in daytime, is also a convenient starting point for such a tour. The distance from Cherbourg to Bayeux, along the N13, is about 37 miles (60km), but a detour via Barfleur, on the north-eastern tip of the Contentin peninsula, is recommended.

Getting there

P&O Portsmouth (☎ 0870 242 4999) run ferries from Portsmouth to Cherbourg. The journey takes about 2 hours 40 minutes by day and about 5 hours by night.

Brittany Ferries (☎ 0870 536 0360) run ferries from Poole to Cherbourg (journey time between 2 hours 15 minutes and 4 hours 15 minutes) and also from Portsmouth to Caen (journey time about 6 hours).

CHERBOURG

Cherbourg came into its own as a major naval base in the nineteenth century. It also developed as a transatlantic port and was a stopping place for large liners such as the QE2. The town was a stronghold in World War II for the Germans, who held out here until late June 1944, after which the port became a major conduit for heavy equipment and supplies to Allied troops fighting in Normandy. Cherbourg was also the terminus of the Pluto pipeline, which ran under the Channel and supplied fuel for Allied equipment. It is now a large industrial town, a ferry port and a major terminal for imported cars. Having been largely rebuilt after wartime damage, Cherbourg is not the prettiest place in France by any means, but it does have some interesting museums, pretty parks, busy quaysides, a huge yachting marina, a pedestrianised shopping area and some good markets.

Not to be missed

- Musée de Libération, Cherbourg
- The harbour at Barfleur
- The view from the jetty at St Vaast
- The Bayeux Tapestry
- Bayeux Cathedral
- Bayeux's unspoilt Old Town
- The artificial harbour at Arromanches
- Musée 6 Juin 1944, Arromanches
- Skeleton of a whale at Luc-sur-Mer
- The Pegasus Bridge
- Duke William's Citadel and its museums, Caen
- The Abbaye-aux-Hommes, Caen
- The Abbaye-aux-Dames, Caen
- Le Mémorial on the Caen ring road

Things to do

- View Cherbourg from the Forte du Roule
- Shop in Cherbourg's street markets
- See the tropical plants in Parc Emmanuel Liais, Cherbourg
- Shop for pottery and antiques in Barfleur
- Travel in an amphibious craft to Ile de Tatihou
- Listen to the story of William and Harold on the earphones in Bayeux's tapestry museum
- Shop for lace and porcelain in Bayeux
- Visit Bayeux's art and war museums
- Visit Gold Beach Musée America at Vers
- Look for crabs and shrimps on the beach at St Aubin
- Look out for the British telephone box at Hermanville
- Observe the Caen skyline from Duke William's Citadel
- Shop in the Rue St Pierre, Caen

Pipe down!

In 1944 Cherbourg became the French terminus of an underwater pipeline known as PLUTO (Pipe Line Under The Ocean), which ran for 65 miles (105km) from the Isle of Wight and was designed to supply fuel to the Allied armies advancing across France.

Planning for the pipeline began in May 1942 and involved expert help from John Augustus Oriel, the chief chemist at Shell, who had been rendered partially sighted by a gas attack in World War I. The technique was first tested by the laying of a pipe from Swansea to Watermouth, near Ilfracombe. This test was beset by problems, not least the severing of the pipe by the anchor of a tanker.

Two pipes were laid to Cherbourg in August 1944 and a further pipe was laid in September. Accounts of the effectiveness of PLUTO differ greatly. Some commentators maintain that it fulfilled its role admirably, but others suggest that it was riddled with problems, including breaks and leaks, and that the troops had reached Belgium before it began to operate in any meaningful way.

The nineteenth-century **Forte du Roule,** in the south-east corner of the town, makes a good starting point for an exploration of Cherbourg because it stands on a 367ft (112m) crag and commands very good views over the town. It was here that the Germans held out until 27 June 1944. The fort now houses the **Musée de la Libération,** an exhibition which covers the years of the occupation of France and the subsequent liberation of Normandy, by means of photographs, maps, scale models and audio-visual presentations. A section devoted to wartime propaganda reveals how truth and honesty become lost in times of conflict.

The **Musée Thomas Henry** lies just beyond the quaysides to the north-west of the Forte du Roule. This is a modern, purpose-built cultural center, which contains paintings by local artists but also work by old masters such as Fra Angelico and Filippo Lippi, as well as paintings by distinguished French artists such as Poussin and David.

The middle of Cherbourg has pedestrianised streets, one or two old buildings, particularly around the Rue du Blé, and street markets on Tuesday, Thursday and Saturday, when stalls are laden with poultry, shellfish, fruit, vegetables and flowers. The Place Napoléon has nice flower beds and a bronze statue of the Emperor himself.

Port Chanteryne, immediately north of the town centre, is always bustling with life, activity and the clinking of masts, because it is one of the largest yacht marinas to be found anywhere.

Parc Emmanuel Liais, slightly south-west of the yachting marina, was created by the naturalist and astronomer Emmanuel Liais. Its plants include some tropical varieties, which are able to survive and even flourish here because the Gulf Stream produces a relatively mild climate. The park contains the **Musée Ethnographie,** which has shells and stuffed birds and mammals, as well as sections devoted to human development. One exhibit traces the life of the Eskimos.

BARFLEUR

Some visitors may wish to take the N13 directly to Bayeux, but a detour via Barfleur is well worthwhile. The D901, which runs along the coast of the Contentin peninsula, has a succession of magnificent viewpoints along the way. The temptation to stop and admire the view is irresistible.

Barfleur is an old fishing port whose quayside is lined with solid, no-nonsense granite houses, which nevertheless form a picturesque whole, especially as they terminate in a seventeenth-century church with a distinctive, squat tower. The church has good stained glass, nice wooden statues and a rather special sixteenth-century Pieta in the south transept.

Richard the Lionheart sailed from Barfleur in 1194 to assume the English throne and it is said that the ship that carried William the Conqueror across the Channel in 1066 was built here. The Barfleur of today has a good collection of potteries and antique shops.

The D1 leads from Barfleur to **St Vaast**.

ST VAAST

St Vaast is a picturesque fishing port, which is now a popular yachting venue. A very long jetty affords views of the various reefs and islands off the shore. The jetty also contains a lighthouse, but it is said that the whitewashed apse of the eleventh-century fishermen's church, at the eastern end of the quay, is also used as a navigational aid.

Amphibious craft take visitors out to **Ile de Tatihou**, which has a maritime museum, with lots of fascinating artefacts recovered from shipwrecks, a nature reserve and a fort by our old friend Vauban.

The D902 now leads, via **Quettehou**, with its thirteenth-century granite church, back to the N13, where it is possible to pick up the direct road to Bayeux. Along the way, the N13 passes through **Carentan**, which has a church with a large octagonal spire, a fourteenth-century arcaded, covered market, and a town hall housed in an old convent.

BAYEUX

Visitors are drawn to **Bayeux** by its great tapestry, which is one of the most interesting and remarkable exhibits in France, but the town itself, which has picturesque but unpretentious houses and a magnificent but slightly odd cathedral, is very worthy of a visit. As we have seen, there are many fascinating and attractive towns throughout northern France, but Bayeux is one of my own favourites, and I am confident that it will be equally appealing to most tourists.

The Tapestry

The first destination for most visitors to Bayeux is the **Musée de la Tapisserie**, otherwise known as **Centre Guillaume le Conquérant**. Parking is free (assuming I have not missed any signs or pay-stations) and the path to the museum passes, rather incongruously, through what appears to be the out-patients department of a hospital, before it enters the courtyard of an eighteenth-century seminary.

When I first saw the tapestry many years ago, I recall trying unsuccessfully to follow a commentary which emanated from a set of dodgy earphones and was almost completely muffled out by the hub-hub from a crowd of other visitors. All has now changed. This great tapestry could not be better housed, better displayed or better interpreted. In fact, Bayeux's splendid museum should be seen as the model for mounting informative and entertaining exhibitions.

Visitors walk up to the first floor interpretation area, where there is an audio-visual presentation, which explains the activities of the Vikings in Normandy, a strip cartoon sequence, which is used to explain the make-up of the tapestry, and an audio-visual interpretation of the Battle of Hastings. Before visitors enter the tapestry room, they are given earphones, which give a very clear guide, in English and at just the right pace, of the contents of the tapestry, which is over 200ft (61m) long.

Elliptical thinking

It is generally agreed that the comet that features so prominently on the Bayeux Tapestry is Halley's Comet.

Edmond Halley was a British astronomer and mathematician who was greatly inspired by Newton's theories of gravity and planetary motion. In fact, Halley not only persuaded Newton to write up his theories, but even put up the money for their publication. By applying Newton's Laws to the motion of comets, Halley was able to prove that comets are part of the solar system and that they move around the sun in elliptical orbits.

Most famously, he correctly predicted that a comet, which had been seen in 1682, would return 76 years later in 1758. By the time the comet made its scheduled appearance, Halley was dead, but he had the posthumous satisfaction of having his name associated with the comet for evermore. Halley's Comet has made regular appearances ever since 1758 and was even penetrated by Russian and European space probes during its last visit.

Anyone who is prepared to idle away a few minutes of their holiday by counting back in multiples of 76 from 1758 will discover that 1066 is not a scheduled date for the comet's appearance. However, astronomers maintain that the combined results of the gravitational pull of planets and the effects of gases boiled off the sun caused sufficient variation in the rotation period to make 1066 a visiting year.

The story unfolds on the tapestry in dramatic fashion. Harold crosses to France for his audience with William and makes his promise that William should accede to the English throne; Edward the Confessor dies and Harold goes back on his word by declaring himself King; William assembles a fleet and sets sail for England; the English armies are defeated at the Battle of Hastings and Harold is killed. Every episode of this story is captured to perfection by the remarkably animated figures and the composition of the tapestry, which is suitably busy where there is action and quiet where there is negotiation. I particularly like the sequence where Harold is warned that the coming of Halley's Comet is a bad omen. The tapestry also gives a clear guide to the military equipment, the fashions and even the hairstyles of the period.

Harold and William

The saga of Harold and William, which is told so graphically on the Bayeux Tapestry, began when Harold was despatched to France by Edward the Confessor to inform the King's cousin, William Duke of Normandy, that he had been chosen as Edward's successor to the English throne. Harold's troubles started when his boat was shipwrecked off the French coast. He was rescued, but held captive by Count Guy of Ponthieu, until he was set free and received by William.

Harold duly swore on oath that he would accept William as King of England, but then went back on his word by assuming the English throne for himself on Edward's death on 5 January 1066.

William set sail for England from Dives on 27 September 1066 and then engaged in battle with Harold's forces at Hastings, where Harold was killed by an arrow which penetrated his eye.

The tapestry tour tour ends in an excellent gift shop, where it is possible to buy many souvenirs and postcards, including pull-out prints of the tapestry – I can assure readers that these elongated prints make ideal friezes for children's bedrooms!

The origins of the tapestry and the identity of the artists who produced it are both unknown. The French insist on calling the embroidery Tapisserie de la Reine Mathilde, but the English believe it was commissioned in Kent and produced by Saxon embroiderers.

Bayeux Cathedral

After leaving the tapestry museum, visitors are drawn to Bayeux's **Cathedral**, which manages to be both a fine example of a large Romanesque church and a building with a highly idiosyncratic exterior. The cathedral is very tall and has emphasized flying buttresses. The west front and twin western towers are surprisingly plain, but the south porch is highly elaborate and has a tympanum depicting the story of St Thomas Becket. The central tower, which is topped by a curious nineteenth-century 'bonnet,' is downright bizarre.

The interior consists of a fine Romanesque nave, with excellent decorations, a splendid chancel, with sixteenth-century choir stalls, an eighteenth-century altar and an array of radiating chapels.

To my eyes, Bayeux's cathedral is not at all like most other French cathedrals. Aside from that weird central tower, it reminds me very much of Truro Cathedral in

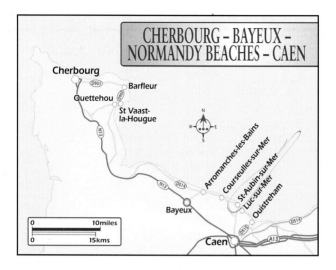

Cornwall. The designers of that nineteenth-century English structure must surely have been influenced by the architecture of Bayeux.

The town

Bayeux was the very first French town to be liberated by the Allies, and General de Gaulle entered the streets to great acclaim on 7 June 1944. Fortunately the town was spared any war damage and many old houses survive in the **Old Town**. Most of the houses with projecting upper floors and timber frameworks have been renovated, but they have not been inappropriately smartened up and embellished. Bayeux' Old Town manages to be both charming and modest; it is an absolute joy to wander its streets. It is probably advisable to explore the area without a set itinerary in mind and simply let the discoveries happen, but Rue des Cuisiniers, Rue St Martin, Rue St Malo, Rue Franche and Rue Bienvenue (to name but five) should not be missed.

Other museums

In addition to the tapestry museum, Bayeux has a number of other museums. Two are particularly worthy of a visit.

The **Musée Baron Gérard**, close to the cathedral, contains archaeological finds, superb Bayeux porcelain and lace, furniture and also paintings, including works by David, Philippe de Champagne and Boudin.

The **Musée Memorial de la Bataille de Normandie**, on the ring road to the south-west of the town, has military equipment, uniforms and personal mementos from all participating nations in the battle for Normandy. There is also a presentation of interesting archive film.

The town is often festooned with flags of many nations, a good number of shops in Bayeux sell lace and porcelain, and there is a Saturday market in Place St Patrice.

ARROMANCHES-LES-BAINS

The D516 leads from Bayeux to a stretch of coast officially known by the French as the **Côte de Nacre** (the

D-Day landings

At meetings in 1943, Churchill and Roosevelt chose the Normandy coast as a point of entry for Allied troops in the projected liberation of western Europe. They felt that the Germans, who were concentrating their defences on the Calais area, would find it quite difficult to repel an invasion from the Calvados region.

After the dreadful failure of the Dieppe raid in 1942 (see Chapter 4), the Allies decided to use landing craft and artificial docks, such as that constructed at Arromanches, rather than use existing ports.

As a preliminary to the landings, the French railway system was attacked by aerial bombardment and by acts of sabotage by the French Resistance. The landings took place at dawn on 6 June 1944. The British and Commonwealth forces landed at Sword, Juno and Gold beaches and airborne troops were landed a little to the north. The Americans came ashore on the Omaha and Utah beaches.

Cherbourg fell to the Allies on 26 June and Caen fell on 9 July. By August, troops were pushing out from Normandy and the recapture of western Europe was well under way.

Mother of Pearl Coast), but now universally known as the site of the D-Day landings in 1944. When the landings took place, the stretch of coast between Arromanches and Ouistreham was given three code names. Reading from west to east, they were Gold Beach, Juno Beach and Sword Beach.

The D516 passes through pleasant countryside and sleepy stone hamlets but, when the sea first becomes visible on the approach to **Arromanches-les-Bains**, a most remarkable vision appears, almost as startling and unexpected as the first sight of an oasis in a desert. A huge array of what seem to be large black logs is seen to be floating on the water in a vast, strictly regular semi-circle. It materialises that this formation is the considerable remnants of an artificial dock, known as a 'Winston', which was towed across the Channel and assembled here in just twelve days

to assist the D-Day landings. Breakwaters, of concrete-filled caissons, formed the outer ring; steel pontoons, held to the bottom of the sea by suction rods, formed pier-heads and they were linked to the beach by floating piers of light metal. A great deal of this remarkable structure remains and can be inspected from telescopes arranged on the promenade.

Until 6 June 1944, when the landings took place, Arromanches was a quiet fishing village. It is now a magnet for tourists, who come to see the artificial dock and visit the **Musée 6 Juin 1944,** which has been constructed at the water's edge and contains equipment, working models, photographs, films and dioramas, all designed to bring to life the story of the D-Day landings. The museum's exhibition is well put together and gives a clear account of the liberation of Normandy, but the **Terrasse de Normandie Café,** on the promenade, has a little display of paintings which act as an even more poignant reminder of those heady days. One picture shows the landings on the beach; another shows troops being welcomed by the local population (especially the girls) and another depicts celebrations on the Champs-Élysées when Paris was liberated.

The landing beaches

After leaving Arromanches, the D516 follows the coast to Courseulles, but it is worth making a short diversion inland to **Vers-sur-Mer**, where the **Gold Beach Musée America** has further graphic descriptions of operations. Vers was the main bridgehead in the Gold Beach sector.

Courseulles-sur-Mer is the spot on the coast where Winston Churchill and General de Gaulle arrived after the landings and where George VI disembarked to visit the troops. It is now an expanding holiday resort with new blocks of flats, a marina and a **Maison de la Mer**, containing an extensive collection of sea-shells.

The next settlement along the coast, which is known as **Bernieres**, was not only the landing place for a French Canadian regiment, but also the spot where members of the press and radio reporters came ashore to cover the battle for Normandy. Bernieres is now a seaside resort with a good beach and a line of beach huts.

The road then passes through **St Aubin-sur-Mer**, a small resort where children can enjoy themselves by looking for crabs and shrimps on the beach. The stretch of landing beach known as Sword Beach begins at **Luc-sur-Mer**, a seaside town that has

a casino, a hydro and the first hint of those eccentric, top-heavy, mock half-timbered Normandy houses which so dominate the Côte Fleurie (Chapter 5). Luc also has a skeleton of a whale that was washed up here in 1885.

There is a surprise in store for British visitors entering **Hermanville**, the next resort along the coast, because a traditional red British telephone box is positioned by the side of the road. Incongruously located in this French coastal resort, the box looks like an object that has landed from another planet. An old French battleship, called *Courbet*, was deliberately sunk at Hermanville to act as a sea-wall during the landings on Sword Beach.

Pegasus Bridge

The road can now be followed to **Bénouville**, where we find the famous **Pegasus Bridge**, or at least a replacement that was built in 1992. The real Pegasus Bridge hides behind **Musée 6 Juin 1944 D-Day**, which recalls the exploits of the British 6th Airborne Division, which landed here from gliders on the 6 June, took the bridge after a four-minute fight and was then joined by commandos led by Lord Lovat, who had fought their way to this spot from Sword Beach.

A World War II tank stands by the bridge, as does the **Café Musée Gondrée**, which has gifts and a small museum.

It is now but a short distance to Caen along the D516.

CAEN

Caen is a port, university city and industrial centre with a very complex set of bridges and roads – beware! A two-month battle in June and July 1944 destroyed the central area of Caen Thousands of people fled from their homes and took refuge in churches, abbeys and even in a nearby quarry. Although the city has been rebuilt, it contains some old steep-gabled, half-timbered houses on the Rue St Pierre, one of the main shopping streets. As befits a university city, Caen has a thriving night life, and it is also a major tourist hub because it contains three very significant buildings.

The Château

The Château, which is often known as **Duke William's Citadel**, was erected in 1060 and used by William the Conqueror. The buildings have been much altered over the centuries and they were damaged in the bombardments of 1944, but the Château has been restored and the grounds are now planted with neat gardens. The castle has curtain wall ramparts, sentry walks, barbicans, a round tower and a great hall. There is a very fine view from the castle grounds of the Caen skyline with its plethora of church towers.

Museums

Within the precincts of the castle there are two museums. The **Musée des Beaux Arts** contains an excellent collection of paintings, including fifteenth- to seventeenth-century Italian works, seventeenth-century pictures by French and Flemish artists, eighteenth- and nineteenth-

century French works by the likes of Boucher, Géricault and Delacroix, and twentieth-century works by French masters, including Dufy and Bonnard. The **Musée de Normandie** uses artefacts and models to trace the history and traditions of Normandy.

Abbaye-aux-Hommes

The greatest building in Caen is the **Abbaye-aux-Hommes** (Abbey for Men), which stands south-west of the Château. Its west front and nave are both in a plain Romanesque style, but very aesthetically pleasing. The western towers are topped by some distinctively-shaped, thirteenth-century spires and the chancel is also thirteenth-century. Significant eighteenth-century additions include an organ at the west end, a clock in the north transept, large candlesticks near the altar and a portrait in the sacristy of William the Conqueror, in which he looks uncannily like Henry VIII. The chancel is closed by a nineteenth-century, wrought-iron screen.

Despite these additions over the centuries, the abbey has a remarkable unity and a very memorable profile. The eighteenth-century monastic buildings, which now house municipal offices and a registry, were designed by Brother Guillaume de la Tremblaye and contain some fine woodwork. From the cloisters, there is a magnificent view of the abbey.

A man and a woman

When William, Duke of Normandy, chose Matilda of Flanders as his bride, she resisted his attentions, but William persisted with his proposal. He is said to have broken into her house and dragged her around the room by her hair and even given her a few kicks on hearing of her obstinacy. Surprisingly, this rough treatment seems to have convinced Matilda that she should marry the Duke. The Pope was less convinced of the suitability of the marriage, because William and Matilda were distant cousins.

The couple were married in spite of the Pope's disapproval but, as penance for marrying against the will of the church, they agreed to found two separate abbeys in Caen, one for men and one for women. The marriage seems to have worked well and Matilda certainly benefited from the marriage in terms of status. She was allowed to rule Normandy while her husband was away fighting and she became Queen of England in 1068.

The **Abbaye-aux-Dames** (Abbey for Women) is situated north-east of the Château and was erected at the bidding of Queen Matilda in 1062. The Romanesque structure has a huge nave and wide transepts, with a thirteenth-century chapter house added to the south transept. The tomb of Queen Matilda is housed in a slab of black marble in the chancel. The abbey buildings include a Great Hall and refectory.

North of the city, on the Dwight Eisenhower Esplanade, there is a new, purpose-built museum for peace, known as **Le Mémorial.** The museum, which was erected on the site of a German bunker, traces the rise of Fascism, the history of World War II and the story of the D-Day landings. Visitors are shown a film that reflects intelligently and movingly on the effects of war and the prospects for peace in the future – a fitting end to this tour of the Normandy landing beaches.

Additional Information

Cherbourg, Bayeux,
D-Day landing beaches and Cean

ACCOMMODATION

There are many hotels in this area that cater for visitors to the Bayeux Tapestry and the Normandy beaches. A small selection follows:

Cherbourg
** Hotel Mercure
Modern, by the quay
Gare Maritime
☎ 0233 440111

** Le Louvre
Reasonably priced, in middle of town
Rue Dunant
☎ 0233 530288

Bayeux
** Lion d'Or
An ancient inn, but modernised
Rue St Jean
☎ 0231 920690

Caen
**** Les Relais des Gourmets
Near chateau, full of atmosphere
Rue de Geole
☎ 0231 860601

*** Hotel Moderne
In middle of town, cable TV, sound-proofed rooms
Boulevard Maréchal Leclerc
☎ 0231 860423

** Hotel Bristol
In middle of town
Rue du 11 Novembre
☎ 0231 845976

** Hotel des Quatrans
Fully renovated, sound-proofed rooms
Rue Gémaire
☎ 0231 862557

ATTRACTIONS

Cherbourg
Musée de la Libération
Open: May–September: 10am–6pm. rest of year: 9.30am–12 noon, 2–5.30pm, not Monday.
Forte du Roule
☎ 0233 201412

Musée Thomas Henry
Open: Tuesday–Saturday: 9am–12 noon, 2–6pm.
Behind Theatre Municipal
☎ 0233 230223

Musée Ethnographie
Open: 10am–12 noon, 2–5pm.
Closed: Sunday am, Monday all day.
Parc E Liais
☎ 0233 535161

Bayeux
Tapisserie de la Reine Mathilde (Bayeux Tapestry)
Open: May–August: 9am–7pm. mid-March–April: and September–mid-October: 9am–6.30pm. Rest of year: 9.30am–12.30pm, 2–6pm.
Rue de Nesmond
☎ 0231 512550

Musée Baron Gérard
Open: June–mid-September: 9am–
7pm. Mid-September–May: 10am–
12.30pm. 2–6pm.
near Cathedral
Combined ticket with tapestry
available
☎ 0231 921421

Musée de la Bataille de Normandie
Open: May–mid-September: 9.30am–
6.30pm. Mid-September–April:
10am-12.30pm. 2–6.30pm.
Boulevard Fabian Ware
☎ 0231 929341

Arromanches
Musée 6 Juin 1944
Open: May–October: 9am–7pm. April
and May: 9am–6pm. Rest of year:
9am–5pm.
Place du 6 Juin
☎ 0231 223431

Caen

Abbaye-aux-Hommes
Guided tours: 9.30am, 11am
2.30pm, 4pm.
Esplanade Jean Marie Louvel
☎ 0231 304281

Abbaye-aux-Dames
Open: 9am–6pm
Place de la Reine Mathilde
☎ 0231 952149

Musée des Beaux Arts
Open: 10am–6pm (free Wednesday)
In Chateau
☎ 0231 852863

Musée de Normandie
Open: April–September: 10am-
12.30pm 1.30–6pm. Weekends and
Mondays in summer and daily rest of
year: 9.30am–12.30pm 2–6pm.
Closed Tuesday. Free Wednesday.
In chateau
☎ 0231 304750

Le Mémorial
Open: July–31 August: 9am–9pm.
Rest of year: 9am–7pm
Esplanade du Géneral Eisenhower
☎ 0231 060644

EATING OUT

Lots to choose from, not only in
Cherbourg, Caen and Bayeux, but
also along the coast. A few
suggestions:

Cherbourg
Café de Paris
Famous for sea food
Quai Caligny
☎ 0233 431236

St Vaast
France et Fuschias
Also famous for sea food
Rue du Maréchal Foch
☎ 0233 544226

Bayeux
Lion d'Or
A noted hotel restaurant
Rue St Jean
☎ 0231 920690

Caen

La Bourride
Superb food in nineteenth-century setting
Rue du Vaugueux
☎ 0231 935076

SHOPPING

Cherbourg

There is a good selection of shops in the pedestrianised shopping area and there are street markets on Tuesday, Thursday and Saturday. There is an Auchan hypermarket on the perimeter.

Barfleur

A good place to buy pottery and antiques.

Bayeux

An excellent centre for lace and porcelain.

Arromanches

One of the obvious places to buy D-Day souvenirs.

Caen

A very wide choice of shops in the extensive shopping area.

TOURIST INFORMATION

Cherbourg
Quai Alexandre III
☎ 0233 935202

Barfleur
Rond-Point Guillaume le Conquérant
☎ 0233 540248

Bayeux
Pont St Jean
☎ 0231 921626

Arromanches
Rue du Maréchal Joffre
☎ 0231 214756

Caen
Place St Pierre
☎ 0231 271414

8 St Malo, Dinard, Dinan and Mont St Michel

INTRODUCTION

St Malo is the most remarkable of all the Channel ports featured in this guide book. The town stands on a peninsula where the Rance estuary meets the sea. Its narrow, grid-like streets of large, somewhat forbidding, granite houses are entirely contained by massive ramparts. Over the centuries, seafarers from St Malo have discovered and plundered large areas of the globe and its people have always been fiercely independent.

Getting there

Brittany Ferries (☎ 0870 536 0360) run ferries from Portsmouth to St Malo. Travelling time is about nine hours. Condor Ferries (☎ 0845 345 2000) operate ferries from Poole to St Malo, either directly or via Guernsey and Jersey. The direct time for the fast ferry is about four and a half hours.

The town has long been fortified, but its current granite ramparts, which are massive and impressively gated, were designed in 1689 by Vauban (Who else could it possibly have been?!). They are so solid and impregnable that they even survived intact after a twentieth-century American attack from land, sea and air!

In August 1944, the Germans took refuge in the walled town and held out against the advancing Americans, who bombarded the place for two weeks before they secured a surrender. The walls survived, but eighty per cent of the Old Town was destroyed.

After the war, some of the more significant buildings were restored but the rest of the Old Town was reconstructed by the erection of very tall granite buildings alongside the narrow, grid-like streets. The reconstructed Old Town is not exactly pretty, but it has an impressive homogeneity.

Exploration of the walled town

There are some parking spaces inside the walled town but there is ample parking just outside the ramparts. The fortified area is entered through Porte St Vincent, an impressive gate with the arms of St Malo and

Not to be missed

- The walled town of St Malo
- Vauban's National Fort on an offshore island
- Chateubriand's lonely grave on an offshore island
- The hydroelectric scheme on the Rance estuary
- The Grande Plage at Dinard
- The Promenade du Clair de Lune, Dinard
- The upper Old Town of Dinan
- The Rue du Zerzual and the Rue du Petit Port, Dinan
- The Tour d'Horloge, Dinan
- Mont St Michel – from a distance, from close-up and by visiting it
- The Abbey and the Merveille on Mont St Michel
- The fishing village of Cancale
- Grouin Point

Things to do

- Visit the Chateau at St Malo
- Walk around the full circuit of town walls, St Malo
- Eat pancakes in St Malo
- Relax on St Malo beach
- Walk along causeways at low tide to the National Fort and the Ile de la Grande Blé
- Take a boat trip to Jersey for the day or a shorter cruise to Dinard
- Visit the Aquarium or Marine Museum at Dinard
- Walk around Pointe du Moulinet and along the Promenade du Clair de Lune, Dinard
- Buy pottery or paintings in Dinan
- Have a refreshment break on the quayside at Dinan
- Ascend the belfry at Dinan for a great view
- Visit the chateau and walk the ramparts at Dinan
- Tour the abbey and monastic buildings at Mont St Michel
- Eat oysters at Cancale
- Enjoy the view of the Baie du Mont St Michel from Grouin Point

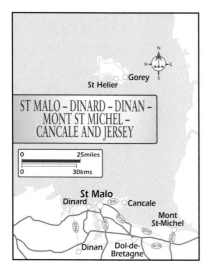

Brittany above its gateway. Immediately right of the gate, there is a fifteenth-century **Château**, which was restored by Vauban. There are superb views from the castle ramparts and, within the building, there is a museum which celebrates St Malo's famous sons, including Jacques Cartier, who discovered the mouth of the St Lawrence, and the poet Chateaubriand. A walk around the complete circuit of walls provides great views in all directions – over the town, out to sea and down the Rance estuary.

The Place Chateaubriand, immediately left of the Château, is a lively open space with cafés and tourist shops. By following Rue Jacques Cartier along the line of the walls and then turning right up the Grand Rue, visitors can gain access to **St Vincent Cathedral**, which was started in the eleventh century but took over 700 years to complete. The church has a huge nave, which is impressively lit by colourful stained glass, and a more delicately-styled chancel.

St Malo may look grey and intimidating, but it is a very lively place, with lots of cafés, bars and clubs, especially in the area around the cathedral. For further exploration, a compass would be useful, because there are rival attractions in different directions.

The **Maison de la Duchesse Anne,** in the extreme north of the old Town, is a fifteenth-century town house; and the **Maison de Corsaire,** in the south-east corner, is an eighteenth-century merchant's house.

St Malo has excellent street markets on Tuesday and Friday, a covered vegetable market and a fish market. Not surprisingly, excellent sea food is served up in the town's many restaurants, but the local pancakes are absolutely delicious.

The beach

The Porte des Bés and the Porte St Pierre, along the western stretch of the wall, open out onto a most unexpected sight: a vast beach, which stretches around the full length of the western and northern walls. In the middle of the beach, there is a walled sea-water swimming pool and the seaward view is made fascinating and picturesque by a litter of small islands and rocks. An island on the northern side of the beach accommodates Vauban's **National Fort**, which has great views and a dungeon, and the **Isle de la Grande Bé**, on the south side of the beach, houses Chateaubriand's lonely granite tomb. Both of these islands can be reached by causeways at low tide.

Boat trips are available from St Malo to Dinard, the Rance valley and to the Channel Islands.

Popping to Britain for the day

The car ferries, which run from St Malo to Jersey, provide an opportunity for a great day out – in Britain! The ferries run to St Helier, which is very congested and not particularly attractive. However, do not despair – an anti-clockwise circumnavigation of the island by car is very rewarding indeed.

The eastern side of the island has some fine beaches and lush countryside, whereas the western side is much more rugged, with a rock-strewn shore. There is a splendid castle on a rocky promontory above Gorey and even some nice British-style pubs in country locations.

Although Jersey has the same latitude as Rouen, it is unmistakably British, with hedgerows, patchwork fields, deep country lanes and chocolate box cottages. Only the street names, which are in French, and the telephone boxes, which are yellow, indicate that Jersey is not simply an extension of the Home Counties. Here is convincing proof that landscapes are largely man-made. Nature provides the canvas, but humans paint the picture!

The Rance hydro-electric scheme

Anyone setting out on a car drive from St Malo in the summer months will need to exercise patience, because the roads which run through the suburbs of the town are very congested. The D168 crosses the Rance to the resort of Dinard, on the western shores of the estuary. As it crosses the wide river, the road runs along the top of a dam wall, which closes the estuary and forms an eight square-mile (21sq km) reservoir. This construction is part of a massive hydro-electric scheme which utilizes the ebb and flow of the tide to make electric power. The road also crosses over two locks that allow boats to pass in and out of the estuary.

Dinard

Dinard was a simple fishing village until it was discovered by the Americans in the middle of the nineteenth century. The British then developed the place as a fashionable resort by erecting large villas and luxurious hotels and planting impressive floral displays. Dinard has managed to retain its rather refined, fashionable character and it is still popular with English visitors, who are now joined in large numbers by French families. There is a casino, an **Aquarium**, with two dozen pools, and a **Marine Museum**, with exhibits from Polar expeditions.

Dinard has the appearance of an English seaside town of the Victorian period, but its main beach, with its rows of cloned, orange beach tents, is unmistakably French. The Grande Plage is separated from the Plage du Prieuré by **Pointe du Moulinet**, from which there are wonderful views, and the Promenade du Clair de Lune, which offers a very pleasant walk along the water's edge. Another beach, the Plage de St Enogat, occupies a cove to the west of the main town.

Clones on the beach

All the beaches in the classier resorts on France's western coast are characterised by their neat rows of large bathing tents. Each resort has a peculiar style of tent. For example, Deauville's are igloo-like, Biarritz's are Arabian and Dinard's cloned, orange-coloured tents are of the Persian variety.

DINAN

The D266 heads southwards from Dinard towards the old town of **Dinan**, which is accessed by joining the N176 for a stretch before taking a slip road to the town.

Dinan, which is one of the best old towns in France, stands on two levels. The higher Old Town occupies a promontory above the river Rance; the lower town and port sit below a great viaduct. The two areas are linked by a steep, cobbled street, known as Rue du Zerzual in its upper reaches and as Rue du Petit Port in its lower reaches. This street is lined with superbly restored half-timbered houses, now mostly occupied by artists, potters and craftspeople. Although the street has been renovated and prettified and is blatantly touristy, it is wonderfully atmospheric and redolent of medieval France.

A long sojourn at the café by the quayside is recommended as an essential preliminary to the exhausting walk back up the Rue du Petit Port and the Rue du Zerzuel. The old town at the summit of the hill is almost as evocative as the steep street of artists and potters, especially in the area around the Place des Merciers and along the Rue de la Cordonnerie and the Rue du Petit Pan. The **Tour d'Horloge** offers great views from the top of its 158 steps and **St Saviour's Church** has a casket in the north transept which contains the heart of Du Guesclin, who was a constant thorn in the flesh of the English occupying armies.

A stretch of town wall survives to the south of the Old Town. A walk along the walls provides wonderful views and there is a **Château** in the southern corner of the ramparts. The Château contains a museum of medieval artefacts, local crafts and nineteenth-century furnishings of the region.

Dinan is quite simply a superb town and a place not to be missed by visitors to this region of France.

MONT ST MICHEL

The N176 leads from Dinan to **Dol-de-Bretagne** and then to **Mont St Michel,** one of the most spectacular and most visited attractions in the whole of France.

The first, distant view of the island abbey in the **Baie du Mont St Michel** is very memorable. On closer approach, the monastic buildings grow ever larger and more impressive. The abbey stands on an offshore crag and is reached at low tide by a causeway, which is lined with parked cars at low tide but is covered very quickly indeed at high tide.

Mirror image

St Michael's Mount, on an offshore island off the coast of Cornwall, is a pale reflection of Mont St Michel, not nearly so spectacular as its French counterpart, but satisfyingly photogenic when viewed from the mainland. In fact, it was a group of monks from Mont St Michel who first established a monastery on the Cornish offshore island in 1044. The Benedictine monks on St Michael's Mount were ejected by the English Crown in 1425, when the site was acquired as a fortress. The abbey was later converted into a castellated mansion by the St Aubyn family.

An oratory was built on the crag in the eighth century by Aubert, Bishop of Avranches, after he had supposedly seen a vision of the Archangel Michael. The oratory was replaced by an abbey, which was extended over the centuries by a succession of Romanesque and Gothic edifices.

The mount has been a place of pilgrimage for many centuries. During the Hundred Years' War, British occupying forces cashed in on the abbey's pulling power by selling safe passages to pilgrims, and tourists now arrive in such numbers that it is often necessary to impose a one-way pedestrian system on the granite rock!

The abbey and its church have been much altered over the years and there is a mix of architecture from Romanesque to early Gothic to Flamboyant to nineteenth-century Revivalism, but the profile of the pile of buildings is superb and there is a surprising unity to the whole assemblage.

The abbey

The abbey is entered through the outer defences, which lead to a guardroom and a great staircase that gives access to Gautier's Leap, a terrace from which a soldier is said to have jumped to his death. Visitors will wish to pause here to admire the fabulous view over Baie du Mont St Michel, before entering the Romanesque nave of the church.

On the north side of the mount there are great thirteenth-century monastic buildings known as the **Merveille** (the Marvel), including the Guests' Hall, the Knights' Hall, the cloister and the refectory. All the buildings are impressive, both from within and from without. The crypt, with its ten great columns, is not to be missed either.

The Grande Rue

The main street, which runs back down from the abbey to the car park, is entirely given over to tourism, with cafés and rather tacky souvenir shops, all swarming with visitors, Most visitors are glad to return to their vehicles after buffeting their way down this crowded thoroughfare, but as they drive away from the mount a vision appears in their rear view mirror to remind them that they have just visited one of the greatest attractions in the western world.

CANCALE

The N176, followed by the N137, provides a direct route for the return to St Malo, but it is worth taking an alternative route along the coast, via the D797 and the D76, in order to visit the fishing port of **Cancale**, where much of the foreshore is covered in oyster beds. There is also a picturesque quayside, a fishermen's quarter, a church tower with a view of Jersey visible from its summit on a clear day and a **Museum** devoted to local arts and traditions.

A further diversion to the rocky **Grouin Point**, at the north-eastern extremity of the headland, is worth making for the great view across the Baie du St Michel.

The return to St Malo through the town's busy suburbs can be very slow going but, as they wait in the traffic queues, drivers and passengers have the consolation of being able to muse over a journey which has taken them from a walled port to a classy resort, a medieval town, a great offshore abbey and a fishing village famous for its oysters.

Additional Information

St Malo, Dinard, Dinan and Mont St Michel

ACCOMMODATION

A good number of hotels exist in this area. Some of the better known ones are listed below:

St Malo
*** Central
44 rooms, near dock
Grand Rue
☎ 0299 408770

*** Elizabeth
Inside town walls, modern rooms
Rue des Cordiers
☎ 0299 562498

Dinard
**** Grand Hotel
Very posh and correspondingly priced
Avenue George V
☎ 0299 882626

Dinan
*** d'Avangour
Traditional furnishings, modern rooms
Place du Champ-Clos
☎ 0296 390749

ATTRACTIONS

St Malo
Chateau de St Malo
Open: October–Easter: Monday, Wednesday, Sunday: 10am–12 noon, 2–6pm. Easter–September: daily: 10am–12 noon, 2–6pm.
☎ 0299 407111

Dinard
Aquarium and Marine Museum
Open: May–September.
For hours consult number below:
☎ 0299 461390

Dinan
Tour d'Horloge
Open: July and August: 10am–7pm. Closed Sundays and holidays.
☎ 0296 397540

Chateau
Rue de Chateau
Open: 10am–6pm
☎ 0296 394520

Mont St Michel

Abbey
Open: May–September: 9am–5.30pm.
October–April: 9am–4.30pm.
☎ 0233 601414

EATING OUT

In this area, there are lots of seafood restaurants and also lots of restaurants offering pancakes and oysters. Visitors could possibly try the following:

St Malo

La Duchesse Anne
Excellent seafood and Cancale oysters
Place Guy la Chambre
☎ 0299 408533

Pomme d'Or
Intimate atmosphere
Place du Poids du Roi
☎ 0299 409024

Dinard

Altair
Good value, terrace seats available
Boulevard Féart
☎ 0299 461358

Dinan

Chez Le Mer Pourcel
Good regional food, very good wine
Place des Mercurs
☎ 0296 390380

Mont St Michel

Auberge St Pierre
Local dishes
Grande Rue
☎ 0233 601403

Cancale

La Cancalaise
A crêperie
Rue de la Vallée Pocon
☎ 0299 897122

SHOPPING

Good street markets in St Malo. Pancakes in St Malo. Some fairly tasteful souvenirs in Dinard. Good local art and pottery in Dinan. Lots of souvenirs (if you really want them) on Mont St Michel. Oysters in Cancale.

TOURIST INFORMATION

St Malo
Esplanade St Vincent
☎ 0299 566448

Dinard
Boulevard Féart
☎ 0299 469412

Dinan
Rue d'Horloge
☎ 0296 397540

Mont St Michel
On the mount
☎ 0233 601430

Cancale
Rue du Port
☎ 0299 896372

Fact File

ACCOMMODATION

Hotels

A selection of the huge range of hotels in northern France is given in the additional information at the end of each chapter. Details of accommodation of all kinds can be obtained from:

French Government Tourist Office
178 Piccadilly, London W1
(☎ 0207 4919 995)
who issue an annual handbook.

Traditional family-run hotels, many of which are very charming, are usually billed as Logis de France, Auberges de France or France Accueil. Modern hotel chains include Novotel, Ibis, Climat, Mercure, Sofitel and Campanile, but it is important to remember that these hotels are used by business people, so tourists may end up paying for facilities, such as faxes, computer and telephone links, which are not needed by holidaymakers who simply want to 'get away from it all.'

Choosing an appropriate hotel from a brochure is not easy. Star ratings are given in this guide, but their value as indicators of quality is limited because they are based on the level of physical provision, including facilities which are important to business people, rather than on quality of service.

Hotels with lifts almost always carry higher ratings, hence higher room charges, but the provision of a lift may not be a prime consideration for fit and healthy visitors. The existence of private parking facilities is likely to be a major consideration for anyone taking their own car to France. Some of the hotels that provide parking levy an extra charge. Plenty of hotels offer free accommodation to young children sharing a room with adults, but others charge a nominal fee. The provision of private bathrooms, showers or saunas is another high priority for many people. Bidets are usually provided, whether you want one or not!

Advanced booking and travel packages

A day spent in a desperate search for a suitable place to stay is an appalling waste of holiday time, so it advisable to book rooms in advance, and many will wish to book accommodation and travel as a single package through a reputable company or travel agent. Companies offering travel packages include:

Magic of France
☎ 0208 741 0208

Bowhills
☎ 0148 987 8567

Brittany Ferries
☎ 0990 143537

Country Cottages in France
☎ 0128 244 5005

French Affair ☎ 0207 381 8519	**Meon** ☎ 0173 023 0370
Crystal ☎ 0123 582 4324	**Something special** ☎ 0199 255 7711
Just France ☎ 0208 780 4480	**Vacances en Campagne** ☎ 0870 078 0185

Camping and caravan sites

There are some excellent caravan and camping sites in France, many with swimming pools, restaurants, evening entertainment and children's play areas. The livelier sites are particularly appreciated by teenagers, who generally prefer socialising to sightseeing, but they are also popular with families who have young children. Visitors who would rather spend a relaxing holiday without the accompaniment of loud and insistent music may wish to opt for a lower rated site. However, visitors who would like a guarantee of reasonable facilities, including an adequate number of shower units and a few English-style toilets, are advised to choose sites with a 4-star rating.

The Caravan Club (☎ 0134 231 6101) and the **Camping and Caravanning Club** (☎ 0120 342 2010) will arrange packages, including Channel crossing and insurance, for people taking their own caravan or tent.

Driving to a set-up tent or mobile home is a popular choice for many people. Companies such as:

Eurocamp ☎ 0160 678 7878	**Canvas Holidays** ☎ 0138 364 4000
Keycamp ☎ 0870 700 0123	**Eurosites** ☎ 0870 751 0000

provide this option and have on-site representatives who will offer advice about local attractions and cater for your every need. They also offer attractive packages, including multiple site holidays. As these companies only use sites with good facilities, their brochures can be used as a good source of suitable sites for campers and caravanners who prefer to travel independently

Gîtes

Gîte accommodation is very popular with visitors to France, especially with those people who like to share their holiday with another family or travel in a small party. Gîtes are usually converted buildings in pleasant country locations. However, it is always advisable to check the exact location of a gîte on a detailed map, because some gîtes are in areas which are a little too remote!

Information on gîtes, including the brochure **Gîtes de France,** is available from the French Government Tourist Office (see above) and many are advertised in newspapers or in magazines such as **France** and **Living France**.

Refuges

Gîtes d'étapes and *refuges* are very basic forms of shelter, with bunk beds and simple kitchen facilities. They are usually located close to walking routes or cycle trails. Details can be found in the **Rando Guide,** available from:

Comité National des Sentiers de la Grande Randonnée, 64 Rue de Gergovie 75014 Paris.

Youth Hostels

If you want a cheap holiday and you are happy to accept dormitory accommodation and basic meals, youth hostels (*auberges de jeunesse*) are the answer. Some town-based hostels are located in unattractive areas, but others are ideally placed, often close to walking routes and attractions.

Information can be obtained from:

YHA
14 Southampton Street
London WC2

DISABLED VISITORS

Some tourist attractions have limited access for disabled visitors. A comprehensive list of facilities for disabled visitors and details of access arrangements are given in **Touristes quand meme! Prom-enades en France pour Voyageurs Handicapés**. This publication can be obtained from:

Comité National Francais de Liaison pour Réadaptiondes Handicapés, 38 Boulevard Respail 75007, Paris.

DRIVING IN FRANCE

All vehicles travelling in France must carry a red warning triangle and a spare headlight bulb. Headlight deflectors for right-hand drive vehicles can be obtained at outlets near the Channel terminals.

It is compulsory for front seat passengers to wear seatbelts, and children below ten are not allowed to travel in the front seats.

Speed limits are as follows;

Motorways (*autoroutes*):	130kph (81mph) in dry conditions; 110kph (68mph) when wet.
N roads (*Routes Nationales*):	110kph (68mph) in dry conditions; 90kph (56mph) when wet.
Other roads:	90kph (56mph) in dry conditions; 80kph (50mph) when wet.
In built-up areas:	50kph (31mph).

There are on-the-spot impositions for speeding and drink-driving. Nationals of EU countries are required to carry a valid driving licence.

The infamous rule of *priorité a droite* (give way to traffic from the right) has disappeared from main roads, but still applies on unmarked junctions, including those in built-up areas. The rule no longer applies at roundabouts, except at L'Etoile in Paris, where traffic coming on to the roundabout has priority over traffic already circulating the traffic island!

Motorway driving in France has its drawbacks, chief of which is the cost of tolls (*péage*). Slip roads are often rather alarmingly short; hard shoulders are ludicrously narrow and so offer little protection for motorists who have breakdowns; most autoroutes are two-lane only and there is often only short advance warning of roadworks, lane switches and motorway splits.

However, French autoroutes also have distinct advantages over their British counterparts. Traffic is relatively light, drivers are well protected against the headlights of oncoming vehicles by barriers, shrubbery or vegetation in the central reservation, and there are lots of rest stops (*aires)* with toilets, picnic areas and telephones.

When leaving the motorway at service stations, it is important to remember that fuel stations precede refreshment areas in French service stations (the reverse of the arrangement in British service stations),

Fuel is sold as *super, sans plomb* (unleaded) and *gazole* (diesel).

There is a good system of N roads (the equivalent of British A roads) but drivers need to take particular care on those N roads which have three lanes, with alternating overtaking priorities. D roads (the third grade of road) are generally well surfaced, but they may be narrow and are quite often flanked by ditches, so it is important to take care when pulling over to allow another vehicle to pass. D roads also change their number designations unexpectedly, so a good map is essential. Michelin maps are excellent and the AA Road Atlas of France covers the rod network in minute detail, but good eyesight is essential for reading it!

One important hint for anyone driving in France: French drivers seem to regard overtaking as a challenge, not least on blind bends. Visiting drivers, and their passenger-navigators, need to have their wits about them at all times.

ELECTRICITY

The French system operates on 220v, 50 Hertz. A few areas still use 110v ac. Round 2-pin plugs are in general use for sockets, so visitors will need to take with them a Continental 2-pin adaptor.

HEALTH

British visitors should obtain a Form E111 from the Department of Health and Social Security. This ensures access to health services in France.

In an emergency, phone 19 or the local police station. Pharmacists always give very helpful advice and stock a comprehensive range of products.

MEASUREMENTS

One mile is equivalent to 1.6 km, so a journey of 100 miles will be signed as 160 km. In order to make a rough conversion of km to miles, multiply by 6 and divide by 10, so 100km is about 60 miles. Thanks to standardisation and European Community regulations, British people are now much more familiar with continental measurements of area, volume and weight but, for the record, conversions are as follows:

2.3lb is equivalent to 1kg (1,000g)
1.75 pints is equivalent to 1 litre
1 gallon is equivalent to 4.5 litres
2.5 acres is equivalent to 1 hectare

MONEY

There is no restriction on the amount of money that can be taken into France, but visitors would be well advised to minimize the amount of cash they carry around with them, by taking Eurocheques and Travellers' Cheques and by using credit cards to pay for fuel and for bills at supermarkets and restaurants. Credit cards are widely accepted

All transactions are now conducted in Euros. At the time of writing, one Euro is worth about 60p.

Banks are normally open from 9am to 12 noon and from 2 to 4pm.

OUTDOOR ACTIVITIES

Opportunities for outdoor activities, such as sailing, water-skiing, horse-riding, swimming and facilities for playing golf are listed in the additional information at the end of each chapter.

France is covered by an excellent network of long-distance footpaths, known as *Grandes Randonnées (GR)*. There is also a series of shorter routes, known as *Petites Randonnées*. Detailed maps usually show these routes, but a *Rando Guide* can be obtained from the French Tourist Office in Piccadilly (☎ 0207 491 9995).

The French take their cycling very seriously and cyclists are very welcome and well catered for in France. Maps with suggested itineraries for cyclists are available from railway stations.

The **Cyclists' Touring Club,** Cotterell House, 69 Meadow house, Goldalming, Surrey GU7 3Hs (☎ 0148 368 7217) can provide details of cycling opportunities.

PASSPORTS FOR PETS

It is now possible to take your pet abroad, but the following procedure must be followed:

Your pet must be injected by a vet with an International Standard Organisation (ISO) approved microchip and vaccinated with an anti-rabies vaccine. 30 days later, the vet should take a blood sample and send this off for analysis at an approved laboratory in order to check that the vaccine has taken effectively.

This will then allow you to receive a Pet Re-entry Certificate (valid for the life of the rabies vaccine).

POSTAGE

Stamps (*timbres)* can be purchased from post offices, which normally open from 8am to 7pm on weekdays and from 8am to 12 noon on Saturdays. Post offices in some smaller places close for lunch.

PUBLIC HOLIDAYS

The following public holidays apply in France:
    New Year's Day
    Easter Monday
    May Day
    Ascension Day
    VE Day (8th May)
    Whit Monday
    Bastille Day (4th July)
    Assumption Day (15th August) Note: some attractions
        close on this day.
    All Saints' Day (1st November) Note: this day marks the end of the
        season for many attractions
    Armistice Day (11th November)
    Christmas Day

TELEPHONES

Most public telephones in France do not take coins, but have to be fed with telephone cards (*télécartes*), which can be obtained from any *tabac.*

To phone home, leave off the first zero of the British area code and then prefix the number with 00 44.

Fact File

TIME

France is one hour ahead of Greenwich Mean Time.

TIPPING

Expectations on tipping in restaurants and hotels are similar to those at home, but guides in castles and museums generally expect a small tip.

TOURIST INFORMATION OFFICES

Every significant town and village in France has a tourist information office. Almost invariably, the staff speak English and the standard of leaflets, guides etc. is excellent. Information offices are listed in the additional information at the end of each chapter.

   The French Tourist Office in Great Britain is located at 178 Piccadilly, London W1V OAL ☎ 0207 491 7622

TRAVELLING ACROSS THE CHANNEL

Details of ferries and rail crossings to France are given at the beginning of each chapter. The companies involved are:

Brittany Ferries
☎ 0990 360360

Eurotunnel
☎ 0990 353535

Eurostar
☎ 0990 186186

Hoverspeed
☎ 0990 240241

P & O European Ferries
☎ 0970 242 4999

P & O Stena
☎ 0990 980980

Sea France
☎ 0990 711711

National Express
coaches operate Euroline coach services to France
☎ 0207 730 8235

Index

A

Abbaye-aux-Dames, *Caen* 170
Abbaye-aux-Hommes, *Caen* 169
Abbeville 82
Abbey of St Riquier 83
Abbey of St Vaast, *Arras* 88
Aire de la Baie de Somme
  service station 81
Alabaster Coast 103
Albert 84
Ambleteuse 29
American Art Museum,
  Giverny 120
Amiens 83
Aqualand,
  Le Touquet-Paris-Plage 77
Aquarium, *Dinard* 177
Aquarium Marin, *Étretat* 111
Aquarium, *Trouville* 134
Ardres 32
Arras 87
Arromanches-les-Bains 166
Audlinghen 29
Aviators' Monument 109

B

Bagatelle 78
Baie du Mont St Michel 178
Barfleur 163
Basilica of Notre Dame,
  St Omer 34
Basilica of Saint-Rémi 60
Basilica of St André,
  St Quentin 50
Bayeux 163
Bayeux Cathedral 165
Beaumont-Hamel 85
Beauvais 120
Belfroi du Gros Horloge,
  Rouen 116
Belfry, *Boulorne-Sur-Mer* 71
Belfry, *Dreux* 139
Bénédictine Museum,
  Fécamp 08
Bénouville 168
Berck-Plage 78
Bergues 36
Bernieres 168
Birthplace of General de Gaulle,
  Lille 47
Bishop's Palace, *St Quentin* 55

Bishop's Residence, *St Quentin* 56
Blériot-Plage 27
Bois des Moutiers,
  Varengeville-sur-Mer 105
Boulevard Jacquard, *Calais* 23
Boulevard Maréchal Foch,
  Dieppe 101
Boulogne 30
Boulogne-sur-Mer 66
British War Cemetery, *Pozières* 87
Bunker d'Eperlecques 32
Burghers of Calais 24

C

Cabourg 136
Caen 168
Café du Tribunaux, *Dieppe* 100
Café Musée Gondrée,
  Pegasus Bridge 168
Calais 17, 22
Cancale 179
Cany-Barville 107
Cap Blanc-Nez 28
Cap de la Hève, *Le Havre* 132
Cap Gris-Nez 29
Carentan 163
Cassel 35
Cathedral, *Boulorne-Sur-Mer* 71
Cathedral of Notre Dame,
  Amiens 83
Cathedral of Notre Dame,
  Evreux 139
Cathedral of Notre Dame,
  St Quentin 53
Cathedral of St Pierre,
  Beauvais 120
Cathédrale Notre-Dame,
  Rouen 114
Centre Guillaume le Conquérant,
  Bayeux 163
Chamber of Commerce, *Lille* 48
Champagne Houses, *Reims* 60
Chapelle des Templiers,
  St Quentin 55
Chartres 137, 138, 139
Chartres Cathedral 140
Château, *Boulorne-Sur-Mer* 71
Chateau de Bizy, *Vernon* 118
Chateau des Aygues, *Étretat* 111
Château, *Dieppe* 100
Château, *Dinan* 178

Château, *St Malo* 176
Cherbourg 160
Church of Notre Dame,
  Dives-sur-Mer 136
Church of Saint Jacques,
  Dieppe 99
Church of St Joseph,
  Le Havre 131
Church of St Martin,
  St Quentin 56
Church of St Pierre, *Gerberoy* 122
Church of St Rémy, *Dieppe* 100
Citadelle, *Calais* 25
Citadelle, *Lille* 47
citadelle, *Montreuil-sur-Mer* 78
Cité Europe 17
Clères 111
Clocher de Ste-Catherine,
  Honfleur 133
Collegiate Church of St Vulfran,
  Abbeville 82
Coquelles 17
Côte de Nacre 166
Côte Fleurie 132
Courseulles-sur-Mer 168

D

Deauville 134
Dieppe 98
Dinan 178
Dinard 177
Dives-sur-Mer 136
Dol-de-Bretagne 178
Dreux 139
Duke William's Citadel, *Caen* 169
Dunkerque 36

E

Église Notre Dame Vernon 118
Église St-Taurin, *Evreux* 139
Église Ste-Catherine,
  Honfleur 133
Entomological Museum,
  St Quentin 51
Eperlecques 32
Escalles 29
Etaples 75
Étretat 109
Euralille, *Lille* 48
Evreux 138

F

Falaise d'Amont	109
Falaise d'Aval	109
Fécamp	107
Field of the Cloth of Gold	32
Fine Arts Museum, *St Omer*	34
Fort Vauban	29
Forte du Roule, *Cherbourg*	162
French Flanders	31, 32

G

Galerie Nationale de Tapisserie,	
Beauvais	121
Gerberoy	121
Giverny	118
Gold Beach Musée America	168
Grand Hotel, *Cabourg*	136
Grand' Place, *Arras*	87
Grande Rue,	
Boulorne-Sur-Mer	70
Grande Rue, *Dieppe*	99
Gravelines	37
Gros Horloge, *Rouen*	116
Grouin Point	180
Guillaume le Conquérant,	
Dives-sur-Mer	136
Guines	32
Guines Forest	32

H

Hardelot	73
Haute Ville, *Boulorne-Sur-Mer*	70
Hautes de Montreuil,	
Montreuil-sur-Mer	78
Hermanville	168
Historal de la Grand Guerre,	
Péronne	87
Honfleur	133
Hortillonnages	84
Hotel de Bailliage, *St Omer*	33
Hôtel de Ville, *Arras*	88
Hôtel de ville,	
Boulorne-Sur-Mer	70
Hôtel de Ville, *Calais*	23
Hôtel de Ville, *Le Havre*	131
Hotel de Ville, *Lille*	48
Hôtel de ville, *St Omer*	33
Hôtel de Ville, *St Quentin*	51
Hôtel de Ville, *St Quentin*	56
Hotel Desandrouins,	
Boulorne-Sur-Mer	70
Houlgate	136

I

Ile de Tatihou	163
Isle de la Grande Bé, *St Malo*	176

L

La Boiselle	85
La Coupole	35
La Forêt Verte	113
La Voix du Nord, *Lille*	47
Laon	52
Le Clos Lupin, *Étretat*	111
Le Crotoy	78
Le Havre	128
Le Mémorial, *Caen*	170
Le Quartier du Pollet, *Dieppe*	102
Le Touquet Museum	77
Le Touquet-Paris-Plage	76
Le Volcan, *Le Havre*	131
Lécuyer Museum, *St Quentin*	51
Les Boves, *Arras*	88
Les Halles, *Dives-sur-Mer*	136
Les Loges	111
Les Planches, *Deauville*	135
Les Tourelles, *Dieppe*	101
lighthouse, *Calais*	25
Lille	43
Longueval	85
Luc-sur-Mer	168

M

Maison de Corsaire, *St Malo*	176
Maison de la Duchesse Anne,	
St Malo	176
Maison de la Mer	168
Maison des Finances, *Rouen*	114
Maison du Temps Jadis,	
Vernon	118
Mammetz	85
Manneporte	110
Manoir d'Ango	106
Manoir de Salamandre,	
Étretat	110
Mareis, *Etaples*	76
Marine Museum, *Dinard*	177
Merlimont	78
Monet's garden, *Giverny*	119
Mont St Michel	178
Montagne de Reims	60
Montreuil-sur-Mer	78
Monument to Auguste Mariette,	
Boulorne-Sur-Mer	71
Musée 6 Juin 1944,	
Arromanches-les-Bains	167
Musée 6 Juin 1944 D-Day,	
Pegasus Bridge	168
Musée Baron Gérard, *Bayeux*	166
Musée Boucher-de-Perthes,	
Abbeville	82
Musée de la Ceramique,	
Rouen	117

Musée de la Ferronerie,	
Rouen	118
Musée de la Libération,	
Cherbourg	162
Musée de la Marine, *Etaples*	76
Musée de la Tapisserie,	
Bayeux	163
Musée de l'Hospice Comtesse,	
Lille	47
Musée de Normandie, *Caen*	169
Musée de Picardie, *Amiens*	84
Musée des Arbris, *Albert*	84
Musée des Arts et de l'Enfance,	
Fécamp	109
Musée des Beaux Arts, *Arras*	88
Musée des Beaux Arts, *Caen*	169
Musée des Beaux Arts,	
Chartres	142
Musée des Beaux Arts,	
Dunkerque	37
Musée des Beaux Arts,	
Le Havre	132
Musée des Beaux Arts, *Reims*	59
Musée des Beaux Arts, *Rouen*	117
Musée du Château, *Dieppe*	100
Musée Ethnographie,	
Cherbourg	162
Musée Eugene Boudin,	
Honfleur	133
Musée Flaubert et d'Histoire de	
Médecine, *Rouen*	118
Musée Memorial de la Bataille de	
Normandie, *Bayeux*	166
Musée Paléontologique,	
Deauville	136
Musée Thomas Henry,	
Cherbourg	162
Musée Villa Montebello,	
Trouville	134
Museum, *Cancale*	180
Museum, *Evreux*	139
Museum of Automobiles and	
Military Vehicles, *Clère*	113
Museum of Fine Arts and Lace,	
Calais	25
Museum of History, Art and	
Folklore, *Cassel*	36
Museum of Natural History,	
St Omer	34
Museum of Newfoundland	
Fishermen, *Fécamp*	109
Museum of the Atlantic Wall	29
Museum of the Second	
World War	29
Museum of War, *Calais*	24
Museum, *St Quentin*	55

N

National Fort, *St Malo* 176
Nausicaa, *Boulorne-Sur-Mer* 69
Neufchâtel-en-Bray 122
Notre Dame, *Calais* 25
Notre Dame de Brebieres,
  Albert 84
Notre Dame de la Treille, *Lille* 47
Notre Dame de Salut,
  Fécamp 109
Notre-Dame-de-la-Garde 109

O

Old Town, *Bayeux* 166
Old Town, *Chartres* 142
Opal Coast 26
Opera House, *Lille* 48

P

Palais de Justice, Beauvais 121
Palais de Justice,
  Boulorne-Sur-Mer 70
Palais de Justice, *Rouen* 117
Palais des Beaux Arts 48
Parc Emmanuel Liais,
  Cherbourg 162
Paris 150
Pegasus Bridge 168
Place des Héros, *Arras* 88
Place du Général de Gaulle,
  Lille 46
Place du Puits Sale, *Dieppe* 99
Place Maréchal Foch, *St Omer* 33
Pointe du Moulinet, *Dinard* 177
Pont d'Aval Arch 110
Pont de Normandie 132
Port Chanteryne, *Cherbourg* 162
Port of Calais 22
Porte de Mars, *Reims* 60
Pourville-sur-Mer 105
Pozières 85
Promenade Concerts, *Reims* 59

Q

Quartier St Leu, *Amiens* 84
Quettehou 163
Quiberville-sur-Mer 107

R

Rancourt 85
Reims 56
Reliquary of St Taurinius,
  Evreux 139
Rouen 113
Royal Chapel of St Louis,
  Dreux 139
Rue 78
Rue de Lille,
  Boulorne-Sur-Mer 71
Rue Royale, *Calais* 25

S

Saint-Pierre, *Dreux* 139
Samer 79
Sangatte 28
Somme battlefields 79
Somme Bay 78
Songeons 121
Sotteville-sur-Mer 107
Square du Canada, *Dieppe* 101
St Aubin 107
St Aubin-sur-Mer 168
St Malo 174
St Marguerite-sur-Mer 107
St Omer 33
St Pierre, *Chartres* 143
St Quentin 48
St Saviour's Church, *Dinan* 178
St Trinité, *Fécamp* 109
St Vaast 163
St Valéry 106
St Valéry-en-Caux 107
St Vincent Cathedral, *St Malo* 176
St-Maclou, *Rouen* 115
St-Pierre 22

Ste-Adresse, *Le Havre* 132
Stella-Plage 78
Surrender Museum, *Reims* 60

T

Tau Museum, *Reims* 58
Terrasse de Normandie Café,
  Arromanches-les-Bains 167
Thiepval 87
Tour d'Horloge, *Dinan* 178
Tour du Buerre, *Rouen* 115
Tour du Guet, *Calais* 23, 25
Tour Jeanne d'Arc, *Rouen* 118
Tour Perret, *Amiens* 84
Tour St-Romain, *Rouen* 115
Town Walls,
  Boulorne-Sur-Mer 71
Tree of Jesse window,
  St Valéry 106
Trouville 133

U

Ulster Tower 85

V

Varengeville-sur-Mer 105
Vernon 118
Vers-sur-Mer 168
Veules-les-Roses 107
Vieille Bourse, *Lille* 47
Vieille Ville, *Lille* 47
Villerville 133
Vimy Ridge 88

W

Wimereux 29
Wissant 29
Wormhout 36

Z

Zoological Park, Clères 113

Published in the UK by
Landmark Publishing Ltd,
Ashbourne Hall, Cokayne Avenue, Ashbourne, Derbyshire DE6 1EJ England
Tel: (01335) 347349 Fax: (01335) 347303
e-mail: sales@landmarkpublishing.co.uk
website: landmarkpublishing.co.uk

ISBN 1 84306 054 X

Print: Gutenberg Press Ltd, Malta
Design & Cartography: Mark Titterton
Editor: Kay Coulson

Front cover: Beach umbrellas, Deauville
Back cover, top: Café culture, Lille
Back cover, bottom: Mont St Michel

Photographs: All by the author except; title page (Honfleur); front cover and page 147
bottom (Beach umbrellas) by Colin Bannon